Not bloody likely

Famous Lines
The Columbia Dictionary of Familiar Quotations
by Robert Andrews

The Columbia Dictionary of Quotations
by Robert Andrews

Women's Words
The Columbia Book of Quotations by Women
by Mary Biggs

Family Wisdom
The 2,000 Most Important Things Ever Said about Parenting,
Children, and Family Life
by Susan Ginsberg

I Can Resist Everything Except Temptation
And Other Quotations from Oscar Wilde
by Karl Beckson

Of the People, By the People, For the People
And Other Quotations from Abraham Lincoln
by Gabor Borritt

When in Doubt, Tell the Truth
And Other Quotations from Mark Twain
by Brian Collins

Hitch Your Wagon to a Star
And Other Quotations from Ralph Waldo Emerson
by Keith Frome

Simplify, Simplify
And Other Quotations from Henry David Thoreau
by K.P Van Anglen

NOT BLOODY LIKELY!

And Other Quotations from
BERNARD SHAW

Bernard F. Dukore

Columbia University Press
New York

Columbia University Press
Publishers Since 1893
New York   Chichester, West Sussex

Quotations from the works of Bernard Shaw © 1997 by the Trustees of the
British Museum, the Governors and Guardians of the National Gallery of
Ireland and Royal Academy of Dramatic Art

Library of Congress Cataloging-in-Publication Data
  Shaw, Bernard,, 1856–1950
  The Columbia book of Bernard Shaw quotations /
edited by Bernard F. Dukore
    p.   cm.
  Includes bibliographical references (p.   ).
  ISBN 0-231-10478-2 (alk. paper)
  1. Shaw, Bernard, 1856–1950—Quotations. 2. Quotations, English—Irish authors.
  3. Literary calendars. I. Dukore, Bernard Frank, 1931—. II. Title.
  PR5361.D84   1997   96-18731
  822'.912—dc20   CIP

∞

Casebound editions of Columbia University Press books are printed on permanent and
durable acid-free paper.

Printed in the United States of America
c 10 9 8 7 6 5 4 3 2 1

Contents

INTRODUCTION

Probably the most quotable and quoted dramatist in the English language after Shakespeare, Bernard Shaw was born in 1856, before the American Civil War began, and died in 1950, after the Korean War began. For some three-quarters of a century, he has been a source of insight and intelligent, witty, and elegantly phrased commentary on numerous subjects. Although his quotations do not literally fall under every letter of the alphabet from A to Z, they cover most of them, including A (America: "A country where every citizen is free to suppress liberty") and Z ("Zola's books, like Voltaire's pamphlets, scandalize thoughtless people; and contain episodes which can have no further or higher effect than to scandalize them. But they are securing the right of way for thinkers who will bring light and fresh air into this sanctuary"). Like the topics of these quotations, their sources are varied, and they include plays, prefaces, letters, interviews, reviews, speeches, and tracts.

Shaw understood that, as Samuel Johnson said in his *Dictionary of the English Language,* "Every quotation contributes to the stability or enlargement of the language." Shaw called literature "the recorded expression of the former consciousness of the race," noting that "in contributing anything new to literature you are adding to that consciousness," which one might also say of quotations. His contributions include neologisms, such as "Bardolatry" (blind or indiscriminate idolatry of Shakespeare) and "Comstockery" (activities of people like Anthony Comstock, secretary and special agent of the New York Society for the Suppression of Vice, who boasted that in thirty years he brought over 3,500 criminals to justice and destroyed 160 tons of obscene literature and pictures).

Shaw is a master wordsmith. His sparkling wit, brilliant style, and ability to create a telling phrase, combined with his originality, distinctive viewpoints about a dazzling variety of subjects, and ability to cut to the heart of the matter, help to explain his quotability. A good quotation is a striking phrase, passage, or exchange that vividly encapsulates an attitude, insight, or idea. Literally, thousands of passages from Shaw's writings and speeches do so. "He who can, does. He who cannot, teaches" and "The conversion of a savage to Christianity is the conversion of Christianity to savagery" are among his commonly quoted phrases. Although many who repeat them may not be aware who their source is, those who cite his retort to movie producer Samuel Goldwyn, who proclaimed himself more interested in art than in money, know it is Shaw: "I'm afraid, Mr. Goldwyn, that we shall not ever be able to do business together. You see, you're an artist, and care only about art, while I'm only a tradesman and care only about money." Notwithstanding the copiousness of Shaw's output, this volume contains one previously unpublished quotation: "Charity feeds misery: that is why I object to it."

American politicians and social reformers have used Shaw's words for effectiveness. When Robert Kennedy sought the Democratic Party's nomination for president, he quoted Shaw: "You see things; and you say 'Why?' But I dream things that never were; and I say 'Why not?'" In the 1960s, members of the radical Free Speech Movement at the University of California, Berkeley turned one of Shaw's maxims, "Every man over forty is a scoundrel," to "Don't trust anyone over thirty." Today, with tax cuts, tax giveaways, and political elections so much in the news, politicians or journalists might discover quotations in this book that they can put to good or bad use. "A government which robs Peter to pay Paul can always depend on the support of Paul." "Mankind, being for the most part incapable of politics, accepts vituperation as an easy and congenial substitute." "Democracy in America has led to the withdrawal of ordinary refined persons from politics; and the same result is coming in England as fast [as] we make Democracy as democratic as it is in America." "We go to the polling station mostly to vote against something instead of for something." "Ninety-nine hundredths of it [government] is unknown to the people, and the remaining hundredth is resented by them as an invasion of their liberty or an increase in their taxation."

Contemporary feminists may find Shaw's words useful. "The domestic career is no more natural to all women than the military career is natural to all men." So may advocates of a traditional role for women: "The really hard position for the moment is that of the domestic woman, whose enormously valuable services, both to society and to her own household are accepted and even exacted as a matter of course, as if they were the least she could do in return for the privilege of being fed and clothed and housed and protected." Yet Shaw can be off-putting as well, since, unblinded by ideology, he avoids idolatry and victimology: "It's usually pointed out that women are not fit for political power, and ought not to be trusted with a vote because they are politically ignorant, socially prejudiced, narrow-minded, and selfish. True enough, but precisely the same is true of men!" He also avoids the pitfall of undiscriminating contemporaneity: "A great deal of the Bible is much more alive than this morning's paper and last night's parliamentary debate."

Shaw's words befit numerous aspects of the world that approaches the millennium. "I am a Millionaire. That is my religion." "It is really an atrocious institution, this Christmas. We must be gluttonous because it is Christmas. We must be drunken because it is Christmas. . . . We must buy things that nobody wants, and give them to people we don't like . . . all because it is Christmas—that is, because the mass of the population, including the all-powerful middle-class tradesman, depends on a week of license and brigandage, waste and intemperance, to clear off its outstanding liabilities by the end of the year." "If you make a single exception to the rule of toleration, you give away your own bigotry." "Democracy substitutes election by the incompetent many for appointment by the corrupt few." "A conquered nation is like a man with cancer: he can think of nothing else." "A political scheme that cannot be carried out except by soldiers will not be a permanent one." "If there was twenty ways of telling the truth and only one way of telling a lie, the Government would find it out. It's in the nature of governments to tell lies." "The colossal proportions [of the movie business] make mediocrity compulsory." "The old differences in speech and dress and manners are much less than they were, partly because the working class is picking up middle class manners, but much more because they are forcing their own manners and speech on the middle class as standards." "Nobody who can see an adequate performance for nothing in comfort at home with his family will dress up, leave his fireside, and pay guineas for theatre stalls and taxis."

Some of Shaw's quotations parody or put familiar quotations to his own use. He goes beyond *Deuteronomy*, 8:3, which he quotes: "Although 'man doth not live by bread alone,' yet until he lives by bread he cannot live by anything else." Playing upon Adam Smith's description of the English as "a nation of shopkeepers," Shaw describes them differently: "We are a nation of governesses." Reversing *Matthew*, 9:13, he declares, "I come not to call sinners, but the righteous, to repentance."

He expresses insights as aphorisms, such as his definition of blasphemy and sedition, "the truth about Church and State," and his description of females in the time of Queen Victoria: "Woman was not dressed in the sense we are familiar with. She was upholstered." One can easily multiply these examples. "Pursue commonplace ideas with all the intensity of which you are capable, and you will reap instant and plentiful applause." "The man of business ... goes on Sunday to the church with the regularity of the village blacksmith, there to renounce and abjure before his God the line of conduct which he intends to pursue with all his might during the following week." "A barrister in England gets an immense reputation as a criminals' advocate when a dozen of his clients have been hanged (the hanging being at once a proof and advertisement of the importance of the cases)." "The fairness of criticism is one thing, its adequacy quite another." "Martyrdom ... is the only way in which a man can become famous without ability." "There is nothing more dangerous than the conscience of a bigot."

Some of Shaw's aphorisms employ metaphor and simile. "He who desires a lifetime of happiness with a beautiful woman desires to enjoy the taste of wine by keeping his mouth always full of it." "First Love is only a little foolishness and a lot of curiosity." "Every dream is a prophecy: every jest is an earnest in the womb of time." "Trade Unionism is not Socialism: it is the Capitalism of the Proletariat." "The nation's morals are like its teeth: the more decayed they are the more it hurts to touch them." In at least one instance, Shaw produces a double whammy: "Contemporary journalism, like democracy, is always a better judge of second-rate than of first-rate."

He is a master of the telling phrase, *le mot juste*. As he says, "My method is to take the utmost trouble to find the right thing to say, and then to say it with the utmost levity." "Patriotism is, fundamentally, a conviction that a particular country is the best in the world because you were born in it." "The fact is, there are no rules, and there never were any rules, and there never will be any rules of musical composition except rules of thumb; and thumbs vary in length, like ears." "Though you cannot walk through Paris without coming at every corner upon some fountain or trophy or monument for which the only possible remedy is dynamite, you can always count upon the design including a female figure free from the defect known to photographers as underexposure." "The manager may not want good plays; but he does not want bad plays: he wants nice ones. Nice plays, with nice dresses, nice drawing rooms and nice people, are indispensable: to be ungenteel is worse than to fail."

"Paradoxes are the only truths," says Shaw, who is a master of paradox. "I claim to be a conscientiously immoral writer." "No question is so difficult to answer as that to which the answer is obvious." "How conventional all you unconventional people are!" "Whenever you wish to do anything against the law, Cicely, always consult a good solicitor first." "To make Democracy work, you need an aristocratic democracy. To make Aristocracy work, you need a democratic aristocracy." "The social rule must be 'Live; and let live,' and people who break this rule persistently must be liquidated."

As the last quotation suggests, and as those familiar with Shaw know, he achieves many effects through anticlimax. "Offenbach's music is wicked. It is abandoned stuff: every accent in it is a snap of the fingers in the face of moral responsibility: every ripple and sparkle on its surface twits me for my teetotalism, and mocks at the early rising of which I fully intend to make a habit some day." "There is not a man living who is not in favor of equality of opportunity, justice, and everything that is proper and sublime, consistently, of course, with an independent income for himself." "There is nothing so insufferable as happiness, except perhaps unhappiness."

Often, Shaw's style befits his subject. Indignantly, he demonstrates what one should not be and what one should be indignant about: "The ballet indecent! Why, it is the most formal, the most punctilious, ceremonious, professor-ridden, pig-headed solemnity that exists." Authoritatively, he insists, "Always contradict an authoritative statement." With his first adverb, he makes his manner suit his matter: "It is always necessary to overstate a case startlingly to make people sit up and listen to it, and to frighten them into acting on it."

His style is elegant, employing antithesis, repetition of key words and phrases, and parallel or neatly balanced language. "Faith in reason as a prime motor is no longer the criterion of the sound mind, any more than faith in the Bible is the criterion of righteous intention." "The weather was warm enough to make anybody play wrong notes—almost warm enough to make me play right ones." "Most men begin to go to the theatre when they arrive at the stage of having a latchkey and pocket money, but no family; and they leave off when they arrive at the stage of a family and (consequently) no pocket money." "As long as you can say that you believe in the sincerity of friendship, you don't believe in friendship, but in sincerity." "The fickleness of the women I love is only equaled by the infernal constancy of the women who love me." "Marriage is popular because it combines the maximum of temptation with the maximum of opportunity." This verbal elegance is especially notable in his dialogue, for instance: "I wouldn't have your conscience, not for all your income." "I wouldn't have your income, not for all your conscience."

"My mission is not to deal with obvious horrors, but to open the eyes of normal respectable men to evils which are escaping their consideration," writes Shaw, who also states: "I am myself what is called an original thinker, my business being to question and test all the established creeds and codes to see how far they are still valid and how far worn out or superseded, and even to draft new creeds and codes." Indeed, he is a genuine original, with strikingly novel perceptions or ways of phrasing his insights. "The French Revolution overthrew one set of rulers and substituted another with different interests and different views. That is what a general election enables the people to do in England every seven years if they choose. Revolution is therefore a national institution in England." "It is a very significant thing, this instinctive choice of the military form of organization, this substitution of the drum for the organ, by the Salvation Army. Does it not suggest that the Salvationists divine that they must actually fight the devil, instead of merely praying at him? At present, it is true, they have not quite ascertained his correct address." "He [Browning] is read by men who regard the reading of most other poetry as a waste of time; and his verse has been declared no verse at all by persons with a turn for 'The Rose is red: the violet, blue' manner of lyric." "Would you insist on cages being put round the Trafalgar Square lions? If not, why do you not apply the same argument to the fig leaf of Hermes?" According to Shaw, who was a vegetarian, "My will contains directions for my funeral, which will be followed not by mourning coaches, but by herds of oxen, sheep, swine, flocks of poultry, and a small travelling aquarium of live fish, all wearing white scarves in honor to the man who perished rather than eat his fellow creatures."

Some of his perceptions involve reversals of conventional values, as in this exchange: "Does anybody want me to flatter and be untruthful?" "Well, since you ask me, I do. Surely it's the very first qualification for tolerable social intercourse." They are not confined to dialogue. "A man of great common sense and good taste, meaning thereby a man without originality or moral courage."

As the reader surely has gathered by this time, Shaw's perceptions can be funny. "The blank verse flowed in at one ear and out at the other without producing any sort of activity between the two." "Elect a world president by universal suffrage, and who would have a chance against Mr. Charles Chaplin?" "When you prevent me from doing anything I want to do, that is persecution; but when I prevent you from doing anything you want to do, that is law, order, and morals." "My method of examining any proposition is to take its two extremes, both of them impracticable; make a scale between them; and try to determine at what point on the scale it can best be put in practice. A mother who has to determine the temperature of her baby's bath has two fixed limits to work between. The baby must not be boiled and must not be frozen."

His comedy includes puns. "I thought it [a popular novel] puerile to the uttermost publishable extreme of jejuniority." "I have 'risen' by sheer gravitation." "A vegetarian is not a person who lives on vegetables, any more than a Catholic is a person who lives on cats."

A writer of comedy, Shaw has views about comedy that complement rather than contradict each other. "The function of comedy . . . is nothing less than the destruction of old-established morals." Humor is "Anything that makes you laugh. But the finest sort draws a tear along with the laugh." "When a thing is funny, search it for a hidden truth." "The truth is sometimes the funniest joke in the world until it is thoroughly found out." He admires revolutionary humor: "The salvation of the world depends on the men who will not take evil good-humoredly, and whose laughter destroys the fool instead of encouraging him."

Despite his imprecation, "I lay my eternal curse on whomseover shall make me hated as Shakespeare is hated. My plays were not designed as instruments of torture," his plays are on the curriculum of many American colleges and universities, and of high schools as well. His insights, his polished prose, and his wit, which the following quotations demonstrate, help to explain why.

$\mathcal{A}$CKNOWLEDGMENTS

First and foremost, I am grateful to Barbara Dukore for her perceptive comments on my introduction. I wish to thank Sidney P. Albert for generously providing me with the one previously unpublished quotation in this collection.

For their help in several ways, let me happily express my indebtedness to other generous Shavians, in alphabetical order: Fred D. Crawford, T.F. Evans, Dan H. Laurence, and Stanley Weintraub.

I also wish to acknowledge Virginia Polytechnic Institution and State University for having provided me with the time to prepare this book.

Abortion

In London, people of good social standing seem to have no difficulty whatever in getting rid of undesirable additions surgically on the flimsiest pretexts. I am of course quite aware of the arguments in favor of legalizing the operation; but . . . it is not my subject; and it is not a man's subject anyhow: the women must handle it, as it is they who claim the right, or repudiate it.

Letter to Muriel F. MacSwiney, June 8, 1931, *Collected Letters*, ed. Dan H. Laurence, vol. 4 (1988).

Abstinence

I'm only a beer teetotaller, not a champagne teetotaller. I don't like beer.

Proserpine, in *Candida*, act 3; *The Bodley Head Bernard Shaw: Collected Plays with their Prefaces*, vol. 1 (1970).

First produced in 1897.

Action

Nothing is ever done in this world until men are prepared to kill one another if it is not done.

Andrew Undershaft, in *Major Barbara*, act 3; *The Bodley Head Bernard Shaw: Collected Plays with their Prefaces*, vol. 3 (1971).

First produced in 1905.

Actors and Acting

The Puritan assumption that every woman on the stage is necessarily a coarse and brazen voluptuary is as offensive as the counter assumption that she is necesarily a fireside angel, supporting a deserving family out of her modest earnings, and never going out without a chaperone.

"Children in Theatres," *Shaw's Music*, vol. 1, ed. Dan H. Laurence (1981).

First published in *The Star*, January 24, 1890.

The function of the actor is to make the audience imagine for the moment that real things are happening to real people.

"From the Point of View of the Playwright," *The Drama Observed*, ed. Bernard F. Dukore; Penn State Press (1993).

First published in *Herbert Beerbohm Tree: Some Memories of Him and His Art* (1920).

*A*DULTERY

ELLIE: Why do women always want other women's husbands?
SHOTOVER: Why do horse thieves prefer a horse that is broken-in to one that is wild?

Heartbreak House, act 2; *The Bodley Head Bernard Shaw: Collected Plays with their Prefaces*, vol. 5 (1972).

First published in 1919.

*A*DVANCED, THE

Those who deliberately and conscientiously profess what are oddly called advanced views by those others who believe them to be retrograde, are often, and indeed mostly, the last people in the world to engage in unconventional adventures of any kind.

Overruled, preface, "The Alleviations of Monogamy"; *The Bodley Head Bernard Shaw: Collected Plays with their Prefaces*, vol. 4 (1972).

First published in 1916.

*A*DVICE

Never take anybody's advice.

Letter to R. Golding Bright, December 2, 1894, *Collected Letters*, vol. 1, ed. Dan H. Laurence (1965).

This admonition comes at the end of a long paragraph of advice.

$\mathcal{A}$IR

BROADBENT: I assure you I like the open air.
AUNT JUDY: Ah galong! How can you like what's not natural?

> *John Bull's Other Island*, act 3; *The Bodley Head Bernard Shaw: Collected Plays with their Prefaces*, vol. 2 (1971).
>
> First produced in 1904.

$\mathcal{A}$LCOHOL AND ALCOHOLISM

The ordinary workman requires a certain quantity of beer to keep him amiable and happy. If he does not get it, he sulks, mopes, beats his wife and children, envies his neighbor, and gets into a state in which it is impossible for him to say a civil word to anyone about him. It is a bad thing to be the wife of a drunkard; but it is ten times worse to be the wife of a man who wants drink and cannot get it.

> Letter to Lady Mary Murray, September 1, 1898, *Collected Letters*, vol. 2, ed. Dan H. Laurence (1972).

UNDERSHAFT: Alcohol is a very necessary article. It heals the sick—
BARBARA: It does nothing of the sort.
UNDERSHAFT: Well, it assists the doctor: that is perhaps a less questionable way of putting it. It makes life bearable to millions of people who could not endure their existence if they were quite sober. It enables Parliament to do things at eleven at night that no sane person would do at eleven in the morning.

> *Major Barbara*, act 2; *The Bodley Head Bernard Shaw: Collected Plays with their Prefaces*, vol. 3 (1971).
>
> First produced in 1905.

$\mathcal{A}$LEXANDRINES

Alexandrines are far worse than English blank verse, which is saying a good deal.

> *Three Plays by Brieux*, preface, "The Pedantry of Paris," *The Drama Observed*, ed. Bernard F. Dukore, vol. 3; Penn State Press (1993).
>
> First published in 1911.

*A*MATEURS

That enormous advantage of the amateur—the unlimited rehearsal which is commercially impossible to the professional.

"The Amateur Orchestra," *Shaw's Music*, vol. 2, ed. Dan H. Laurence (1981).

First published in *The World*, April 26, 1893.

*A*MERICA AND AMERICANS

Decidedly the American woman is the woman of the future.

Letter to Mrs. T.P. O'Connor, May 17, 1888, *Collected Letters*, vol. 1, ed. Dan H. Laurence (1965).

Yet another foreign language: that of Amurrica!

"Mr. Daly Fossilizes," *The Drama Observed*, vol. 2, ed. Bernard F. Dukore; Penn State Press (1993).

First published in *Saturday Review*, June 17, 1895.

Any difference which exists between American methods and English ones must necessarily present itself to the American as an inferiority on the part of the English, and to the Englishman as an inferiority on the part of the Americans; for it is obvious that if the two nations were agreed as to the superiority of any particular method, they would both adopt it, and the difference would disappear.

"The Theatres," *The Drama Observed*, vol. 3, ed. Bernard F. Dukore; Penn State Press (1993).

First published in *Saturday Review*, October 16, 1897.

Of course America will influence the drama of the twentieth century. Already it pays an English dramatist better to take the American view of a question than the English one. Given international copyright and a common language, the rest is merely a counting of heads. The nation that pays the piper will call the tune.

"The New Tendencies in Dramatic Art," *The Drama Observed*, vol. 3, ed. Bernard F. Dukore; Penn State Press (1993).

FIrst published in *The World* (New York), December 30, 1900.

People get funny ideas when they go to America.

"Shaw Answers James Bryce," *The Drama Observed*, ed. Bernard F. Dukore, vol. 3; Penn State Press (1993).

First published in *The New York Times*, May 5, 1907.

A country where every citizen is free to suppress liberty.

> *The Sanity of Art*, preface; *Major Critical Essays*; Constable (1948).
>
> First published in 1908.

What keeps America today the purest of the nations is that when she's not working she's too drunk to hear the voice of the tempter.

> Elder Daniels, in *The Shewing-up of Blanco Posnet*; *The Bodley Head Bernard Shaw: Collected Plays with their Prefaces*, vol. 3 (1971).
>
> First produced in 1909.

Democracy in America has led to the withdrawal of ordinary refined persons from politics; and the same result is coming in England as fast [as] we make Democracy as democratic as it is in America.

> *Misalliance*, preface, "The Provocation to Anarchism"; *The Bodley Head Bernard Shaw: Collected Plays with their Prefaces*, vol. 4 (1972).
>
> First published in 1914.

The Atlantic is no longer an ocean, but a bridge.

> "Appeal for the Second U.S. Liberty Loan, 1917," *SHAW: The Annual of Bernard Shaw Studies*, vol. 16, ed. Dan H. Laurence and Margot Peters; Penn State Press (1996).
>
> Untitled, written on October 12, 1917.

What has been happening during my lifetime is the Americanization of the whole world.

> "What About the Middle Class? A Lay Sermon," *Practical Politics*, ed. Lloyd J. Hubenka; U of Nebraska Press (1976).
>
> First published in *Daily Citizen*, October 19, 1912.

America has the morals and the outlook of a seventeenth-century village with a development of capitalism which only a very highly organized Socialism and an ultramodern freedom of thought could control.

> Letter to Frank Harris, January 4, 1918, *Collected Letters*, ed. Dan H. Laurence, Vol. 3 (1985).

He poses as Jefferson Davis to please the Disruptionists. He . . . poses as Lincoln to please the Unionists. . . . Why does he not visit America, and learn the cult of the man who can look his fellow man (or newspaper) in the eye, and tell him to go to hell?

> "The Betrayal of Ulster"; *The Matter with Ireland*; Rupert Hart-Davis (1962), ed. David H. Greene and Dan H. Laurence.
>
> First published in *Irish Statesman*, January 10, 1920; Shaw refers to Prime Minster David Lloyd George.

We cannot silence the American—who can silence an American?

> Confucius, in *Back to Methuselah*, "The Thing Happens"; *The Bodley Head Bernard Shaw: Collected Plays with their Prefaces*, vol. 5 (1972).
> First published in 1921.

I am not an American, but I am the next worst thing—an Irishman.

> "Look, You Boob! A Little Talk on America," *Platform and Pulpit*, ed. Dan H. Laurence; Hill and Wang (1961).
> Shortwave broadcast to the U.S. from London, October 11, 1931.

I used to feel personally complimented by the amazing warm-hearted hospitality showered on me by Americans. But its scope is so boundless that I now perceive that it lies in the nature of the host rather than in the quality of the guest.

> "The Political Madhouse in America and Nearer Home," *The Political Madhouse in America and Nearer Home*; Constable (1933).
> Speech broadcast on NBC from the Metropolitan Opera House, New York, April 11, 1933.

Talk about liberty in America is a well known symptom of an incurable delusion.

> "Shaw Stands Firm on Censor Charge," self-drafted interview, *The New York Times*, September 27, 1936.

$\mathcal{A}$NARCHY

It is easy to say, Abolish the State; but the State will sell you up, lock you up, blow you up, knock you down, bludgeon, shoot, stab, hang—in short, abolish you, if you lift a hand against it.

> *The Impossibilities of Anarchism*, "The Anarchist Spirit," *Essays in Fabian Socialism*; Constable (1949).
> Paper read to the Fabian Society, October 16, 1891.

All men are anarchists with regard to laws which are against their consciences, either in the preamble or in the penalty.

> *Major Barbara*, preface, "Sane Conclusions," *The Bodley Head Bernard Shaw: Collected Plays with their Prefaces*, vol. 3 (1971).
> First published in 1907.

Anarchism is a game at which the police can beat you.

> Lord Summerhays, in *Misalliance*; *The Bodley Head Bernard Shaw: Collected Plays with their Prefaces*, vol. 4 (1972).
> First produced in 1910.

The ordinary man—we have to face it: it is every bit as true of the ordinary Englishman as of the ordinary American—is an Anarchist. He wants to do as he likes. He may want his neighbor to be governed, but he himself doesn't want to be governed.

The Political Madhouse in America and Nearer Home; Constable (1933).

Speech broadcast on NBC from the Metropolitan Opera House, New York, April 11, 1933.

*A*NIMALS

When I was a child and was told that our dog and our parrot, with whom I was on intimate terms, were not creatures like myself, but were brutal whilst I was reasonable, I not only did not believe it, but quite consciously and intellectually formed the opinion that the distinction was false.

Back to Methuselah, preface, "How One Touch of Darwin Makes the Whole World Kin"; Constable (1949).

First published in the 1921 Standard Edition but omitted by Shaw when he revised the work for the Oxford World's Classics edition [Oxford University Press], printed in 1945, published in 1946; not in *The Bodley Head Bernard Shaw: Collected Plays with their Prefaces*, vol. 5 or in *Complete Prefaces*, vol. 2

*A*NTI-SEMITISM

Take the case of the anti-Dreyfus people. What is it they do? Why, pick out all the general vices of humanity—all its greed and ambition and sensuality—and denounce the Jews for them, as if Christians were any less greedy, ambitious and sensual.

Letter to A.J. Marriott, May 1, 1899, *Collected Letters*, vol. 2, ed. Dan H. Laurence (1972).

*A*RGUMENT

The way to get at the merits of a case is not to listen to the fool who imagines himself impartial, but to get it argued with reckless bias for and against. To understand a saint, you must hear the devil's advocate.

The Sanity of Art, preface; *Major Critical Essays*, Constable (1948).

First published in 1908.

ARISTOCRACY

We are the only real aristocracy in the world: the aristocracy of money.

Epifania, in *The Millionairess*, act 2; *The Bodley Head Bernard Shaw: Collected Plays with their Prefaces*, vol. 6 (1973).

First produced (in German) in 1936.

ARMS RACE, THE

It is utter nonsense to say that if you keep guns they will go off: people can wear boots without kicking their wives.

Letter to Austin Harrison, November 24, 1914, *Collected Letters*, ed. Dan H. Laurence, vol. 3 (1985).

ART AND ARTISTS

Avoid the worship of Art as you would avoid opium.

Quoted in Dan H. Laurence, "Katie Samuel: Shaw's Flameless 'Old Flame,'" *SHAW*, vol. 15 (1995).

Letter to Katie Samuel, June 4, 1884.

An artist's powers are partly native, partly acquired. Some people can do easily at the first challenge what costs other long training and teaching. But it is probable that, though the degree of skill that men and women are born with varies a good deal, the utmost additional skill that they can acquire by study is a constant quality.

"Singing, Past and Present," *Shaw's Music* (1981), vol. 1, ed. Dan H. Laurence.

First published in *Dramatic Review*, August 1, 1885.

If he [the artist] attempts the highest art, which . . . is necessarily the most significant with regard to humanity, he had better either inherit a property first, or else make haste to become popular whilst he is young and does not know enough to be dangerous.

"Art and Society," *Bernard Shaw on the London Art Scene 1885-1950*, ed. Stanley Weintraub; Penn State Press (1989).

Lecture to the Bedford Debating Society, December 10, 1885.

In discussing Socialism, societies of ladies and gentlemen usually emancipate themselves from the sway of reason and humanity, and debate briskly, if not wisely. In discussing Art, they are equally untrammeled; but they unfortunately assume an attitude of supersititious approval towards Art, which they suppose to be a good thing just as they suppose Socialism to be a bad thing. The result is that a discussion on Art has all the insane irrelevance of a debate on Socialism, without the hostilities and personalities which make the later stimulating, if not edifying.

"Art and Society," *Bernard Shaw on the London Art Scene 1885-1950*, ed. Stanley Weintraub; Penn State Press (1989).

Lecture to the Bedford Debating Society, December 10, 1885.

The word Art cannot be defined, because the majority of the people who use it do not understand the matters to which they apply it, sufficiently to determine its function with even moderate exactness.

"Art and Society," *Bernard Shaw on the London Art Scene 1885-1950*, ed. Stanley Weintraub; Penn State Press (1989).

Lecture to the Bedford Debating Society, December 10, 1885.

Mere protest against inferior work never educates the public. The only way to make them intolerant of bad work is to show them better.

"The Opera Season," *Shaw's Music*, vol. 1 ed. Dan H. Laurence (1981).

First published in *Scottish Art Review*, September 1889.

The law of traditional performances is "Do what was done last time": the law of all living and fruitful performance is "Obey the innermost impulse which the music gives, and obey it to the most exhaustive satisfaction." And as that impulse is never, in a fertile artistic nature, the impulse to do what was done last time, the two laws are incompatible, being laws respectively of death and life in art.

"Wagner in Bayreuth," *Shaw's Music*, vol. 1, ed. Dan H. Laurence (1981).

First published in *English Illustrated Magazine*, October 1889.

The artist must be at once his own master and everybody's pupil. If he cannot learn from all that he sees and hears, and then teach himself the practical application of what he has learnt, art is not his affair, and he had better remain an amateur.

"Two Anonymous Communications," *Shaw's Music*, vol. 1, ed. Dan H. Laurence (1981).

First published in *The Star*, November 22, 1889.

There is no more to prevent you or me from turning out a string of bars in the form of a sonata than to prevent us from turning out a string of lines in the form of a sonnet or a tragedy in five acts and in blank verse. It is not the form that baulks us of a Shakespearean immortality, but the inordinate quantity of first-class stuffing that is required to make these forms, long, severe, and tedious as they are in themselves, interesting, or even endurable, to any but the performers or the author.

"Stuffing a Sonata," *Shaw's Music*, vol. 2, ed. Dan H. Laurence (1981).

First published in *The Star*, March 21, 1890.

Art wants a freeing from commercial considerations. . . . There is no theoretical reason why a Government which provides a National Gallery should not also give us a State theatre.

"Concerning State-Aided Amusements," *The Drama Observed*, vol. 1, ed. Bernard F. Dukore; Penn State Press (1993).

Interview by or revised by Shaw, first published in *Sunday Times*, December 9, 1894.

A work of art is no more above the law than anything else. An old bridge may be a beautiful work of medieval art; but if it obstructs navigation, causes the river to silt up, or becomes insufficient for the traffic, it must come down.

"The Living Pictures," *The Drama Observed*, vol. 1, ed. Bernard F. Dukore; Penn State Press (1993).

First published in *Saturday Review*, April 6, 1895.

The artist's rule must be Cromwell's: "Not what they want, but what is good for them."

"Two Bad Plays," *The Drama Observed*, vol. 1, ed. Bernard F. Dukore; Penn State Press (1993).

First published in *Saturday Review*, April 20, 1895.

In art, as in politics, there is no such thing as gratitude.

"Mr John Hare," *The Drama Observed*, vol. 2, ed. Bernard F. Dukore; Penn State Press (1993).

First published in *Saturday Review*, December 21, 1895.

When I see that the nineteenth century has crowned the idolatry of Art with the deification of Love, so that every poet is supposed to have pierced to the holy of holies when he has announced that Love is the Supreme, or the Enough, or the All, I feel that Art was safer in the hands of the most fanatical of Cromwell's major generals than it will be if ever it gets into mine.

Three Plays for Puritans, preface; *The Bodley Head Bernard Shaw: Collected Plays with their Prefaces*, vol. 2 (1971).

First published in 1901.

The artist's work is to show us ourselves as we really are.

John Tanner, in *Man and Superman*, act 1, *The Bodley Head Bernard Shaw: Collected Plays with their Prefaces*, vol. 2 (1971).

First published in 1903.

The true artist will let his wife starve, his children go barefoot, his mother drudge for his living at seventy, sooner than work at anything but his art.

John Tanner, in *Man and Superman*, act 1; *The Bodley Head Bernard Shaw: Collected Plays with their Prefaces*, vol. 2 (1971).

First published in 1903.

No man's intellect and character can hold out against a prolonged and exclusive preoccupation with the fine arts. A man might as well expect to be healthy on a diet of confectionery and liqueurs.

"G.B.S. and the Trust," *The Drama Observed*, ed. Bernard F. Dukore, vol. 3; Penn State Press (1993).

Letter to the *Daily News*, July 28, 1905.

I believe in Michael Angelo, Velasquez, and Rembrandt; in the might of design, the mystery of color, the redemption of all things by Beauty everlasting, and the message of Art that has made these hands blessed.

Louis Dubedat, in *The Doctor's Dilemma*, act 4; *The Bodley Head Bernard Shaw: Collected Plays with their Prefaces*, vol. 3 (1971).

First produced 1906.

The artist is a man who forms the human mind.

"Socialism and the Artistic Professions," *Practical Politics*, ed. Lloyd J. Hubenka; University of Nebraska Press (1976).

Lecture for the Fabian Society, November 23, 1906, first published in the *New York Evening Post*, December 24, 1906.

If your parents approve of your embracing an artistic career, take my advice and get some new parents as soon as you can.

"Art and Public Money," *The Drama Observed*, ed. Bernard F. Dukore, vol. 3; Penn State Press (1993).

Speech at Brighton, March 6, 1907.

There has been no period in the history of the world in which a great school of art has been first produced in for the purpose of pleasure. Art has always grown up as the expression of a great religious movement.

"Art and Public Money," *The Drama Observed*, ed. Bernard F. Dukore, vol. 3; Penn State Press (1993).

Speech at Brighton, March 6, 1907.

I say, not in the spirit of vulgar abuse, but in the solemnest Scriptural use of the terms, that the man who believes in art for art's sake is a fool; that is to say, a man in a state of damnation. It is possible for a man to be a fool, and yet to be an accurate observer, even to be an artist of considerable power.

"Literature and Art," *Platform and Pulpit*, ed. Dan H. Laurence; Hill and Wang (1961).

Lecture from the pulpit of the City Temple, London, October 8, 1908.

I say that all art at the fountainhead is didactic, and that nothing can produce art except the necessity of being didactic.

"Literature and Art," *Platform and Pulpit*, ed. Dan H. Laurence; Hill and Wang (1961).

Lecture from the pulpit of the City Temple, London, October 8, 1908.

Fine art is the only teacher except torture.

Misalliance, preface, "Art Teaching"; *The Bodley Head Bernard Shaw: Collected Plays with their Prefaces*, vol. 4 (1972).

First published in 1914.

In Beethoven's day the business of art was held to be "the sublime and beautiful." In our day it has fallen to be the imitative and voluptuous.

Back to Methuselah, preface, "The Artist-Prophets"; *The Bodley Head Bernard Shaw: Collected Plays with their Prefaces*, vol. 5 (1972).

Frst published in 1921.

The artist divines by inspiration all the truths that the so-called scientist grubs up in his laboratory slowly and stupidly long afterwards.

Ecrasia, in *Back to Methuselah*, "As Far as Thought Can Reach"; *The Bodley Head Bernard Shaw: Collected Plays with their Prefaces*, vol. 5 (1972).

First published in 1921.

I'm afraid, Mr. Goldwyn, that we shall not ever be able to do business together. You see, you're an artist, and care only about art, while I'm only a tradesman and care only about money.

"Shaw in Film Debut Derides Movies," *New York American*, October 9, 1926.

$\mathcal{A}$SCETICISM

Everybody who does not live in a prostitute's bed and on a diet of cocaine snow is called an ascetic nowadays.

Quoted in Frank Harris, *Bernard Shaw*, ch. 17; Garden City Publishing Co.(1931).

${\cal A}$THEISM

As the freethinking will gradually grows and supplants the superstitious will, there is a period in which the conflict of the two produces a very painful struggle in the man, the forces being sometimes so evenly balanced that the slightest circumstance will turn the scale, the same man being a sceptic at 2 o'clock on a fine afternoon and a remorseful Christian at 2 in the morning with a thunderstorm raging.

Letter to E.C. Chapman, July 29, 1891, *Collected Letters*, ed. Dan H. Laurence, vol. 1 (1965).

To the pious man the newly made freethinker, suddenly renouncing supernatural revelation, and denying all obligation to believe the Bible and obey the commandments as such, appears to be claiming the right to rob and murder at large.

The Quintessence of Ibsenism, "The Two Pioneers," *The Drama Observed*, vol. 1, ed. Bernard F. Dukore; Penn State Press (1993).

First published in 1891.

The disciples of Voltaire and Tom Paine do not pick pockets or cut throats oftener than your even Christian.

The Quintessence of Ibsenism, "The Two Pioneers," *The Drama Observed*, vol. 1, ed. Bernard F. Dukore; Penn State Press (1993).

First published in 1891.

Secularism is not a philosophy of life: it is only an attempt to leave life out of the question because no rationalistic, materialistic explanation of it has been found.

Letter to Cliff Keane, April 2, 1904; *Collected Letters*, ed. Dan H. Laurence, vol. 2 (1972).

Have I not told you that he is an atheist, and, like all atheists, an inflexible moralist?

Aubrey, in *Too True to be Good*, act 2; *The Bodley Head Bernard Shaw: Collected Plays with their Prefaces*, vol. 6 (1973).

First produced in 1932.

${\cal A}$TOMIC BOMB

As long as atomic bomb manufacture remains a trade secret known to only one State, it will be the mainstay of Peace because all the States (including this one) will be afraid of it. When the secret is out atomic warfare will be barred as poison gas was in 1938-45; and war will be possible as before.

Farfetched Fables, preface; *The Bodley Head Bernard Shaw: Collected Plays with their Prefaces*, vol. 7 (1974).
First published in 1951, written in 1949.

*A*UDIENCES

Most men begin to go to the theatre when they arrive at the stage of having a latchkey and pocket money, but no family; and they leave off when they arrive at the stage of a family and (consequently) no pocket money.

"*Madame Angot* Returns," *Shaw's Music*, vol. 2, ed. Dan H. Laurence (1981).
First published in *The World*, July 27, 1893.

*A*UTHORITY

If you demand my authorities for this and that, I must reply that only those who have never hunted up the authorities as I have believe that there is any authority who is not contradicted flatly by some other authority.

"Androcles and the Lion," *Complete Prefaces*, ed. Dan H. Laurence and Daniel J. Leary, vol. 2 (1995).
Program of *Androcles and the Lion*, St. James's Theatre, London, September 1, 1913.

Always contradict an authoritative statement.

Misalliance, preface, "The Abuse of Docility"; *The Bodley Head Bernard Shaw: Collected Plays with their Prefaces* , vol. 4 (1972).
First published in 1914.

There must be some ground for attaching authority to an order. A child will obey its parents, a soldier his officer, a philosopher a railway porter, and a workman a foreman, all without question, because it is generally accepted that those who give the orders understand what they are about, and are duly authorized and even obliged to give them, and because, in the practical emergencies of daily life, there is no time for lessons and explanations, or for arguments as to their validity.

Saint Joan, preface, "The Conflict Between Genius and Discipline"; *The Bodley Head Bernard Shaw: Collected Plays with their Prefaces*, vol. 6 (1973).
First published in 1924.

When a railway porter directs me to number ten platform I do not strike him to earth with a shout of "Down with tyranny!" and rush violently to number one platform. I accept his direction because I want to be directed, and want to get into the right train.

The Intelligent Woman's Guide to Socialism, Capitalism, Sovietism, and Fascism, ch. 70; Constable (1949).
First published in 1928 as *The Intelligent Woman's Guide to Socialism and Capitalism*.

$\mathcal{A}$UTOBIOGRAPHY

All autobiographies are lies. I do not mean unconscious, unintentional lies: I mean deliberate lies.

Sixteen Self Sketches, "In the Days of My Youth"; Constable (1949).
First published in *M.A.P.* (Mainly About People), September 17, 1898.

$\mathcal{B}$ACHELORS

PATIOMKIN: Have you a college education, darling? *I* have.
EDSTASTON: Certainly. I am a Bachelor of Arts.
PATIOMKIN: It is enough that you are a bachelor, darling: Catherine will supply the arts.

Great Catherine, scene 1; *The Bodley Head Bernard Shaw: Collected Plays with their Prefaces*, vol. 4 (1972).
First produced in November 1918; Catherine is Queen Catherine the Great of Russia.

$\mathcal{B}$ALLET

An ordinary ballet is no more a true dance than an ordinary Church of England service is a true act of worship.

"A Defence of Ballet," *Shaw's Music*, vol. 1, ed. Dan H. Laurence (1981).
First published in *The Star*, October 4, 1889.

The ballet indecent! Why, it is the most formal, the most punctilious, ceremonious, professor-ridden, pig-headed solemnity that exists.

"A Defence of Ballet," *Shaw's Music*, vol. 1, ed. Dan H. Laurence (1981).

First published in *The Star*, October 4, 1889.

ℬANJOS

I found Mr. Shortis playing the banjo with a delicacy and conscientiousness that ought to have been devoted to some musical instrument.

"Impervious to Counterpoint," *Shaw's Music*, vol. 2, ed. Dan H. Laurence (1981).

First published in *The World*, July 5, 1893.

ℬEHAVIOR

LADY BRITOMART: He [Undershaft] never does a proper thing without giving an improper reason for it.
CUSINS: He convinced me that I have all my life been doing improper things for proper reasons.

Major Barbara, act 3; *The Bodley Head Bernard Shaw: Collected Plays with their Prefaces*, vol. 3 (1971).

First produced in 1905.

The difference between a lady and a flower girl is not how she behaves, but how she's treated.

Eliza Doolittle, in *Pygmalion*, act 5; *The Bodley Head Bernard Shaw: Collected Plays with their Prefaces*, ed. Dan H. Laurence, vol. 4 (1972).

First produced (in German) in 1913.

ℬELIEF

What a man believes may be ascertained, not from his creed, but from the assumptions on which he habitually acts.

Man and Superman, The Revolutionist's Handbook, "Maxims for Revolutionists"; *The Bodley Head Bernard Shaw: Collected Plays with their Prefaces*, vol. 2 (1971).

First published in 1903.

If you cannot have what you believe in you must believe in what you have.

> *The Doctor's Dilemma*, preface, "Doctors' Consciences"; *The Bodley Head Bernard Shaw: Collected Plays with their Prefaces*, vol. 3 (1971).
>
> First published in 1911.

I cannot tell why people who will not believe in baptism on any terms believe in vaccination with the cruel fanaticism of inquisitors.

> *Androcles and the Lion*, preface, "Credibility of the Gospels"; *The Bodley Head Bernard Shaw: Collected Plays with their Prefaces*, vol. 4 (1972).
>
> First published in 1916.

Are we any the less obsessed with a belief when we are denying it than when we were affirming it?

> Aubrey, in *Too True to be Good*, act 3; *The Bodley Head Bernard Shaw: Collected Plays with their Prefaces*, vol. 6 (1973).
>
> First produced in 1932.

*B*ETRAYAL

CLEOPATRA: I have not betrayed you, Caesar: I swear it.
CAESAR: I know that. I have not trusted you.

> *Caesar and Cleopatra*, act 4; *The Bodley Head Bernard Shaw: Collected Plays with their Prefaces*, vol. 2 (1971).
>
> First published in 1901.

*B*IBLE, THE

I . . . once read the Old Testament and the four Gospels straight through, from a vainglorious desire to do what nobody else had done.

> "*Olivia*," *The Drama Observed*, vol. 2, ed. Bernard F. Dukore; Penn State Press (1993).
>
> First published in *Saturday Review*, February 6, 1897.

Like all highly developed literatures, the Bible contains a great deal of sensational fiction, imagined with intense vividness, appealing to the most susceptible passions, and narrated with a force which the ordinary man is not able to resist.

> "The Board School," *The Drama Observed*, vol. 3, ed. Bernard F. Dukore; Penn State Press (1993).
>
> First published in *Saturday Review*, November 27, 1897.

The trouble taken to impress me with the duty of reading it (with the natural result of filling me with a conviction that such an occupation must be almost as disagreeable as going to church).

"*Olivia*," *The Drama Observed*, vol. 2, ed. Bernard F. Dukore; Penn State Press (1993).

First published in *Saturday Review*, February 6, 1897.

The difference, so far, between the Pentateuch and the scriptures of the scientific materialism of the sixties, is the difference between shrewd nonsense and DAMNED nonsense.

Letter to H.G. Wells, 12 December 1901, *Selected Correspondence of Bernard Shaw: Bernard Shaw and H.G. Wells*, ed. J. Percy Smith; University of Toronto Press (1995).

You cannot read the Bible if you have no sense of literary art. The reason why the continental European is, to the Englishman or American, so surprisingly ignorant of the Bible, is that the authorized English version is a great work of literary art, and the continental versions are comparatively artless.

Misalliance, preface, "Art Teaching"; *The Bodley Head Bernard Shaw: Collected Plays with their Prefaces*, vol. 4 (1972).

First published in 1914.

At worst the Bible gives a child a better start in life than the gutter.

"The Black Girl in Search of God," preface, *The Black Girl in Search of God and Some Lesser Tales*; Constable (1948).

First published in 1932.

A great deal of the Bible is much more alive than this morning's paper and last night's parliamentary debate.

"The Black Girl in Search of God," preface, *The Black Girl in Search of God and Some Lesser Tales*; Constable (1948).

First published in 1932.

*B*IRTH

It is long and hard and painful to create life: it is short and easy to steal the life others have made.

Eve, in *Back to Methuselah*, "In the Beginning," act 2; *The Bodley Head Bernard Shaw: Collected Plays with their Prefaces*, vol. 5 (1972).

First published in 1921.

It was Lilith who did wrong when she shared the labor of creation so unequally between man and wife. If you, Cain, had had the trouble of making Abel, or had had to make another man to replace him when he was gone, you would not have killed him; you would have risked your life to save his. . . . That is why there is enmity between Woman the creator and Man the destroyer.

Eve, in *Back to Methuselah*, "In the Beginning," act 2; *The Bodley Head Bernard Shaw: Collected Plays with their Prefaces*, vol. 5 (1972).

First published in 1921.

*B*LANK VERSE

Our feeling that blank verse is artificial and flat is based on blank verse that *is* artificial and flat, or that is unskillfully uttered as to appear so.

Letter to William Archer, April 16, 1886, *Collected Letters*, vol. 1, ed. Dan H. Laurence (1965) .

The blank verse flowed in at one ear and out at the other without producing any sort of activity between the two.

"Two Easter Pieces," *The Drama Observed*, vol. 2, ed. Bernard F. Dukore; Penn State Press (1993).

First published in *Saturday Review*, April 18, 1896.

*B*LASPHEMY

All great truths begin as blasphemies.

Annajanska, in *Annajanska, The Bolshevik Empress*; *The Bodley Head Bernard Shaw: Collected Plays with their Prefaces*, vol. 5 (1972).

First produced in 1918.

Blasphemy and sedition (meaning the truth about Church and State).

Back to Methuselah, Preface, "Homeopathic Education"; *The Bodley Head Bernard Shaw: Collected Plays with their Prefaces*, vol. 5 (1972).

First published in 1921.

Boasting

I leave the delicacies of retirement to those who are gentlemen first and literary workmen afterwards. The cart and trumpet for me.

Three Plays for Puritans, preface; *The Bodley Head Bernard Shaw: Collected Plays with their Prefaces*, vol. 2 (1971).

First published in 1901.

Books

A book is like a child: it is easier to bring it into the world than to control it when it is launched there.

Cashel Byron's Profession, preface; Constable (1950).

Preface written in 1901.

THEODOTUS: Caesar: once in ten generations of men, the world gains an immortal book.

CAESAR: If it did not flatter mankind, the common executioner would burn it.

Caesar and Cleopatra, act 2; *The Bodley Head Bernard Shaw: Collected Plays with their Prefaces*, vol. 2 (1971) .

First published in 1901.

The lesson intended by an author is hardly ever the lesson the world chooses to learn from his book.

Man and Superman, Epistle Dedicatory; *The Bodley Head Bernard Shaw: Collected Plays with their Prefaces*, vol. 2 (1971).

First published in 1903.

Boredom

People get tired of everything, and of nothing sooner than of what they most like.

"Ibsen Ahead!" *The Drama Observed*, vol. 2, ed. Bernard F. Dukore; Penn State Press (1993).

First published in *Saturday Review*, November 7, 1896.

*B*ORROWING *AND* LENDING

It is perfectly easy to be poor so long as you don't borrow money. You can never borrow enough to pay you for the friends you lose by the transaction.

"George Bernard Shaw," *Shaw: Interviews and Recollections*, ed. A.M. Gibbs (1990).

Questionnaire-Interview by Clarence Rook, first published in *Chap Book*, November 1, 1896.

*B*REEDING

The test of a man's or woman's breeding is how they behave in a quarrel. Anybody can behave well when things are going smoothly.

Craven, in *The Philanderer*, act 3; *The Bodley Head Bernard Shaw: Collected Plays with their Prefaces*, vol. 1 (1970).

First published in 1898.

*B*ROWNING, ROBERT

He is read by men who regard the reading of most other poetry as a waste of time; and his verse has been declared no verse at all by persons with a turn for "The rose is red: the violet, blue" manner of lyric.

"Richter Waxes Stout," *Shaw's Music*, vol. 1, (1981), ed. Dan H. Laurence.

First published in *Dramatic Review*, October 31, 1885.

*B*USINESS *AND* COMMERCE

If life is crowned by its success and devotion in industrial organization and ingenuity, we had better worship the ant and the bee.

Caesar and Cleopatra, "Notes"; *The Bodley Head Bernard Shaw: Collected Plays with their Prefaces*, vol. 2 (1971).

First published in 1901.

The public need is greatest where the purchasing power is least: the commercial incentive is strongest where purchasing power is heaped up in ridiculous superfluity. . . . Even if we grant that the desire to make money is a stronger incentive than public spirit and public need, we must admit that it is strongest at the wrong end, and dwindles to nothing at the right end, whereas public spirit and public need are strongest at the right end and are not wanted at the other except for repressive purposes.

The Common Sense of Municipal Trading, ch. 6, Essays in Fabian Socialism; Constable (1949). First published in 1904.

CANDOR

Please do not revile me for telling you what I felt instead of what I ought to have felt.

Preface to Killing for Sport, ed. Henry S. Salt; Complete Prefaces, ed. Dan H. Laurence and Daniel J. Leary, vol. 2 (1995). First published in 1914.

CAPITALISM

If there is a burglar present I beg him to believe that I cast no reflection upon his profession. I am not unmindful of his great skill and enterprise . . . nor do I overlook his value to the community as an employer on a large scale in view of the criminal lawyers, policemen, turnkeys, gaol-builders. . . . I hope any shareholders and landlords who may be present will accept my assurance that I have no more desire to hurt their feelings . . . I merely wish to point out that all three inflict on the community an injury of precisely the same nature.

Quoted in Hesketh Pearson, Bernard Shaw: His Life and Personality, ch. 10 (1942). Speech before the Industrial Remuneration Conference, January 1885.

Production and the development of the social instincts are alike hindered by each man's consciousness that the more he stings the community the more he benefits himself, the justification, of course, being that when every man has benefited himself at the expense of the community, the community will benefit by every man in it being benefited.

"The Economic Basis of Socialism," Essays in Fabian Socialism; Constable (1949). First published in December 1889.

I am also a Capitalist, by the way; you will not find many Socialists who are not.

"Socialist Politics," *Practical Politics*, ed. Lloyd J. Hubenka; U of Nebraska Press (1976).
Lecture delivered before the Liverpool Fabian Society, October 28, 1908.

A poor person cannot become a capitalist. . . . Imagine a woman, without enough money to feed her children properly and clothe them decently and healthily, letting them starve still more, and go still more ragged and naked, to buy Savings Certificates, or to put her money in the Post Office Savings Bank and keep it there until there is enough of it to buy stocks and shares!

The Intelligent Woman's Guide to Socialism, Capitalism, Sovietism, and Fascism, ch. 33; Constable (1949).
First published in 1928 as *The Intelligent Woman's Guide to Socialism and Capitalism*.

Capitalism . . . means that the only duty of the Government is to maintain private property in land and capital, and to keep on foot an efficient police force and magistracy to enforce all private contracts made by individuals in pursuance of their own interests, besides, of course, keeping civil order.

The Intelligent Woman's Guide to Socialism, Capitalism, Sovietism, and Fascism, ch. 28; Constable (1949).
First published in 1928 as *The Intelligent Woman's Guide to Socialism and Capitalism*.

Private enterprise will do nothing that is not profitable to its little self, and the very existence of civilization now depends on the swift and unhampered public execution of enterprises that supersede private enterprise and are not merely profitable but vitally necessary to the whole community.

The Apple Cart, preface; *The Bodley Head Bernard Shaw: Collected Plays with their Prefaces*, vol. 6 (1973).
First published in 1930.

*C*APITAL PUNISHMENT

Murder and capital punishment are not opposites that cancel one another, but similars that breed their kind.

Man and Superman, The Revolutionist's Handbook, "Maxims for Revolutionists"; *The Bodley Head Bernard Shaw: Collected Plays with their Prefaces*, vol. 2 (1971).
First published in 1903.

CENSORSHIP

You cannot attack the freedom of the plays you do not like without equally endangering the freedom of those you like.

"Church and Stage," *The Drama Observed*, vol. 2, ed. Bernard F. Dukore; Penn State Press (1993).

First published in *Saturday Review*, January 25, 1896.

Comstockery is the world's standing joke at the expense of the United States.

Letter to Robert W. Welch, c. September 22-23, 1905, *Collected Letters*, vol. 2, ed. Dan H. Laurence (1972).

Shaw coined the term "Comstockery" for activities of people like Anthony Comstock, secretary and special agent of the New York Society for the Suppression of Vice, who boasted that in thirty years he had brought over 3,500 criminals to justice and destroyed 160 tons of obscene literature and pictures.

Assassination is the extreme form of censorship.

The Shewing-up of Blanco Posnet, preface, "The Limits to Toleration"; *The Bodley Head Bernard Shaw: Collected Plays with their Prefaces*, vol. 3 (1971).

First published in 1911.

A censor pretending to protect morality is like a child pushing the cushions of a railway carriage to give itself the sensation of making the train travel at sixty miles an hour.

The Shewing-up of Blanco Posnet, preface, "The Definition of Immorality"; *The Bodley Head Bernard Shaw: Collected Plays with their Prefaces*, vol. 3 (1971).

First published in 1911.

Consider whether we can weed out from the great mass of desirable films those which are detrimental to public morals. The censorship method . . . is that of handing the job over to some frail and erring mortal man, and making him omnipotent on the assumption that his official status will make him infallible and omniscient.

"Mr. G.B. Shaw on Film Censorship," *The Drama Observed*, ed. Bernard F. Dukore; Penn State Press (1993).

Speech on BBC radio, January 20, 1935 .

CHANGE

Fashions change more quickly than manners, manners more quickly than morals, morals more quickly than passions, and, in general, the conscious, reasonable, intellectual life more quickly than the instinctive, willful, affectionate one. The dramatist who deals with the irony and humor of the relatively durable sides of life, or with their pity and terror, is the one whose comedies and tragedies will last longer.

"The Second Dating of Sheridan," *The Drama Observed*, vol. 2, ed. Bernard F. Dukore; Penn State Press (1993).

First published in *Saturday Review*, June 27, 1896.

History, as far as we are capable of history (which is not saying much as yet) shows that all changes from crudity of social organization to complexity, and from mechanical agencies in government to living ones, seem anarchic at first sight.

The Perfect Wagnerite, "Not Love, But Life," *Shaw's Music*, vol. 3, ed. Dan H. Laurence (1981).

First published in 1898.

The law of God is a law of change, and . . . when the Churches set themselves against change as such, they are setting themselves against the law of God.

Saint Joan, preface; *The Bodley Head Bernard Shaw: Collected Plays with their Prefaces*, vol. 6 (1973).

First published in 1924.

CHAPMAN, GEORGE

Chapman was an intolerable boaster, paraded his knowledge of dead languages, scorned the writers of his day, and asserted that his dramas were dictated to him by a spirit. This spirit, judged by his fruits, was not at all so clever a playwright as Shakespeare.

"*Troilus and Cressida*," *The Drama Observed*, vol. 1, ed. Bernard F. Dukore; Penn State Press (1993).

Speech for the New Shakespeare Society, read in Shaw's absence, February 29, 1884.

CHARACTER

What a man is depends on his character; but what he does, and what we think of what he does, depends on his circumstances.

Major Barbara, preface, "Weaknesses of the Salvation Army," *The Bodley Head Bernard Shaw: Collected Plays with their Prefaces*, vol. 3 (1971).

First published in 1907.

CHARITY

Ordinary charity is ludicrously inadequate. . . . No plaster will be of any avail here, for there is no external ailment. The cure, if cure there be, must be radical.

"The Gospel According to St. Jude's," *Bernard Shaw's Book Reviews*, ed. Brian Tyson; Penn State Press (1991).

First published in *Pall Mall Gazette*, December 26, 1888.

Like all persons in sound mental health, I hate charity, whether as giver or receiver, asker or asked. . . . I have no patience with the people who think that social evils can be cured by a little gush of sympathy and a dip of their hands into all the pockets within their reach.

"On Charity," *Shaw's Music*, vol. 3, ed. Dan H. Laurence (1981).

First published in *The World*, March 21, 1894.

There is no getting over the fact that the moment an attempt is made to organize almsgiving by entrusting the funds to a permanent body of experts, it is invariably discovered that beggars are perfectly genuine persons: that is to say, not "deserving poor," but people who have discovered that it is possible to live by simply impudently asking for what they want until they get it, which is the essence of beggary.

"Socialism for Millionaires," *Essays in Fabian Socialism*; Constable (1949).

First published in the *Contemporary Review*, February 1896.

I am the sort of man who devotes his life to the salvation of humanity in the abstract, and can't bear to give a penny to a starving widow.

Letter to Sister Ethna, October 1, 1920, *Collected Letters*, ed. Dan H. Laurence, Vol. 3 (1985).

Charity feeds misery: that is why I object to it.

Handwritten statement on paper presented by Shaw to Prince Christopher Radiwill, signed and dated Feb 18, 1925.

Previously unpublished; in Sidney P. Albert Collection, Brown University.

CHEKHOV, ANTON PAVLOVICH

Everything we write in England seems sawdust after Chekhov.

Letter to H.G. Wells, December 7, 1916, *Selected Correspondence of Bernard Shaw: Bernard Shaw and H.G. Wells*, ed. J. Percy Smith; U of Toronto Press (1995).

Chess

He hates chess. He says it is a foolish expedient for making idle people believe they are doing something clever when they are only wasting their time.

Marian, in *The Irrational Knot*, ch. 14; Constable (1950).

First published in 1885.

Children

You will find that the grandchildren, like all children, have the qualities conventionally ascribed to old age. The ideal old person is a child, the ideal child is forty, the ideal woman is a man, though women lie low and let that secret keep itself.

Letter to Ellen Terry, 21 September 1896, *Collected Letters*, vol. 1, ed. Dan H. Laurence (1965).

Children, like grown-up people, get on well enough together if they are not pushed down one another's throats.

Misalliance, preface, "Family Affection"; *The Bodley Head Bernard Shaw: Collected Plays with their Prefaces*, vol. 4 (1972).

First published in 1914.

If you must hold yourself up to your children as an object lesson (which is not at all necessary), hold yourself up as a warning and not as an example.

Misalliance, preface, "The Manufacture of Monsters"; *The Bodley Head Bernard Shaw: Collected Plays with their Prefaces*, vol. 4 (1972).

First published in 1914.

Most children can be, and many are, hopelessly warped and wasted by parents who are ignorant and silly enough to suppose that they know what a human being ought to be, and who stick at nothing in their determination to force their children into their moulds.

Misalliance, preface, "The Manufacture of Monsters"; *The Bodley Head Bernard Shaw: Collected Plays with their Prefaces*, vol. 4 (1972).

First published in 1914.

CHRIST, JESUS

The record that Jesus said certain things is not invalidated by a demonstration that Confucius said them before him.

Androcles and the Lion, preface, "Why Jesus More Than Another?" *The Bodley Head Bernard Shaw: Collected Plays with their Prefaces*, vol. 4 (1972).

First published in 1916.

We have always had a curious feeling that though we crucified Christ on a stick, he somehow managed to get hold of the right end of it, and that if we were better men we might try his plan.

Androcles and the Lion, preface, "Why Not Give Christianity a Trial?" *The Bodley Head Bernard Shaw: Collected Plays with their Prefaces*, vol. 4 (1972).

First published in 1916.

CHRISTIANITY

The early Christian rules of life were not made to last, because the early Christians did not believe that the world itself was going to last.

Hotchkiss, in *Getting Married*; *The Bodley Head Bernard Shaw: Collected Plays with their Prefaces*, vol. 3 (1971).

First produced in 1908.

I am a Christian. That obliges me to be a Communist.

Father Soames, in *Getting Married*; *The Bodley Head Bernard Shaw: Collected Plays with their Prefaces*, vol. 3 (1971).

First produced in 1908.

I loathe the mess of mean superstitions and misunderstood prophecies which is still rammed down the throats of children in this country under the name of Christianity.

"Shaw Explains His Religion," *Agitations*, ed. Dan H. Laurence and James Rambeau; Ungar (1985).

Letter to The Freethinker, November 1, 1908.

THE CAPTAIN: Lavinia: do Christians know how to love?
LAVINIA: Yes, Captain: they love even their enemies.
THE CAPTAIN: Is that easy?

LAVINIA: Very easy, Captain, when their enemies are as handsome as
you.

Androcles and the Lion, act 1; *The Bodley Head Bernard Shaw: Collected Plays with their Prefaces*, vol. 4
(1972).

First produced in 1913.

I shall have no time for Christian polemics. And will you just tell me why
the Old Man waited until the year 1 A.D. to reveal himself with credentials
of a totally unconvincing and acutely ridiculous kind? Did the people who
lived before that time not matter?

Letter to Frederick H. Evans, October 6, 1916, *Collected Letters*, ed. Dan H. Laurence, vol. 3.

Why not give Christianity a trial?

Androcles and the Lion, preface, "Why Not Give Christianity a Trial?" *The Bodley Head Bernard Shaw:
Collected Plays with their Prefaces*, vol. 4 (1972).

First published in 1916.

Have you ever read St. Augustine? If you have, you will remember that he
had to admit that the early Christians were a very mixed lot, and that some
of them were more addicted to blackening their wives' eyes for tempting
them, and wrecking the temples of the pagans, than to carrying out the
precepts of the Sermon on the Mount. Indeed you must have noticed that
we modern Christians are still a very mixed lot.

The Intelligent Woman's Guide to Socialism, Capitalism, Sovietism, and Fascism, ch. 26; Constable (1949).

First published in 1928 as *The Intelligent Woman's Guide to Socialism and Capitalism*.

*C*HRISTMAS

To sit up working until two or three in the morning, and then, just as I am
losing myself in my first sleep, to hear Venite adoremus, more generally
known as Ow, cam let Huz adore Im, welling forth from a cornet (English
pitch), a saxhorn (Society of Arts pitch, or thereabouts), and a trombone
(French pitch), is the sort of thing that breaks my peace and destroys my
good will towards men.

"Christmas in Broadstairs," *Shaw's Music*, vol. 1, ed. Dan H. Laurence (1981).

First published in *The Star*, December 27, 1889.

It is really an atrocious institution, this Christmas. We must be gluttonous because it is Christmas. We must be drunken because it is Christmas. . . . We must buy things that nobody wants, and give them to people we don't like . . . all because it is Christmas—that is, because the mass of the population, including the all-powerful middle-class tradesman, depends on a week of license and brigandage, waste and intemperance, to clear off its outstanding liabilities by the end of the year.

"Mrs. Tanqueray Plays the Piano," *Shaw's Music*, vol. 3, ed. Dan H. Laurence (1981).

First published in *The World*, December 6, 1893.

On Christmas day it is proclaimed that Christianity established peace on earth and good will towards men. Next day the Christian, with refreshed soul, goes back to the manufacture of submarines and torpedoes.

"The Solidarity of Social-Democracy," *Practical Politics*, ed. Lloyd J. Hubenka; U of Nebraska Press (1976).

English version of an article written for the May 1, 1906 "Labor Day" issue of the German *Vorwärts* but not published in this newspaper.

*C*HURCHES AND CHURCHGOING

Our insular conception of a church as a place where we must on no account enjoy ourselves, and where ladies are trained in the English art of sitting in rows for hours, dumb, expressionless, and with the elbows uncomfortably turned in.

"On the Godliness of Dancing," *Shaw's Music*, vol. 1, ed. Dan H. Laurence (1981).

First published in *The Star*, April 14, 1888.

Of the irreligious majority of the English people I notice that great numbers go to church because it is one of the duties which are included in what is called "respectability."

Letter to the editor of *The Star*, written September 20, 1888, *Collected Letters*, vol. 1, ed. Dan H. Laurence (1965).

Written above the pseudonym Shendar Brwa, an anagram, first published November 20, 1957 in *The Flying Dutchman*, Hofstra College student newspaper.

The majority of churchgoing workmen, probably, are heathens like the rest of us, going as a matter of habit, just as they wear neckties, because their respectability would be doubted if they omitted the observance.

"Working Men and Sacred Music," *Shaw's Music*, vol. 1, ed. Dan H. Laurence (1981).

First published in *The Star*, November 8, 1889.

The man of business . . . goes on Sunday to the church with the regularity of the village blacksmith, there to renounce and abjure before his God the line of conduct which he intends to pursue with all his might during the following week.

Essays in Fabian Socialism, "The Economic Basis of Socialism"; Constable (1949).

First published in *Fabian Essays,* December 1889.

One becomes eminent in the Church through capacity for business more easily than by capacity for religion.

Letter to Laurentia McLachlan, April 12, 1935, *Collected Letters*, ed. Dan H. Laurence, vol. 4 (1988).

CIRCUMSTANCES

People are always blaming their circumstances for what they are. I don't believe in circumstances. The people who get on in this world are the people who get up and look for the circumstances they want, and, if they can't find them, make them.

Vivie Warren, in *Mrs. Warren's Profession*, act 2; *The Bodley Head Bernard Shaw: Collected Plays with their Prefaces*, vol. 1 (1970).

First published in 1898.

CIVILIZATION

Civilization is at present an imposture: we are a crowd of savages on whom a code of makeshift regulations is forced by penalties for breaking them.

Back to Methuselah, "Postscript: After Twenty-five Years"; *The Bodley Head Bernard Shaw: Collected Plays with their Prefaces*, vol. 5 (1972).

First published in World Classics Edition, 1944.

CLASSES, SOCIAL

To persist in showing the classes repulsive pictures of evils which they are powerless to abolish, without ever striving to show the masses the better conditions which they have the power to make real as soon as they have the will, is shallow policy put forward as an excuse for coarse art.

"Realism, Real and Unreal," *Bernard Shaw's Book Reviews*, ed. Brian Tyson; Penn State Press (1991).

First published in *Pall Mall Gazette*, September 29, 1887

My rank is the highest known in Switzerland: I am a free citizen.

Bluntschli, in *Arms and the Man*, act 3, *The Bodley Head Bernard Shaw: Collected Plays with their Prefaces*, vol. 1 (1970).

First produced in 1894.

Everyone is ill at ease until he has found his natural place, whether it be above or below his birthplace. The overrated inheritor of a position for which he has no capacity, and the underrated nobody who is a born genius, are alike shy because they are alike out of place.

Immaturity, preface; Constable (1950).

First published in 1921.

CLERGY

If you want to find the man who is weak in conduct, go to a clergyman.

"Life, Literature, and Political Economy"; *Practical Politics*, ed. Lloyd J. Hubenka, U of Nebraska Press (1976).

Speech to the Students' Union at the London School of Economics and Political Science, December 13, 1905, revised for publication in the *Clare Market Review*, January 1906.

What is wrong with priests and popes is that instead of being apostles and saints, they are nothing but empirics who say "I know" instead of "I am learning," and pray for credulity and inertia as wise men pray for scepticism and activity.

The Doctor's Dilemma, preface, "The Latest Theories"; *The Bodley Head Bernard Shaw: Collected Plays with their Prefaces*, vol. 3 (1971).

First published in 1911.

The average clergyman is an official who makes his living by christening babies, marrying adults, conducting a ritual, and making the best he can (when he has any conscience about it) of a certain routine of school superintendence, district visiting, and organization of almsgiving, which does not necessarily touch Christianity at any point except the point of the tongue.

Androcles and the Lion, epilogue; *The Bodley Head Bernard Shaw: Collected Plays with their Prefaces*, vol. 4 (1972).

First published in 1916.

In reading the Bible—you have heard it read in churches, and you have perhaps had it imparted to you by an ordained clergyman—you have derived an impression that the prophets of whom you read were only a sort of old-fashioned clergy. You are entirely wrong in that; they were prophets who were stoned by the old-fashioned clergy.

"Modern Religion," *Platform and Pulpit*, ed. Dan H. Laurence; Hill & Wang (1961).

Lecture at Hampstead Conservatoire, November 13, 1919.

The average parson does not teach honesty and equality in the village school: he teaches deference to the merely rich, and calls that loyalty and religon. He is the ally of the squire, who, as magistrate, administers the laws made in the interests of the rich by the parliaments of rich men, and calls that justice.

The Intelligent Woman's Guide to Socialism, Capitalism, Sovietism, and Fascism, ch. 19; Constable (1949).

First published in 1928 as *The Intelligent Woman's Guide to Socialism and Capitalism.*

Colonialism

A conquered nation is like a man with cancer: he can think of nothing else.

John Bull's Other Island, preface, "The Curse of Nationalism"; *The Bodley Head Bernard Shaw: Collected Plays with their Prefaces*, vol. 3 (1971).

First published in 1907.

To deprive a dyspeptic of his dinner and hand it over to a man who can digest it better is a highly logical proceeding; but it is not a sensible one. To take the government of Ireland away from the Irish and hand it over to the English on the ground that they can govern better would be a precisely parallel case if the English had managed their own affairs so well as to place their superior faculty for governing beyond question.

John Bull's Other Island, preface, "The Curse of Nationalism"; *The Bodley Head Bernard Shaw: Collected Plays with their Prefaces*, vol. 3 (1971).

First published in 1907.

Comedy

All genuinely intellectual work is humorous.

> Letter to Florence Farr, January 28, 1892, vol. 1, *Collected Letters*, ed. Dan H. Laurence (1965).

You are wrong to scorn farcical comedy. It is by jingling the bells of a jester's cap that I, like Heine, have made people listen to me.

> Letter to Florence Farr, January 28, 1892, vol. 1, *Collected Letters*, ed. Dan H. Laurence (1965).

Unless comedy touches me as well as amuses me, it leaves me with a sense of having wasted my evening. I go to the theatre to be moved to laughter, not to be tickled or bustled into it.

> "An Old New Play and a New Old One," *The Drama Observed*, vol. 1, ed. Bernard F. Dukore, Penn State Press (1993).
>
> First published in *Saturday Review,* February 23, 1895.

The function of comedy is to dispel . . . unconsciousness by turning the searchlight of the keenest moral and intellectual analysis right on to it.

> "Meredith on Comedy," *The Drama Observed*, vol. 3, ed. Bernard F. Dukore, Penn State Press (1993).
>
> First published in *Saturday Review,* March 27, 1897.

The function of comedy . . . is nothing less than the destruction of old-established morals.

> "Meredith on Comedy," *The Drama Observed*, vol. 3, ed. Bernard F. Dukore; Penn State Press (1993).
>
> First published in *Saturday Review,* March 27, 1897.

My way of joking is to tell the truth. It's the funniest joke in the world.

> Father Keegan, in *John Bull's Other Island*, act 2; *The Bodley Head Bernard Shaw: Collected Plays with their Prefaces*, vol. 2 (1971).
>
> First produced in 1904.

Fortunately there is one outlet for the truth. We are permitted to discuss in jest what we may not discuss in earnest. A serious comedy about sex is taboo: a farcical comedy is privileged.

> *Overruled*, preface, "Artificial Retribution"; *The Bodley Head Bernard Shaw: Collected Plays with their Prefaces*, vol. 4 (1972).
>
> First published in 1916.

When a thing is funny, search it for a hidden truth.

The He-Ancient, in *Back to Methuselah*, "As Far as Thought Can Reach"; *The Bodley Head Bernard Shaw: Collected Plays with theirPrefaces*, vol. 5 (1972).

First published in 1921.

Common sense

A man of great common sense and good taste, meaning thereby a man without originality or moral courage.

Caesar and Cleopatra, "Notes"; *The Bodley Head Bernard Shaw: Collected Plays with their Prefaces*, vol. 2 (1971).

First published in 1901.

Communism

Most people will tell you that Communism is known only in this country as a visionary project advocated by a handful of amiable cranks. Then they will stroll off across the common bridge, along the common embankment, by the light of the common gas lamp shining alike on the just and the unjust, up the common street, and into the common Trafalgar Square.

The Impossibilities of Anarchism, "Communist Anarchism," *Essays in Fabian Socialism*; Constable (1949).

Paper read to the Fabian Society, October 16, 1891; Shaw parodies Matthew, 5:45: "He maketh his sun to rise on the evil and on the good, and sendeth rain on the just and on the unust."

All the time we are denouncing Communism as a crime, every street lamp and pavement and water tap and police constable is testifying that we could not exist for a week without it.

The Intelligent Woman's Guide to Socialism, Capitalism, Sovietism, and Fascism, ch. 62; Constable (1949).

First published in 1928 as *The Intelligent Woman's Guide to Socialism and Capitalism*.

Communism can spread only as Capitalism spread: that is, as a development of existing economic civilization and not by a sudden wholesale overthrow of it. What it proposes is not a destruction of the material utilities inherited from Capitalism, but a new way of managing them and distributing the wealth they produce.

The Intelligent Woman's Guide to Socialism, Capitalism, Sovietism, and Fascism, ch. 75; Constable (1949).

First published in 1928 as *The Intelligent Woman's Guide to Socialism and Capitalism.*

Communism is neither a melodrama in which every Communist is a hero and every Plutocrat a villain, nor a Utopia in which everything is done by the State and nothing by private enterprise.

"Bernard Shaw on Peace (1950)," *SHAW: The Annual of Bernard Shaw Studies*, vol. 16, ed. Dan H. Laurence and Margot Peters; Penn State Press (1996).

Written in 1950.

COMPETITION

I have no competitive instinct; nor do I crave for prizes and distinctions: consequently I have no interest in competitive examinations: if I won, the disappointment of my competitors would distress me instead of gratifying me: if I lost, my self-esteem would suffer.

Immaturity, preface; Constable (1950).

First published in 1921.

CONCEIT

If you tell a conceited man that he is juvenile and thoughtless, you must expect him to have it out with you.

Letter to Francis Hueffer, January 19, 1883; *Collected Letters*, ed. Dan H. Laurence, vol. 1 (1965).

CONDUCTING

Might we venture to suggest the establishment of a prize for conducting, to be awarded by a committee of deaf men? We in London do not lack variety and picturesqueness in the action of our our favorite conductors. As practised by Mr. August Manns, conducting is a vigorous broadsword exercise. Herr [Hans] Richter fingers his baton as delicately as a fine fencer fingers his foil, or a fine violinist his bow, moving his arm gently and evenly from the elbow joint. Mr. Carl Rosa slashes from his wrist.

"Motets and Madrigals," vol. 1, ed. Dan H. Laurence, *Shaw's Music* (1981).

First published in *Dramatic Review,* September 5, 1885.

CONFORMITY

There is a period in life which is called the age of disillusion, which means the age at which a man discovers that his generous and honest impulses are incompatible with success in business; that the institutions he has reverenced are shams; and that he must join the conspiracy or go to the wall.

The Impossibilities of Anarchism, "The Anarchist Spirit," *Essays in Fabian Socialism;* Constable, 1949).

Paper read to the Fabian Society, October 16, 1891.

CONFUSION

My business is not to make confusion worse confounded, but to clear it up.

Misalliance, preface, "The Child is Father to the Man"; *The Bodley Head Bernard Shaw: Collected Plays with their Prefaces* , vol. 4 (1972).

First published in 1914.

CONSCIENCE

My conscience is the genuine pulpit article: it annoys me to see people comfortable when they ought to be uncomfortable; and I insist on making them think in order to bring them to conviction of sin.

Man and Superman, Epistle Dedicatory, *The Bodley Head Bernard Shaw: Collected Plays with their Prefaces,* vol. 2 (1971).

First published in 1903.

There is nothing more dangerous than the conscience of a bigot.

Quoted in A. Emil Davies, "G.B.S. and Local Government," *G.B.S. 90*, ed. S. Winsten; Dodd, Mead (1946).

Election speech, Spring 1904.

SHIRLEY: I wouldn't have your conscience, not for all your income.

UNDERSHAFT: I wouldn't have your income, not for all your conscience.

Major Barbara, act 2; *The Bodley Head Bernard Shaw: Collected Plays with their Prefaces*, vol. 3 (1971).

First produced in 1905.

"Act according to your conscience" is a rule no sooner applied than we find that its validity depends altogether on what sort of conscience you have.

The W.E.A. [Workers' Educational Association] Education Year Book, preface to Part 1; *Complete Prefaces*, ed. Dan H. Laurence and Daniel J. Leary, vol. 2 (1995).

First published in 1918.

A world without conscience: that is the horror of our condition.

Franklyn Barnabas, in *Back to Methuselah*, "The Gospel of the Brothers Barnabas"; *The Bodley Head Bernard Shaw: Collected Plays with their Prefaces*, vol. 5 (1972).

First published in 1921.

You cannot divide my conscience into a war department and a peace department. Do you suppose that a man who will commit murder for political ends will hesitate to commit theft for personal ends? Do you supose you can make a man the mortal enemy of sixty million of his fellow creatures without making him a little less scrupulous about his next door neighbor?

Aubrey, in *Too True to be Good*, act 3; *The Bodley Head Bernard Shaw: Collected Plays with their Prefaces*, vol. 6 (1973).

First produced in 1932.

CONSEQUENCES

Nothing is worth doing unless the consequences may be serious.

Hypatia, in *Misalliance*; *The Bodley Head Bernard Shaw: Collected Plays with their Prefaces*, vol. 4 (1972).

First produced in 1910.

CONSIDERATION

It is this consideration of other people—or rather this cowardly fear of them which we call consideration—that makes us the sentimental slaves we are.

John Tanner, in *Man and Superman*, act 1, *The Bodley Head Bernard Shaw: Collected Plays with their Prefaces*, vol. 2 (1971).

First published in 1903.

CONSTITUTIONS

The American Constitution, one of the few modern political documents drawn up by men who were forced by the sternest circumstances to think out what they really had to face instead of chopping logic in a university classroom.

Getting Married, preface, "Divorce Without Asking Why"; *The Bodley Head Bernard Shaw: Collected Plays with their Prefaces*, vol. 3 (1971).

First published in 1911.

CONTRADICTION

A man never tells you anything until you contradict him.

Letter to Ellen Terry, August 28, 1896, *Collected Letters*, vol. 1, ed. Dan H. Laurence (1965).

CONTROVERSY

He who knows only the offical side of a controversy knows less than nothing of its nature.

Misalliance, preface, "What We Do Not Teach, and Why"; *The Bodley Head Bernard Shaw: Collected Plays with their Prefaces*, vol. 4 (1972).

First published in 1914.

Controversy is educational in itself: a controversially educated person with an open mind is better educated than a dogmatically educated one with a closed mind. The student should hear the case, but should never be asked for a verdict. It may take him forty years to arrive at one.

> *The W.E.A. [Workers' Educational Association] Education Year Book*, preface to Part 1; *Complete Prefaces*, ed. Dan H. Laurence and Daniel J. Leary, vol. 2 (1995).
>
> First published in 1918.

CONVENTIONALITY

How conventional all you unconventional people are!

> Candida, in *Candida*, act 2; *The Bodley Head Bernard Shaw: Collected Plays with their Prefaces*, vol. 1 (1970).
>
> First produced in 1897.

The reason why sensible people are as conventional as they can bear to be is that conventionality saves so much time and thought and trouble and social friction of one sort or another that it leaves them much more leisure for freedom than unconventionality does.

> *The Intelligent Woman's Guide to Socialism, Capitalism, Sovietism, and Fascism*, ch. 79; Constable (1949).
>
> First published in 1928 as *The Intelligent Woman's Guide to Socialism and Capitalism*.

CONVERSION

The conversion of a savage to Christianity is the conversion of Christianity to savagery.

> *Man and Superman*, The Revolutionist's Handbook, "Maxims for Revolutionists"; *The Bodley Head Bernard Shaw: Collected Plays with their Prefaces*, vol. 2 (1971).
>
> First published in 1903.

CORRESPONDENCE

The old rule was, Never write a letter and never burn one. Mine is, Never keep a letter and never answer one.

> Letter to John Burns, 12 August 1892, vol. 1, *Collected Letters*, ed. Dan H. Laurence (1965).

CORRUPTION

The corruption of society today is caused by evils which can be remedied only by the aspiration of the masses towards better things, and not by the shrinking of the classes from horrors known to them only by clever descriptions. Besides, one cannot help suspecting that those who shrink do not read, and that the rest dreadfully enjoy, the paper sensation.

"Realism, Real and Unreal," *Bernard Shaw's Book Reviews*, ed. Brian Tyson; Penn State Press (1991).

First published in *Pall Mall Gazette*, September 29, 1887.

CREDULITY

In the Middle Ages people believed that the earth was flat, for which they had at least the evidence of their senses: we believe it to be round, not because as many as one per cent of us could give the physical reasons for so quaint a belief, but because modern science has convinced us that nothing that is obvious is true, and that everything that is magical, improbable, extraordinary, gigantic, microscopic, heartless, or outrageous is scientific.

Saint Joan, preface, "The Real Joan Not Marvelous Enough for Us"; *The Bodley Head Bernard Shaw: Collected Plays with their Prefaces*, vol. 6 (1973).

First published in 1924.

CRIME

Death, it is said, is irrevocable; and after all, they [convicted criminals] may turn out to be innocent. But really you cannot handle criminals on the assumption that they may be innocent. You are not supposed to handle them at all until you have convinced yourself by an elaborate trial that they are guilty.

Imprisonment, "The Lethal Chamber," *Doctors' Delusions, Crude Criminology, and Sham Socialism*; Constable (1950).

First published in 1922.

How can a prison chaplain appeal with any effect to the conscience of a professional criminal who knows quite well that his illegal and impecunious modes of preying on society are no worse morally, and enormously less mischievous materially, than the self-legalized plutocratic modes practised by the chaplain's most honored friends with the chaplain's full approval?

Imprisonment, "Man in Society Must Justify His Existence," *Doctors' Delusions, Crude Criminology, and Sham Socialism*; Constable (1950).

First published in 1922.

Society has a right of self-defence, extending to the destruction or restraint of lawbreakers. This right is separable from the right to revenge or punish: it need have no more to do with punishment or revenge than the caging or shooting of a man-eating tiger.

Imprisonment, "Recapitulation," *Doctors' Delusions, Crude Criminology, and Sham Socialism*; Constable (1950).

First published in 1922.

CRIMINALS

The only one insufferable and unpardonable thing for a criminal to do is to confess before he is found out. When a man goes to a police station and gives himself up for an undiscovered murder, the first uncontrollable impulse of every healthy person is one of impatient exasperation with a fool who cannot bear his cross and hold his tongue, but must tear open a healed wound for the sake of having his miserable conscience soothed by the hangman.

"More Masterpieces," *The Drama Observed*, vol. 2, ed. Bernard F. Dukore; Penn State Press (1993).

First published in *Saturday Review*, October 26, 1895.

CRITICISM

Critics are only human, and they will attribute their anguish whilst listening to the tenor to anything sooner than to his defects. If they can see no excellences, they will invent some.

"Vocalists of the Season," *Shaw's Music*, vol. 1 (1981), ed. Dan H. Laurence.

First published in *The Hornet*, June 27, 1877.

Dramatic criticism is the quintessence of art criticism, which is itself the essence of human folly and ignorance.

"Acting, by One Who Does not Believe In It," *The Drama Observed*, vol. 1, ed. Bernard F. Dukore; Penn State Press (1993).

Paper read at a meeting of the Church and Stage Guild, February 5, 1889.

Reviewing has one advantage over suicide. In suicide you take it out of yourself: in reviewing you take it out of other people.

"Canterbury Kinfreederl and a Lighthouse," *Shaw's Music*, vol. 1, ed. Dan H. Laurence (1981).

First published in *The Star*, January 3, 1890.

The fairness of criticism is one thing, its adequacy quite another.

"Bernard Shaw Replies to the Critics of *Widowers' Houses*," *The Drama Observed*, vol. 1, ed. Bernard F. Dukore; Penn State Press (1993).

Letter to the editor, *The Star*, December 19, 1892.

The critic stands between popular authorship, for which he is not silly enough, and great authorship, for which he has not genius enough.

"The Author to the Dramatic Critics," *The Drama Observed*, vol. 1, ed. Bernard F. Dukore; Penn State Press (1993).

Appendix 1 to *Widowers' Houses* (1893).

My critics (whom I pass over in dignified silence only when they happen to have the best of the argument).

"A Reply to Mr. Lunn," *Shaw's Music*, vol. 2, ed. Dan H. Laurence (1981).

First published in *The World*, January 18, 1893.

Criticism is not only medicinally salutary: it has positive popular attractions in its cruelty, its gladiatorship, and the gratification given to envy by its attacks on the great, and to enthusiasm by its praises.

Preface, *Plays Unpleasant*; *The Bodley Head Bernard Shaw: Collected Plays with their Prefaces*, vol. 1 (1970).

First published in 1898.

There are twenty-four concerts this week. Consequently I give myself a holiday; for if anyone asks me what I thought of this or that performance, I reply, "How can I possibly be in twenty-four places at the same time? The particular concert you are curious about is one of those which I was unable to attend."

"An Embarrassment of Riches," *Shaw's Music*, vol. 1, ed. Dan H. Laurence (1981).

First published in *The Star*, March 1, 1889.

Never insult an author or artist by sparing his feelings. That is the one thing he will never forgive. If you are going to hit him, hit him straight in the face—exuberantly, as if you enjoyed it—and give him credit for being able to stand up to it.

"On Criticism," *The Drama Observed*, vol. 1, ed. Bernard F. Dukore; Penn State Press (1993).

Statement first published in G. Burgin, "Some Literary Critics," *The Idler*, June 1894.

No man sensitive enough to be worth his salt as a critic could for years wield a pen which, from the nature of his occupation, is scratching somebody's nerves at every stroke, without becoming conscious of how monstrously indefensible the superhuman attitude of impartiality is for him.

"On Musical Criticism," *Shaw's Music*, vol. 3, ed. Dan H. Laurence (1981).

First published in *The World*, June 13, 1894.

Critics, like other people, see what they look for, not what is actually before them.

Three Plays for Puritans, preface; *The Bodley Head Bernard Shaw: Collected Plays with their Prefaces*, vol. 2 (1971).

First published in 1901.

Criticism, dramatic

It is the business of the dramatic critic to educate . . . dunces, not to echo them.

"Two New Plays," *The Drama Observed*, vol. 1, ed. Bernard F. Dukore; Penn State Press (1993).

First published in *Saturday Review*, January 12, 1895.

He is the policeman of dramatic art; and it is his express business to denounce its delinquencies.

"On the Living and the Dead," *The Drama Observed*, vol. 3, ed. Bernard F. Dukore; Penn State Press (1993).

First published in *Saturday Review*, December 25, 1897.

Every time one of my new plays is first produced the critics declare it is rotten, though they are always willing to admit that the next to the last play is the greatest thing I've done. I have educated the critics up to an appreciation of the next to the last of my plays.

"Shaw Answers James Bryce," *The Drama Observed*, ed. Bernard F. Dukore, vol. 3; Penn State Press (1993).

First published in *The New York Times*, May 5, 1907.

Criticism is, has been, and eternally will be as bad as it can possibly be.

"On Drama Critics and Drama Criticism," *The Drama Observed*, ed. Bernard F. Dukore, vol. 4; Penn State Press (1993).

Speech, London Critics Circle Annual Luncheon, October 11, 1929.

CRITICISM, MUSIC

If criticism is to have any effect on concerts, it must clearly be published before they come off.

"Lucifer and Richter," *Shaw's Music*, vol. 1, ed. Dan H. Laurence (1981).

First published in *The Star*, April 5, 1889.

CRUCIFIXION

Unfortunately, the crucifixion was a complete political success.

Androcles and the Lion, preface, "After the Crucifixion"; *The Bodley Head Bernard Shaw: Collected Plays with their Prefaces*, vol. 4 (1972).

First published in 1916.

CURSES

Not bloody likely.

Eliza Doolittle, in *Pygmalion*, act 3; *The Bodley Head Bernard Shaw: Collected Plays with their Prefaces*, vol. 4 (1972).

First produced (in German) in 1913.

CUSTOMS

When will we realize that the fact that we can become accustomed to anything, however disgusting at first, makes it necessary for us to examine carefully everything we have become accustomed to? Before motor cars became common, necessity had accustomed us to a foulness in our streets which would have horrified us had the street been our drawing-room carpet.

> *Misalliance*, preface, "Under the Whip"; *The Bodley Head Bernard Shaw: Collected Plays with their Prefaces*, vol. 4 (1972).
>
> First published in 1914.

DANGER

Everything is dangerous unless you take it at the right time. An apple at breakfast does you good: an apple at bedtime upsets you for a week.

> B.B., in *The Doctor's Dilemma*, act 1; *The Bodley Head Bernard Shaw: Collected Plays with their Prefaces*, vol. 3 (1971).
>
> First produced in 1906.

DARWINISM

There is no place in Darwinism for free will, or any other sort of will.

> *Back to Methuselah*, preface, "The Greatest of These Is Self-Control"; *The Bodley Head Bernard Shaw: Collected Plays with their Prefaces*, vol. 5 (1972).
>
> First published in 1921.

DEATH

In the arts of life man invents nothing; but in the arts of death he outdoes Nature herself, and produces by chemistry and machinery all the slaughter of plague, pestilence, and famine.

> The Devil, in *Man and Superman*, act 3; *The Bodley Head Bernard Shaw: Collected Plays with their Prefaces*, vol. 2 (1971).
>
> First published in 1903.

It is not death that matters, but the fear of death. It is not killing and dying that degrades us, but base living, and accepting the wages and profits of degradation. Better ten dead men than one live slave or his master.

> Don Juan, in *Man and Superman*, act 3, *The Bodley Head Bernard Shaw: Collected Plays with their Prefaces*, vol. 2 (1971).
>
> First published in 1903.

Life levels all men: death reveals the eminent.

> *Man and Superman, The Revolutionist's Handbook*, "Maxims for Revolutionists," *The Bodley Head Bernard Shaw: Collected Plays with their Prefaces*, vol. 2 (1971).
>
> First published in 1903.

Life does not cease to be funny when people die any more than it ceases to be serious when people laugh.

> Dr. Colenso Ridgeon, in *The Doctor's Dilemma*, act 5; *The Bodley Head Bernard Shaw: Collected Plays with their Prefaces*, vol. 3 (1971).
>
> First produced in 1906.

I cannot tell you the exact date of my death. It has not yet been settled. When it is, I shall be settled too.

> Letter to Hannen Swaffer, February 26, 1938, *Collected Letters*, ed. Dan H. Laurence, vol. 4 (1988).

*D*ECENCY

No child would ever dream of a statue being indecent if it had not been taught so.

> Letter to the Evacustus Phipson, Jr., March 8, 1892; *Bernard Shaw on the London Art Scene 1885-1950*, ed. Stanley Weintraub; Penn State Press (1989).
>
> First published in *Cat's Paw Utopia* by Ray Reynolds (1972).

*D*EFINITIONS

CONRAD: If she shut *you* up, she is a woman in a thousand.

IMMENSO: That is an almost perfect example of a modern scientific definition. It has the air of exactitude which arithmetic alone can give. Yet as, from the moment the population exceeds nine hundred and ninety-nine, every woman is a woman in a thousand, it means absolutely nothing whatever.

> "A Glimpse of the Domesticity of Franklyn Barnabas"; *The Bodley Head Bernard Shaw: Collected Plays with their Prefaces*, vol. 5 (1972).
>
> Originally intended to be act 2 of *The Gospel of the Brothers Barnabas*, first published in *Short Stories, Scraps and Shavings*, 1930.

DEMOCRACY

A Socialist who thinks that the opinions of Mr. Gladstone on Socialism are unsound and his own sound, is within his rights; but a Socialist who thinks that his opinions are virtuous and Mr. Gladstone's vicious, violates the first rule of morals and manners in a Democratic country; namely, that you must not treat your political opponent as a moral delinquent.

"The Illusions of Socialism," *Shavian Tract* No. 4 (1956).
First published in September 1896.

Democracy substitutes election by the incompetent many for appointment by the corrupt few.

Man and Superman, The Revolutionist's Handbook, "Maxims for Revolutionists"; *The Bodley Head Bernard Shaw: Collected Plays with their Prefaces,* vol. 2 (1971).
First published in 1903.

Democracy has given us a power which we have neither been bred to use nor schooled to understand: the vote, flung at us as if it were a talisman that would make magicians of us, is but the latest quack remedy for ailments that only the profoundest political science can treat successfully. In this controversy the number of even our legislators who have shown any knowledge of its merest ABC can be counted on the fingers of one of the hands of an employee in an American sawmill.

Fabianism and the Fiscal Question, preface; *Complete Prefaces,* ed. Dan H. Laurence and Daniel J. Leary, vol. 1 (1993).
First published in 1904.

To make Democracy work, you need an aristocratic democracy. To make Aristocracy work, you need a democratic aristocracy.

Tarleton, in *Misalliance; The Bodley Head Bernard Shaw: Collected Plays with their Prefaces,* vol. 4 (1972).
First produced in 1910.

As another famous American said, "You can fool some of the people all the time, and you can fool all the people some of the time, but you cannot fool all the people all the time," whereas an autocrat need not fool the people: he can oppress all the people all the time.

Letter to Maxim Gorky, December 28, 1915, *Collected Letters,* ed. Dan H. Laurence, vol. 3 (1985).
The American of this slight misquotation is Abraham Lincoln.

Elect a world president by universal suffrage, and who would have a chance against Mr. Charles Chaplin?

> *The W.E.A. [Workers' Educational Association] Education Year Book*, preface to Part 1; *Complete Prefaces*, ed. Dan H. Laurence and Daniel J. Leary, vol. 2 (1995).
>
> First published in 1918.

Democracy prefers second best always.

> "The Drama, the Theatre, and the Films," *The Drama Observed*, ed. Bernard F. Dukore, vol. 4; Penn State Press (1993).
>
> First published in *Fortnightly Review*, September 1, 1924.

What is it now when every fool and every flapper has a vote? Government by the unqualified, chosen by the if possible less qualified.

> Letter to Alfred Douglas, August 28, 1940, *Collected Letters*, ed. Dan H. Laurence, vol. 4 (1988).

Government by Anybodies elected by Everybody, calling itself Democracy, has given us rulers who, without taking the trouble to understand what they are doing or considering its inevitable consequences, decree anything that will tide them over an immediate difficulty.

> *Everybody's Political What's What?* ch. 35; Constable (1944).

We are clamoring for Democracy, by which we mean the British parliamentary system, under which real democracy is impossible.

> Letter to Lady Rhondda, January 1, 1945, *Collected Letters*, ed. Dan H. Laurence, vol. 4 (1988).

Democracy means government in the interest of everybody. It most emphatically does not mean government BY everybody.

> *Farfetched Fables*, preface; *The Bodley Head Bernard Shaw: Collected Plays with their Prefaces*, vol. 7 (1974).
>
> First published in 1951, written in 1948-49.

*D*ESIRE

Take care to get what you like or you will be forced to like what you get.

> *Man and Superman, The Revolutionist's Handbook*, "Maxims for Revolutionists," *The Bodley Head Bernard Shaw: Collected Plays with their Prefaces*, vol. 2 (1971).
>
> First published in 1903.

DETERRENCE

In a purely deterrent system . . . it matters not a jot who is punished provided somebody is punished and the public persuaded that he is guilty. The effect of hanging or imprisoning the wrong man is as deterrent as hanging or imprisoning the right one.

Imprisonment, "Deterrence a Function of Certainty, Not of Severity," *Doctors' Delusions, Crude Criminology, and Sham Socialism*; Constable (1950).

First published in 1922.

DEVIL, THE

When you give the devil fair play he loses his case.

The Bishop, in *Getting Married*; *The Bodley Head Bernard Shaw: Collected Plays with their Prefaces*, vol. 3 (1971).

First produced in 1908.

DIPSOMANIA

That most horrible form of dipsomania, the craving for afternoon tea.

"Too Long," *Shaw's Music*, vol. 2, ed. Dan H. Laurence (1981).

First published in *The World*, March 1, 1893.

DISCIPLINE, MILITARY

The real object of the demand for discipline is to make soldiering so stupidly mechanical that it can be worked by officers without sufficient brains and character to make them respected and obeyed.

"Why Not Abolish the Soldier?" *SHAW: The Annual of Bernard Shaw Studies*, vol. 16, ed. Dan H. Laurence and Margot Peters; Penn State Press (1996).

Letter, written on April 20, 1899, to the editor of *The Chronicle*, which did not publish it.

*D*ISCOVERY

Any fool can make a discovery. Every baby has to discover more in the first years of its life than Roger Bacon ever discovered in his laboratory.

The Elderly Gentleman, in *Back to Methuselah*, "Tragedy of an Elderly Gentleman," act 1; *The Bodley Head Bernard Shaw: Collected Plays with their Prefaces*, vol. 5 (1972).

First published in 1921.

*D*ISCUSSION DRAMA

Formerly you had in what was called a well-made play an exposition in the first act, a situation in the second, and unraveling in the third. Now you have exposition, situation, and discussion; and the discussion is the test of the playwright.

The Quintessence of Ibsenism, "The Technical Novelty in Ibsen's Plays," *The Drama Observed*, ed. Bernard F. Dukore, vol. 4; Penn State Press (1993).

First published in revised edition, 1913.

*D*ISEASE

I've known over thirty men that found out how to cure consumption. Why do people go on dying of it, Colly?

Sir Patrick Cullen, in *The Doctor's Dilemma*, act 1; *The Bodley Head Bernard Shaw: Collected Plays with their Prefaces*, vol. 3 (1971).

First produced in 1906.

*D*ISSENTERS

The Nonconformist can quote the prayer book for his own purposes, I see.

Lubin, in *Back to Methuselah*, "The Gospel of the Brothers Barnabas"; *The Bodley Head Bernard Shaw: Collected Plays with their Prefaces*, vol. 5 (1972).

First published in 1921; parody of *The Merchant of Venice*, Act I, Scene iii: "The devil can cite Scripture for his purpose."

*D*IVORCE

If we adopt the common romantic assumption that the object of marriage is bliss, then the very strongest reason for dissolving a marriage is that it shall be disagreeable to one or other or both of the parties. If we accept the view that the object of marriage is to provide for the production and rearing of children, then childlessness should be a conclusive reason for dissolution.

> *Getting Married*, preface, "Survivals of Sex Slavery"; *The Bodley Head Bernard Shaw: Collected Plays with their Prefaces*, vol. 3 (1971).
>
> First published in 1911.

*D*OCTORS

The average doctor is a walking compound of natural ignorance and acquired witchcraft.

> "Henry IV," *The Drama Observed*, vol. 2, ed. Bernard F. Dukore; Penn State Press (1993).
>
> First published in *Saturday Review*, May 16, 1896.

Doctors all think that science is knowledge instead of being the very opposite of knowledge: to wit, speculation.

> Letter to H.G. Wells, December 12, 1901, *Selected Correspondence of Bernard Shaw: Bernard Shaw and H.G. Wells*, ed. J. Percy Smith; U of Toronto Press (1995).

He said that private practice in medicine ought to be put down by law. When I asked him why, he said that private doctors were ignorant licensed murderers.

> Jennifer Dubedate, paraphrasing Dr. Blenkinsop, in *The Doctor's Dilemma*, act 5; *The Bodley Head Bernard Shaw: Collected Plays with their Prefaces*, vol. 3 (1971).
>
> First produced in 1906.

The only evidence that can decide a case of malpractice is expert evidence: that is, the evidence of other doctors, and every doctor will allow a colleague to decimate a whole countryside sooner than violate the bond of profesional etiquet by giving him away.

> *The Doctor's Dilemma*, preface, "Recoil of the Dogma of Medical Infallibility on the Doctor"; *The Bodley Head Bernard Shaw: Collected Plays with their Prefaces*, vol. 3 (1971).
>
> First published in 1911.

It will do you no good if I get over this. A doctor's reputation is made by the number of eminent men who die under his care.

Quoted in *Bernard Shaw: The Lure of Fantasy 1918-1951* by Michael Holroyd (1991).

Statement (at age 94) to his doctor, September 14, 1950.

DOGMA

A basis of physical science no more justifies dogmatism than a metaphysical basis does.

Letter to E.C. Chapman, July 29, 1891, *Collected Letters*, ed. Dan H. Laurence, vol. 1 (1965).

Nothing can save us from a perpetual headlong fall into a bottomless abyss but a solid footing of dogma; and we no sooner agree to that than we find that the only trustworthy dogma is that there is no dogma.

The Elder, in *Too True to be Good*, act 3; *The Bodley Head Bernard Shaw: Collected Plays with their Prefaces*, vol. 6 (1973).

First produced in 1932.

DOLL'S HOUSE, A

A Doll's House will be as flat as ditchwater when *A Midsummer Night's Dream* will still be as fresh as paint; but it will have done more work in the world; and that is enough for the highest genius, which is always intensely utilitarian.

"The Problem Play," *The Drama Observed*, vol. 1, ed. Bernard F. Dukore; Penn State Press (1993).

First published in *The Humanitarian*, May 1895.

DRAMA AND DRAMATISTS

I avoid plots like the plague.

"The Drama, the Theatre, and the Films," *The Drama Observed*, ed. Bernard F. Dukore, vol. 4; Penn State Press (1993).

First published in *Fortnightly Review*, September 1, 1924.

For me the play is not the thing, but its thought, its purpose, its feeling, and its execution. And as most modern plays have no thought, and are absurdly vulgar in purpose and feeling, I am mainly interested in their execution.

"Mr. William Archer's Criticisms," *The Drama Observed*, vol. 1, ed. Bernard F. Dukore; Penn State Press (1993).

First published in *Saturday Review*, April 13, 1895.

Every play which is a criticism of contemporary life, must, if it is an honest play, involve a certain struggle with the public.

"The Two Latest Comedies," *The Drama Observed*, vol. 2, ed. Bernard F. Dukore; Penn State Press (1993).

First published in *Saturday Review*, May 18, 1895.

In order to realize fully how bad a popular play can be, it is necessary to see it twice.

"More Masterpieces," *The Drama Observed*, vol. 2, ed. Bernard F. Dukore; Penn State Press (1993).

First published in *Saturday Review*, October 26, 1895.

The ordinary dramatist only neglects social questions because he knows nothing about them.

"The Problem Play," *The Drama Observed*, vol. 1, ed. Bernard F. Dukore; Penn State Press (1993).

First published in *The Humanitarian*, May 1895.

Social questions are too sectional, too topical, too temporal to move a man to the mighty effort which is needed to produce great poetry. Prison reform may nerve Charles Reade to produce an effective and businesslike prose melodrama; but it could never produce *Hamlet*, *Faust*, or *Peer Gynt*.

"The Problem Play," *The Drama Observed*, vol. 1, ed. Bernard F. Dukore; Penn State Press (1993).

First published in *The Humanitarian*, May 1895.

If you bring on the stage the Englishman who lives in a single-room tenement, as many Englishmen do, and who beats his wife, as all Englishmen do under such circumstances except when their wives beat them, you will be denounced as the author of "a problem play."

"Told You So," *The Drama Observed*, vol. 2, ed. Bernard F. Dukore; Penn State Press (1993).

First published in *Saturday Review*, December 7, 1895.

The second-rate dramatist always begins at the beginning of his play; the first-rate one begins in the middle; and the genius—Ibsen, for instance— begins at the end.

"Boiled Heroine," *The Drama Observed*, vol. 2, ed. Bernard F. Dukore; Penn State Press (1993).

First published in *Saturday Review*, March 26, 1896.

It is the privilege of drama to make life intelligible, at least hypothetically, by introducing moral design into it, even if that design be only to show that moral design is an illusion, a demonstration which cannot be made without some counter-demonstration of the laws of life with which it clashes.

"Satan Saved at Last," *The Drama Observed*, vol. 2, ed. Bernard F. Dukore; Penn State Press (1993).
First published in *Saturday Review*, January 16, 1897.

There is only one way of dramatizing an idea; and that is by putting on the stage a human being possessed by that idea, yet nonetheless a human being with all the human impulses which make him akin and therefore interesting to us.

The Perfect Wagnerite, "Wagner as Revolutionist," (*Shaw's Music*, vol. 3 (1981).
First published in 1898.

The obvious conflicts of unmistakable good with unmistakable evil can only supply the crude drama of villain and hero, in which some absolute point of view is taken, and the dissentients are treated by the dramatist as enemies to be piously glorified or indignantly vilified. In such cheap wares I do not deal.

Plays Pleasant, preface; *The Bodley Head Bernard Shaw: Collected Plays with their Prefaces*, vol. 1 (1970).
First published in 1898.

The manager may not want good plays; but he does not want bad plays: he wants nice ones. Nice plays, with nice dresses, nice drawing rooms and nice people, are indispensable: to be ungenteel is worse than to fail.

Three Plays for Puritans, preface; *The Bodley Head Bernard Shaw: Collected Plays with their Prefaces*, vol. 2 (1971).
First published in 1901.

The great dramatist has something better to do than to amuse either himself or his audience. He has to interpret life.

Three Plays by Brieux, preface, "The Interpreter of Life"; *The Drama Observed*, ed. Bernard F. Dukore; Penn State Press (1993).
First published in 1911.

An interesting play cannot in the nature of things mean anything but a play in which problems of conduct and character of personal importance to the audience are raised and suggestively discussed.

The Quintessence of Ibsenism, "The Technical Novelty in Ibsen's Plays"; *The Drama Observed*, ed. Bernard F. Dukore, Penn State Press(1993).
First published in revised edition, 1913.

The drama was born of old from the union of two desires: the desire to have a dance and the desire to hear a story.

The Quintessence of Ibsenism, "The Technical Novelty in Ibsen's Plays"; *The Drama Observed*, ed. Bernard F. Dukore, vol. 4; Penn State Press (1993).

First published in revised edition, 1913.

*D*REAMS

Every dream is a prophecy: every jest is an earnest in the womb of Time.

Father Keegan, in *John Bull's Other Island*, act 4; *The Bodley Head Bernard Shaw: Collected Plays with their Prefaces*, vol. 2 (1971).

First produced in 1904.

Live in contact with dreams and you will get something of their charm: live in contact with facts and you will get something of their brutality. I wish I could find a country to live in where the facts were not brutal and the dreams not real.

Larry Doyle, in *John Bull's Other Island*, act 1; *The Bodley Head Bernard Shaw: Collected Plays with their Prefaces*, vol. 2 (1971).

First produced in 1904.

You see things; and you say "Why?" But I dream things that never were; and I say "Why not?"

The Serpent, in *Back to Methuselah*, "In the Beginning," act 1; *The Bodley Head Bernard Shaw: Collected Plays with their Prefaces*, vol. 5 (1972).

First published in 1921.

*D*RESS

We don't bother much about dress and manners in England, because, as a nation, we don't dress well and we've no manners.

Valentine, in *You Never Can Tell*, act 1; *The Bodley Head Bernard Shaw: Collected Plays with their Prefaces*, vol. 1 (1970).

First published in 1898.

[Victorian] Woman was not dressed in the sense we are familiar with. She was upholstered.

"Woman—Man in Petticoats," *Platform and Pulpit*, ed. Dan H. Laurence; Hill and Wang (1961).

Speech at a meeting in behalf of the Cecil Houses Fund (which provided housing for indigent women), May 20, 1927.

*D*RUGS

Alcohol . . . is a very mild drug compared with the most effective modern happiness producers. These give you no mere sodden self-satisfaction and self-conceit: they give you ecstasy. It is followed by hideous wretchedness; but then you can cure that by taking more and more of the drug until you become a living horror to all about you, after which you become a dead one, to their great relief.

The Intelligent Woman's Guide to Socialism, Capitalism, Sovietism, and Fascism, ch. 79; Constable (1949).

First published in 1928 as *The Intelligent Woman's Guide to Socialism and Capitalism.*

*D*UTY

When a stupid man is doing something he is ashamed of, he always declares that it is his duty.

Apollodorus, in *Caesar and Cleopatra*, act 3; *The Bodley Head Bernard Shaw: Collected Plays with their Prefaces*, vol. 2 (1971).

First published in 1901.

*D*YING

Those who do not know how to live must make a merit of dying.

Heartbreak House, preface, "Those Who Do Not Know How to Live Must Make a Merit of Dying"; *The Bodley Head Bernard Shaw: Collected Plays with their Prefaces*, vol. 5 (1972).

First published in 1919.

*E*ARNESTNESS

Sang-froid can be acquired: earnestness is the gift of the gods.

"A Defence of Ballet," *Shaw's Music*, vol. 1, ed. Dan H. Laurence (1981).

First published in *The Star*, October 4, 1889.

Economics

You will find quite a number of professional economists who know nothing of political economy, and never will. They are attracted to it by their natural incapacity for it, just as, on the stage, the man who is naturally a comedian craves for the tragedian's part.

"Life, Literature, and Political Economy"; *Practical Politics*, ed. Lloyd J. Hubenka; U of Nebraska Press (1976).

Speech to the Students' Union at the London School of Economics and Political Science, December 13, 1905, revised for publication in *Clare Market Review*, January 1906.

Education

What we call education and culture is for the most part nothing but the substitution of reading for experience, of literature for life, of the obsolete fictitious for the contemporary real.

Man and Superman, Epistle Dedicatory; *The Bodley Head Bernard Shaw: Collected Plays with their Prefaces*, vol. 2 (1971).

First published in 1903.

Children must be taught some sort of religion. Secular education is an impossibility. Secular education comes to this: that the only reason for ceasing to do evil and learning to do well is that if you do not you will be caned. This is worse than being taught in a church school that if you become a dissenter you will go to hell; for hell is presented as the instrument of something eternal, divine, and inevitable: you cannot evade it at the moment the schoolmaster's back is turned.

Misalliance, preface, "The Impossibility of Secular Education"; *The Bodley Head Bernard Shaw: Collected Plays with their Prefaces*, vol. 4 (1972).

First published in 1914.

It is a monstrous thing to force a child to learn Latin or Greek or mathematics on the ground that they are an indispensable gymnastic for the mental powers. It would be monstrous even if it were true.

Misalliance, preface, "Technical Instruction"; *The Bodley Head Bernard Shaw: Collected Plays with their Prefaces*, vol. 4 (1972).

First published in 1914.

Without living experiences no person is educated. With nothing but academic degrees, even when overloaded by a smattering of dead languages and twopennorth of algebra, the most erudite graduates may be noodles and ignoramuses. The vital difference between reading and experience is not measurable by examination marks.

"Am I an Educated Person?" *Sixteen Self Sketches*; Constable (1949).

Written August 3, 1947.

*E*LECTIONS

Your pious mob fills up ballot papers and imagines it is governing its masters; but the ballot paper that really governs is the paper that has a bullet wrapped up in it.

Andrew Undershaft, in *Major Barbara*, act 3; *The Bodley Head Bernard Shaw: Collected Plays with their Prefaces*, vol. 3 (1971).

First produced in 1905.

An election is a moral horror, as bad as a battle except for the blood: a mud bath for every soul concerned in it.

Franklyn Barnabas, in *Back to Methuselah*, "The Gospel of the Brothers Barnabas"; *The Bodley Head Bernard Shaw: Collected Plays with their Prefaces*, vol. 5 (1972).

First published in 1921.

We go to the polling station mostly to vote against something instead of for something.

The Intelligent Woman's Guide to Socialism, Capitalism, Sovietism, and Fascism, ch. 28; Constable (1949).

First published in 1928 as *The Intelligent Woman's Guide to Socialism and Capitalism*.

If I were seeking your votes, if I wanted to become a popular statesman, I should stand on a platform, I should make a collection of the grossest platitudes I know, things that no person could possibly have avoided thinking for themselves, and I should repeat those with an air of conviction. I should deliver every one of them as an ultimatum; and at the end of a very short time I would have the crowd madly cheering on that account.

"The Future of Western Civilization," *Practical Politics*, ed. Lloyd J. Hubenka; U of Nebraska Press (1976).

Lecture at the Fabian Society, November 22, 1928, first published as "Civilizations," *Newcastle Journal and North Star*, January 19, 1929.

I stand for the future and the past, for the posterity that has no vote and the tradition that never had any. I stand for the great abstractions: for

conscience and virtue; for the eternal against the expedient; for the
evolutionary appetite against the day's gluttony; for intellectual integrity
for humanity, for the rescue of industry from commercialism and of
science from professionalism.

> King Magnus, in *The Apple Cart*, act 1; *The Bodley Head Bernard Shaw: Collected Plays with their Prefaces*, vol. 6 (1973).
>
> First produced in 1929.

Let em [the electorate] have a voice. Let em have a choice. They've neither
at present. But let it be a voice to squeal with when they're hurt, and not to
pretend they know more than God Almighty does. Give em a choice
between qualified men: there's always more than one pebble on the beach;
but let them be qualified men and not windbags and movie stars and
soldiers and rich swankers and lawyers on the make.

> Hipney, in *On the Rocks*, act 2; *The Bodley Head Bernard Shaw: Collected Plays with their Prefaces*, vol. 6 (1973).
>
> First produced in 1933.

EMINENCE

I never climbed any ladder: I have achieved eminence by sheer gravitation.

> *The Irrational Knot*, preface; Constable (1950).
>
> First published in 1905.

EMOTION

It is feeling that sets a man thinking, and not thought that sets him feeling.

> "The Religion of the Pianoforte," *Shaw's Music*, vol. 3, ed. Dan H. Laurence (1981).
>
> First published in *Fortnightly Review*, February 1894.

ENDURANCE

Bear it like a man, Tavy, even if you feel it like an ass.

> John Tanner, in *Man and Superman*, act 2, *The Bodley Head Bernard Shaw: Collected Plays with their Prefaces*, vol. 2 (1971).
>
> First published in 1903.

ENGLAND AND THE ENGLISH

It is the birthright of an Englishman to do as he likes; and if he chooses to pay through the nose for the privilege of hearing a French baritone sing through the nose, he can adduce in his defence the natural fitness of the transaction, and the fact that the national taste rarely gives itself the slightest trouble about artistic excellence.

"Vocalists of the Season," *Shaw's Music*, vol. 1 (1981), ed. Dan H. Laurence.
First published in *The Hornet*, August 22, 1877.

Let no Englishman regret what in Ireland is called his stupidity—meaning his congenital incapacity to talk brilliantly about subjects and practise adroitly arts of which he knows next to nothing.

"Cornelius's *Barber*," *Shaw's Music*, vol. 2, ed. Dan H. Laurence (1981).
First published in *The World*, December 16, 1891.

It has taken me nearly twenty years of studied self-restraint, aided by the natural decay of my faculties, to make myself dull enough to be accepted as a serious person by the British public; and I am not sure that I am not still regarded as a suspicious character in some quarters.

"Irish Patriotism and Italian Opera," *Shaw's Music*, vol. 3, ed. Dan H. Laurence (1981).
First published in *The World*, November 15, 1893.

No man in these islands ever believes that the Bible means what it says: he is always convinced that it says what he means.

"The Living Pictures," *The Drama Observed*, vol. 1, ed. Bernard F. Dukore; Penn State Press (1993).
First published in Saturday Review, April 6, 1895.

Every Englishman is born with a certain miraculous power that makes him master of the world. When he wants a thing, he never tells himself that he wants it. He waits patiently until there comes into his mind, no one knows how, a burning conviction that it is his moral and religious duty to conquer those who possess the thing he wants. Then he becomes irresistible.

Napoleon, in *The Man of Destiny*, *The Bodley Head Bernard Shaw: Collected Plays with their Prefaces*, vol. 1 (1970).
First produced in 1897.

There is nothing so bad or so good that you will not find Englishmen doing it; but you will never find an Englishman in the wrong. He does everything on principle. He fights you on patriotic principles; he robs you on business principles; he enslaves you on imperial principles; he bullies you on manly principles; he supports his king on loyal principles and cuts off his king's head on republican principles. His watchword is always Duty; and he never forgets that the nation which lets its duty get on the opposite side to its interest is lost.

Napoleon, in *The Man of Destiny*; *The Bodley Head Bernard Shaw: Collected Plays with their Prefaces*, vol. 1 (1970).

First produced in 1897 .

The Englishman is the most successful man in the world simply because he values success—meaning money and social precedence—more than anything else.

"Meredith on Comedy," *The Drama Observed*, vol. 3, ed. Bernard F. Dukore; Penn State Press (1993).

First published in *Saturday Review*, March 27, 1897.

Intellectual subtlety is not their [Englishmen's] strong point. In dealing with them you must make them believe that you are appealing to their brains when you are really appealing to their senses and feelings. With Frenchmen the case is reversed: you must make them believe that you are appealing to their senses and feelings when you are really appealing to their brains.

"Shakespeare's Merry Gentlemen," *The Drama Observed*, vol. 3, ed. Bernard F. Dukore; Penn State Press (1993).

First published in *Saturday Review*, February 26, 1898.

The English do not know what to think until they are coached, laboriously and insistently for years, in the proper and becoming opinion.

"Valedictory," *The Drama Observed*, vol. 3, ed. Bernard F. Dukore; Penn State Press (1993).

First published in *Saturday Review*, May 21, 1898.

An Englishman thinks he is moral when he is only uncomfortable.

The Devil, in *Man and Superman*, act 3; *The Bodley Head Bernard Shaw: Collected Plays with their Prefaces*, vol. 2 (1971).

First published in 1903.

Englishmen never will be slaves: they are free to do whatever the Government and public opinion allow them to do.

The Devil, in *Man and Superman*, act 3; *The Bodley Head Bernard Shaw: Collected Plays with their Prefaces*, vol. 2 (1971).

First published in 1903.

Standing between you the Englishman, so clever in your foolishness, and this Irishman, so foolish in his cleverness, I cannot in my ignorance be sure which of you is the more deeply damned.

Father Keegan, in *John Bull's Other Island*, act 4; *The Bodley Head Bernard Shaw: Collected Plays with their Prefaces*, vol. 2 (1971).

First produced in 1904.

There is a saying in the Scripture which runs—so far as the memory of an oldish man can carry the words—Let not the right side of your brain know what the left side doeth. I learnt at Oxford that this is the secret of the Englishman's strange power of making the best of both worlds.

Father Keegan, in *John Bull's Other Island*, act 4; *The Bodley Head Bernard Shaw: Collected Plays with their Prefaces*, vol. 2 (1971).

First produced in 1904; the scriptural paraphrase is of *Matthew*, 6:3: "But when thou doest alms, let not thy left hand know what thy right hand doeth"; Father Keegan is ironic in two ways: not only substituting brain for hand, but also exploitation for almsgiving.

Every true Englishman detests the English. We are the wickedest nation on earth; and our success is a moral horror.

Cusins, in *Major Barbara*, act 3; *The Bodley Head Bernard Shaw: Collected Plays with their Prefaces*, vol. 3 (1971).

First produced in 1905.

We are a nation of governesses.

"The Muddle Over the Irish Grant," *New Statesman*, April 12, 1913.

In part, a parody of Adam Smith's description of the English as "a nation of shopkeepers."

The alleged aptitude of the English for self-government . . . is contradicted by every chapter of their history.

Androcles and the Lion, preface, "Christianity and the Empire"; *The Bodley Head Bernard Shaw: Collected Plays with their Prefaces*, vol. 4 (1972).

First published in 1916.

We are . . . fortunate in that an overwhelming majority of our subjects are Hindoos, Mahometans, and Buddhists: that is, they have, as a prophylactic against salvationist Christianity, highly civilized religions of their own.

Androcles and the Lion, preface, "Christianity and the Empire"; *The Bodley Head Bernard Shaw: Collected Plays with their Prefaces*, vol. 4 (1972).

First published in 1916.

The English face is not an adult face, just as the English mind is not an adult mind.

> Confucius, in *Back to Methuselah*, "The Thing Happens"; *The Bodley Head Bernard Shaw: Collected Plays with their Prefaces*, vol. 5 (1972).
>
> First published in 1921.

Anglo-American relations have always been strained. . . . No quarrels are as frequent and angry as family quarrels.

> Archibald Henderson, *Table-Talk of G.B.S.*, "On Things in General"; Harper (1925).

An English crowd will never do anything, mischievous or the reverse, while it is listening to speeches. And the fellows who make the speeches can be depended on never to do anything else.

> Basham, in *On the Rocks*, act 1; *The Bodley Head Bernard Shaw: Collected Plays with their Prefaces*, vol. 6 (1973).
>
> First produced in 1933.

The English will not be ruled; and there is nothing they hate like brains.

> Charles II, in *"In Good King Charles's Golden Days,"* act 2; *The Bodley Head Bernard Shaw: Collected Plays with their Prefaces*, vol. 7 (1974).
>
> First produced in 1939.

*E*QUALITY

There is not a man living who is not in favor of equality of opportunity, justice, and everything that is proper and sublime, consistently, of course, with an independent income for himself.

> Letter to E.D. Girdlestone, April 12, 1892, *Collected Letters*, vol. 1, ed. Dan H. Laurence (1965).

*E*RROR

As the American Vigilance Committee said to the widow, when they had lynched her husband for a horse stolen by somebody else, the laugh is with you.

> "Bernard Shaw Abashed," *The Drama Observed*, ed. Bernard F. Dukore, vol. 3; Penn State Press (1993).
>
> Letter to *Daily News*, April 17, 1905.

ℰSTEEM

Haven't you noticed that people always exaggerate the value of the things they haven't got? The poor think they need nothing but riches to be quite happy and good. Everybody worships truth, purity, unselfishness, for the same reason: because they have no experience of them.

The Strange Lady, in *The Man of Destiny; The Bodley Head Bernard Shaw: Collected Plays with their Prefaces*, vol. 1 (1970).

First produced in 1897.

ℰTHICS

We see the same ethical systems producing the extremes of maleficent and beneficent conduct as applied by different men under the same circumstances; and we see the same conduct referred to the most widely different materialist and idealist systems; and yet you tell me that these systems are our only refuge from moral chaos.

Letter to E.G. Girdlestone, 13 October 1890, *Collected Letters*, vol. 1 (1965).

ℰVIL

Men are always thinking that they are going to do something grandly wicked to their enemies; but when it comes to the point, really bad men are just as rare as really good ones.

Lady Cicely, in *Captain Brassbound's Profession*, act 2; *The Bodley Head Bernard Shaw: Collected Plays with their Prefaces*, vol. 2 (1971).

First produced in 1900.

Those who understand evil pardon it: those who resent it destroy it.

Man and Superman, The Revolutionist's Handbook, "Maxims for Revolutionists," *The Bodley Head Bernard Shaw: Collected Plays with their Prefaces*, vol. 2 (1971).

First published in 1903.

If a man cannot look evil in the face without illusion, he will never know what it really is, or combat it effectually.

Major Barbara, preface, "Sane Conclusions," *The Bodley Head Bernard Shaw: Collected Plays with their Prefaces*, vol. 3 (1971).

First published in 1907.

EVOLUTION

No doubt it is natural to a snail to think that any evolution which threatens to do away with shells will result in general death from exposure.

The Perfect Wagnerite, "Not Love, But Life," *Shaw's Music,* vol. 3, ed. Dan H. Laurence (1981).

First published in 1898.

What damns Darwinian Natural Selection as a creed is that it takes hope out of evolution, and substitutes a paralysing fatalism which is utterly discouraging.

Back to Methuselah, "Postscript: After Twenty-five Years"; *The Bodley Head Bernard Shaw: Collected Plays with their Prefaces,* vol. 5 (1972).

First published in World Classics Edition, 1944.

If the weight lifter, under the trivial stimulus of an athletic competition, can "put up a muscle"; it seems reasonable to believe that an equally earnest and convinced philosopher could "put up a brain." Both are directions of vitality to a certain end.

Back to Methuselah, preface, "Creative Evolution"; *The Bodley Head Bernard Shaw: Collected Plays with their Prefaces,* vol. 5 (1972).

First published in 1921.

The pursuit of omnipotence and omniscience. Greater power and greater knowledge: these are what we are all pursuing even at the risk of our lives and the sacrifice of our pleasures. Evolution is that pursuit and nothing else. It is the path to godhead. A man differs from a microbe only in being further on the path.

Franklyn Barnabas, in *Back to Methuselah,* "The Gospel of the Brothers Barnabas"; *The Bodley Head Bernard Shaw: Collected Plays with their Prefaces,* vol. 5 (1972).

First published in 1921.

EXPERIMENT

You do not settle whether an experiment is justified or not by merely showing that it is of some use. If that were the only thing to be considered we should kill our soldiers and sailors in time of peace simply to find out what our new guns and explosives could do.

"The Dynamitards of Science," *Platform and Pulpit;* Hill & Wang (1961).

Speech before the London Anti-Vivisection Society, May 30, 1900.

Attention and activity lead to mistakes as well as to successes; but a life spent in making mistakes is not only more honorable but more useful than a life spent doing nothing.

> *The Doctor's Dilemma*, preface, "The Technical Problem"; *The Bodley Head Bernard Shaw: Collected Plays with their Prefaces*, vol. 3 (1971).
>
> First published in 1911.

EXPLANATION

You mistake explanations for facts: all you sciencemongers do.

> Godfrey Kneller, in *"In Good King Charles's Golden Days,"* act 1; *The Bodley Head Bernard Shaw: Collected Plays with their Prefaces*, vol. 7 (1974).
>
> First produced in 1939.

EXPLOITATION

There is the eternal war between those who are in the world for what they can get out of it and those who are in the world to make it a better place for everybody to live in.

> Sir Arthur Chavender, in *On the Rocks*, act 2; *The Bodley Head Bernard Shaw: Collected Plays with their Prefaces*, vol. 6 (1973).
>
> First produced in 1933.

FACTS

No fact is ever attended to by the average citizen until the neglect of it has killed enough of his neighbors to thoroughly frighten him.

> "Ballet at the Alhambra," *Shaw's Music*, vol. 3, ed. Dan H. Laurence (1981).
>
> First published in *The World*, January 24, 1894.

Facts mean nothing by themselves. All the people at present crowding the Strand are facts. Nobody can possibly know the facts. Naturalists collect a few. Men of genius select a fewer few, and lo! a drama or a hypothesis. Genius is a sense of values and significances (the same thing). Without this sense facts are useless mentally. With it a Goethe can do more with ten facts than an encyclopedia compiler with ten thousands

Letter to H.G. Wells, August 2, 1929, *Selected Correspondence of Bernard Shaw: Bernard Shaw and H.G. Wells*, ed. J. Percy Smith; U of Toronto Press (1995).

$\mathcal{F}_{AITH}$

My own faith is clear: I am a resolute Protestant; I believe in the Holy Catholic Church; in the Holy Trinity of Father, Son (or Mother, Daughter) and Spirit; in the Communion of Saints, the Life to Come, the Immaculate Conception, and the everyday reality of Godhead and the Kingdom of Heaven.

"On Going to Church," *Shaw on Religion*, ed. Warren S. Smith; Dodd Mead (1967).

First published in *The Savoy*, January 1896.

$\mathcal{F}_{AMILY}$

The Family is a petty despotism; . . . a school in which men learn to despise women and women to mistrust men (much more than is necessary); a slaughterhouse for children (the firstborn succumbing to unskilled treatment, the lastborn to neglect). . . . Unfortunately, we cannot ask yet do without it; and therefore we put a good face on the matter by conferring upon it the conventional attribute of sacredness, and impudently proclaiming it the source of all the virtues it has well-nigh killed in us.

"Socialism and the Family," *SHAW: The Annual of Bernard Shaw Studies*, vol. 16, ed. Dan H. Laurence and Margot Peters; Penn State Press (1996).

Read to the Fabian Society on October 1, 1886.

I hate the Family, I loathe the Family, I entirely detest and abominate the Family as the quintessence of Tyranny, Sentimentality, Inefficiency, Hypocrisy, and Humbug.

"Socialism and the Family," *SHAW: The Annual of Bernard Shaw Studies*, vol. 16, ed. Dan H. Laurence and Margot Peters; Penn State Press (1996).

Read to the Fabian Society on October 1, 1886.

Has it occurred to you . . . that the prospect of Socialism destroying the family might not be altogether unattractive?

> Sir Arthur Chavender, in *On the Rocks*, act 1; *The Bodley Head Bernard Shaw: Collected Plays with their Prefaces*, vol. 6 (1973).
>
> First produced in 1933.

The difficulty about our family system remains: adults need quiet, order, and cleanliness; and children need noise, dirt, and destructiveness; yet they both need one another's company to some extent.

> Letter to E. Margaret Wheeler, March 1, 1945, *Collected Letters*, ed. Dan H. Laurence, vol. 4 (1988).

*F*ASCISM

Fascism is nothing but State-financed private enterprise.

> Letter to Lady Rhondda, January 1, 1945, *Collected Letters*, ed. Dan H. Laurence, vol. 4 (1988).

*F*EAR

There is only one universal passion: fear. Of all the thousand qualities a man may have, the only one you will find as certainly in the youngest drummer boy in my army as in me, is fear. It is fear that makes men fight: it is indifference that makes them run away: fear is the mainspring of war.

> Napoleon, in *The Man of Destiny*; *The Bodley Head Bernard Shaw: Collected Plays with their Prefaces*, vol. 1 (1970).
>
> First produced in 1897.

*F*EMINISM

I don't see that armies are exclusively men's province. . . . People imagine that women don't fight; but they do, when they get the chance, as the history of every revolution proves.

> "Interview with a Suffragist," *Fabian Feminist*, ed. Rodelle Weintraub; Penn State Press (1977).
>
> Interview with Maud Churton Braby, first published in *The Tribune*, March 12, 1906.

If I were a woman, I'd simply refuse to speak to any man or do anything for men until I'd got the vote. I'd make my husband's life a burden, and everybody miserable generally. Women should have a revolution—they should shoot, kill, maim, destroy—until they are given a vote.

"Interview with a Suffragist," *Fabian Feminist*, ed. Rodelle Weintraub; Penn State Press (1977). Interview with Maud Churton Braby, first published in *The Tribune*, March 12, 1906.

What sort of Bill would I introduce, did you say? Simply a short Act to have the word "men" in all the relevant statutes construed as human beings—as mankind—though, as you hear people talking of womankind, I suppose even that would not be understood. It's one of the many drawbacks to our ridiculous language. We have no word which includes men and women.

"Interview with a Suffragist," *Fabian Feminist*, ed. Rodelle Weintraub; Penn State Press (1977). Interview with Maud Churton Braby, first published in *The Tribune*, March 12, 1906.

It's usually pointed out that women are not fit for political power, and ought not to be trusted with a vote because they are politically ignorant, socially prejudiced, narrow-minded, and selfish. True enough, but precisely the same is true of men!

"Interview with a Suffragist," *Fabian Feminist*, ed. Rodelle Weintraub; Penn State Press (1977). Interview with Maud Churton Braby, first published in *TheTribune*, March 12, 1906.

The vote will never be won by speeches made by men on behalf of women. Every time you ask a man to apear on your platform, you confess the insufficiency of women to plead their own cause.

Letter to Miss Pogány, February 1, 1909, *Collected Letters*, ed. Dan H. Laurence, vol. 2 (1972).

The essence of drama is conflict, either with circumstances or with others . . . and if I have not dramatized the comradeship of women, it is for the same reason as I have not dramatized those of men.

Letter to Lady Rhondda, March 16, 1930, *Collected Letters*, ed. Dan H. Laurence, vol. 4 (1988). Margaret Haig Thomas, Viscountess Rhondda, an ardent feminist, was editor of *Time and Tide*, which from March 7 to April 11, 1930 serialized her articles, "Shaw's Women."

The House of Lords is more representative than the House of Commons because its members are there as the sons of their fathers, which is the reason for all of us being in the world; but it would be a much more human body if it were half-and-half sons and daughters.

"*In Good King Charles's Golden Days*," preface; *The Bodley Head Bernard Shaw: Collected Plays with their Prefaces*, vol. 7 (1974). First published in 1939.

*F*ICKLENESS

The fickleness of the women I love is only equalled by the infernal constancy of the women who love me.

Charteris, in *The Philanderer*, act 2; *The Bodley Head Bernard Shaw: Collected Plays with their Prefaces*, vol. 1 (1970).

First published in 1898.

*F*ICTION

All fiction should be founded on real characters. All good fiction is. The rottenness of most books is due to the fact that the authors are too lazy to observe and describe the people they meet: hence romantic invention, ending in hideous monotony, because every man makes an ass of himself in exactly the same way, whereas no two real persons are quite alike.

Letter to Sidney Dark, 20 March 1902, *Collected Letters*, vol. 2, ed. Dan H. Laurence (1972).

*F*IGHTS

Beware of the man who does not return your blow: he neither forgives you nor allows you to forgive yourself.

Man and Superman, *The Revolutionist's Handbook*, "Maxims for Revolutionists"; *The Bodley Head Bernard Shaw: Collected Plays with their Prefaces*, vol. 2 (1971).

First published in 1903.

*F*INANCIERS

The faults of the burglar are the qualities of the financier: the manners and habits of a duke would cost a city clerk his situation.

Major Barbara, preface, "Weaknesses of the Salvation Army"; *The Bodley Head Bernard Shaw: Collected Plays with their Prefaces*, vol. 3 (1971).

First published in 1907 .

*F*LATTERY

I delight in flattery. Even when there is no mistaking it for sincere admiration, I am pleased to find that anybody attaches sufficient importance to my opinion to spend a postage stamp on an attempt to humbug me. . . . Flatter by all means; and remember that you cannot lay it on too thick.

"A Critics' Trade Union," *Shaw's Music*, vol. 2, ed. Dan H. Laurence (1981).

First published in *The Star*, May 9, 1890.

I am proof against all illusions except illusions which flatter me.

"The Younger Generation," *Shaw's Music*, vol. 2, ed. Dan H. Laurence (1981).

First published in *The World*, March 29, 1893.

What really flatters a man is that you think him worth flattering.

Broadbent, in *John Bull's Other Island*, act 4; *The Bodley Head Bernard Shaw: Collected Plays with their Prefaces*, vol. 2 (1971).

First produced in 1904.

*F*OOD

There is no love sincerer than the love of food.

John Tanner, in *Man and Superman*, act 1, *The Bodley Head Bernard Shaw: Collected Plays with their Prefaces*, vol. 2 (1971).

First published in 1903.

Although "man doth not live by bread alone," yet until he lives by bread he cannot live by anything else.

"Life, Literature, and Political Economy," *Practical Politics*, ed. Lloyd J. Hubenka; U of Nebraska Press (1976).

Speech to the Students' Union at the London School of Economics and Political Science, December 13, 1905, revised for publication in *Clare Market Review*, January 1906; the quotation is from Deuteronomy 8:3.

*F*OOLS *AND FOLLY*

Do you think that the things people make fools of themselves about are any less real and true than the things they behave sensibly about?

Marchbanks, in *Candida*, act 1; *The Bodley Head Bernard Shaw: Collected Plays with their Prefaces*, vol. 1 (1970).

First produced in 1897.

I'm not a fool in the ordinary sense: only in the Scriptural sense of doing all the things the wise man declared to be folly, after trying them himself on the most extensive scale.

Frank Gardner, in *Mrs. Warren's Profession*, act 4; *The Bodley Head Bernard Shaw: Collected Plays with their Prefaces*, vol. 1 (1970).

First published in 1898.

Any fool can hang the wisest man in the country. Nothing he likes better.

Blanco, in *The Shewing-up of Blanco Posnet*; *The Bodley Head Bernard Shaw: Collected Plays with their Prefaces*, vol. 3 (1971).

First produced in 1909.

PROLA: It is dangerous to educate fools.
PRA: It is still more dangerous to leave them uneducated.

The Simpleton of the Unexpected Isles, act 2; *The Bodley Head Bernard Shaw: Collected Plays with their Prefaces*, vol. 6 (1973).

First produced in 1935.

*F*RANCE AND THE FRENCH

To my mind, the French would be a very tolerable nation if only they would let art alone. It is the one thing for which they have no sort of capacity; and their perpetual affectation of it is in them what hypocrisy is in the English, an all-pervading falsehood which puts one out of patience with them in spite of their realities and efficiencies.

"No Rules," *Shaw's Music*, vol. 3, ed. Dan H. Laurence (1981).

First published in *The World*, February 28, 1894.

*F*REEDOM

Freedom, my good girl, means being able to count on how other people will behave.

Joey Percival, in *Misalliance*; *The Bodley Head Bernard Shaw: Collected Plays with their Prefaces*, vol. 4 (1972).

First produced in 1910.

*F*RIENDS AND FRIENDSHIP

I only value friends for what they can give me: if you can only give me one thing, I shall value you only for that.

Letter to Alice Lockett, October 8, 1885, *Collected Letters*, ed. Dan H. Laurence, vol. 1 (1965).

As long as you can say that you believe in the sincerity of friendship, you don't believe in friendship, but in sincerity.

Letter to Robert Blatchford, c. February 7, 1897, *Collected Letters*, vol. 1, ed. Dan H. Laurence (1965).

*F*UGUES

To the average Briton the fugue is still an acute phase of a disease of dullness which occasionally breaks out in drawing rooms, and is known there as classical music.

"Fugue Out of Fashion," *Shaw's Music*, vol. 1 (1981), ed. Dan H. Laurence.

First published in *Magazine of Music*, November 1885.

*F*UNDAMENTALISM

Be on your guard against the idolatry of art—the spirit which says, "This is the absolute, inspired truth, and we will burn anybody who questions it." This is at the bottom of the idolatry of the Bible which would like to burn people who do not believe that the story of the Garden of Eden is a record of literal fact.

"Literature and Art," *Platform and Pulpit*, ed. Dan H. Laurence; Hill and Wang (1961).

Speech at the City Temple, London, October 8, 1908.

Legends and parable and drama: they are the natural vehicles of dogma; but woe to the Churches and rulers who substitute the legend for the dogma, the parable for the history, the drama for the religion!

Back to Methuselah, preface, "A Touchstone for Dogma"; *The Bodley Head Bernard Shaw: Collected Plays with their Prefaces*, vol. 5 (1972).

First published in 1921.

What are called wars of religion are always wars to destroy religion by affirming the historical truth or material substantiality of some legend, and killing those who refuse to accept it as historical or substantial. But who has ever refused to accept a good legend with delight as a legend?

> *Back to Methuselah*, preface, "A Touchstone for Dogma"; *The Bodley Head Bernard Shaw: Collected Plays with their Prefaces*, vol. 5 (1972).
>
> First published in 1921.

I do not, like the Fundamentalists, believe that creation stopped six thousand years ago after a week of hard work. Creation is going on all the time.

> *The Political Madhouse in America and Nearer Home*; Constable (1933).
>
> Speech broadcast on NBC from the Metropolitan Opera House, New York, April 11, 1933.

*F*UTURE, THE

My roots are in the past: my hopes are in the future.

> Mrs. Eteen, in "A Glimpse of the Domesticity of Franklyn Barnabas"; *The Bodley Head Bernard Shaw: Collected Plays with their Prefaces*, vol. 5 (1972).
>
> Originally intended to be act 2 of *The Gospel of the Brothers Barnabas*, first published in *Short Stories, Scraps and Shavings*, 1930.

*G*AMES

Games are for people who can neither read nor think.

> The Lady, in *On the Rocks*, act 1; *The Bodley Head Bernard Shaw: Collected Plays with their Prefaces*, vol. 6 (1973).
>
> First produced in 1933.

*G*ENIUS

There is little connection between the appearance of genius and its recognition.

> "Shaw Answers James Bryce," *The Drama Observed*, ed. Bernard F. Dukore, vol. 3; Penn State Press (1993).
>
> First published in *The New York Times*, May 5, 1907.

The common man does not want to live the life of a man of genius: he would much rather live the life of a pet collie if that were the only alternative.

Major Barbara, preface, "The Gospel of St. Andrew Undershaft"; *The Bodley Head Bernard Shaw: Collected Plays with their Prefaces*, vol. 3 (1971).

First published in 1907.

A man of genius is not a man who sees more than other men do. . . . The man of genius understands the importance of the few things he sees.

"Smoke and Genius," *Platform and Pulpit*, ed. Dan H. Laurence; Hill & Wang (1961).

Speech delivered before the annual meeting of the Coal Smoke Abatement Society, London, June 13, 1911.

I prefer nincompoops. I can always depend on them to do what was done last time. But I never know what a genius will be up to next, except that it will be something upsetting.

The Matron, in *Farfetched Fables*, third fable; *The Bodley Head Bernard Shaw: Collected Plays with their Prefaces*, vol. 7 (1974).

First published in 1951, completed in 1948.

GENRES

A classification is not necessarily a disparagement. When I deny that a certain piece is a comedy, it is much as if I denied that a certain man is a Swede or an Italian: he might be all the better for being neither.

Letter to William S. Douglas, March 18, 1898, *Collected Letters*, vol. 2, ed. Dan H. Laurence (1972).

GENTLEMEN

The essence of gentility is that you should never exploit your views (which may be of the highest Platonic or Christian kind—the higher the better) for political purposes, or allow them to make you socially disagreeable to other gentlemen. Everybody knows that the rich live by robbing the poor. That is why no gentleman ever mentions it.

"A Socialism Program: The Gentle Art of Unpleasantness," *Practical Politics*, ed. Lloyd J. Hubenka, U of Nebraska Press (1976).

First published in *The Clarion*, August 9, 1907.

The idle gentleman understands that the burglar who comes after his spoons is a thief; but he does not understand that he himself bought those spoons out of money stolen from the poor. He sees all the faults of the Labor Party, and none of the faults of the House of Lords.

"Why a Labor Year Book?" *Complete Prefaces*, ed. Dan H. Laurence and Daniel J. Leary, vol. 2 (1995). Preface to *The Labour Year Book*, 1916.

Goᴅ

Beware of the man whose god is in the skies.

Man and Superman, The Revolutionist's Handbook, "Maxims for Revolutionists"; *The Bodley Head Bernard Shaw: Collected Plays with their Prefaces*, vol. 2 (1971). First published in 1903.

We are told that when Jehovah created the world he saw that it was good. What would he say now?

Man and Superman, The Revolutionist's Handbook, "Maxims for Revolutionists"; *The Bodley Head Bernard Shaw: Collected Plays with their Prefaces*, vol. 2 (1971). First published in 1903.

Let God's work be done for its own sake: the work he had to create us to do because it cannot be done except by living men and women. When I die, let him be in my debt, not I in his; and let me forgive him as becomes a woman of my rank.

Barbara Undershaft, in *Major Barbara*, act 3; *The Bodley Head Bernard Shaw: Collected Plays with their Prefaces*, vol. 3 (1971). First produced in 1905.

UNDERSHAFT: You shall have your five thousand pounds.
MRS. BAINES: Thank God!
UNDERSHAFT: You don't thank me?

Major Barbara, act 2; *The Bodley Head Bernard Shaw: Collected Plays with their Prefaces*, vol. 3 (1971). First produced in 1905.

God (as you would put it) fulfills himself in many ways; and he also reveals himself in many ways; so that you can count on nothing but the way being unexpected. First it is generally a joke. Next it is a blasphemy. The third time it is a troublesome call to work. It is never solemn until its time is past and it is nothing but a formula reverberating in hollow hats,

Letter to Rev. H. Montagu Villiers," November 3, 1905, *Collected Letters*, ed. Dan H. Laurence, vol. 2 (1972).

The first phrase is from Tennyson's *Idylls of the King,* "The Passing of Arthur."

If we keep a god at all, we keep him as we keep a watchdog: he may bite everybody else—indeed that is what he is for—but he must not bite us.

"The Critics of the White Prophet," *Complete Prefaces*, ed. Dan H. Laurence and Daniel J. Leary, vol. 1 (1993).

Preface to the second edition of *The Critics of the White Prophet* by Hall Caine, which was not issued; published instead as a pamphlet, 1909.

The current theory that God already exists in perfection involves the belief that God deliberately created something lower than Himself when He might just as easily have created something equally perfect.

Letter to Count Leo Tolstoy, February 14, 1910, *Collected Letters*, ed. Dan H. Laurence, vol. 2 (1972).

In the old Hebrew legend, God lost patience with the world as Nero did with Rome, and drowned everybody except a single family. But the result was that the progeny of that family reproduced all the vices of their predecessors so exactly that the misery caused by the flood might just as well have been spared.

The Doctor's Dilemma, preface, "A False Alternative"; *The Bodley Head Bernard Shaw: Collected Plays with their Prefaces*, vol. 3 (1971).

First published in 1911.

The notion that inspiration is something that happened thousands of years ago, and was then finished and done with, never to occur again: in other words, the theory that God retired from business at that period and has not since been heard from, is as silly as it is blasphemous. He who does not believe that revelation is continuous does not believe in revelation at all, however familiar the parrot's tongue and pewsleepy ear may be with the word.

The Quintessence of Ibsenism, "Needed: An Ibsen Theatre," *The Drama Observed*, ed. Bernard F. Dukore, vol. 4; Penn State Press (1993).

First published in revised edition, 1913.

THE CAPTAIN: What is God?

LAVINA: When we know that, Captain, we shall be gods ourselves.

> *Androcles and the Lion*, act 2; *The Bodley Head Bernard Shaw: Collected Plays with their Prefaces*, vol. 4 (1972).
>
> First produced in 1913.

If he [the Creator] cannot make something out of nothing what was he himself made out of? All evolution is a process of making something out of nothing. What was Shakespeare's genius made out of? His father's tripe, perhaps.

> Letter to Frederick H. Evans, 6 October 1916, *Collected Letters*, ed. Dan H. Laurence, vol. 3 (1985).

LADY UTTERWORD: What a lovely night! It seems made for us.

HECTOR: The night takes no interest in us. What are we to the night?

> *Heartbreak House*, act 3; *The Bodley Head Bernard Shaw: Collected Plays with their Prefaces*, vol. 5 (1972).
>
> First published in 1919.

Better by far declare the throne of God empty than set a liar and a fool on it.

> *Back to Methuselah*, preface, "A Touchstone for Dogma"; *The Bodley Head Bernard Shaw: Collected Plays with their Prefaces*, vol. 5 (1972).
>
> First published in 1921.

My first childish doubt as to whether God could really be a good Protestant was suggested by my observation of the deplorable fact that the best voices available for combination with my mother's in the works of the great composers had been unaccountably vouchsafed to Roman Catholics.

> Quoted in Hesketh Pearson, *Bernard Shaw: His Life and Personality*, ch. 5; Atheneum (1963).
>
> First published in 1942.

We speak of war gods, but not of mathematician gods, poet or painter gods, or inventor gods. Nobody has ever called me a god: I am at best a sage. We worship all the conquerors, but have only one Prince of Peace, who was horribly put to death, and if he lived in these islands, would have some difficulty in getting exempted from military service as a conscientious objector.

> *Everybody's Political What's What?*, ch. 16; Constable (1944).

GOLDEN RULE, THE

Do not do unto others as you would that they should do unto you. Their tastes may not be the same.

> *Man and Superman, The Revolutionist's Handbook*, "Maxims for Revolutionists"; *The Bodley Head Bernard Shaw: Collected Plays with their Prefaces*, vol. 2 (1971).
>
> First published in 1903; Shaw reverses "the golden rule."

GOODNESS

The proper way to keep teeth good is to . . . wash them every day with soap: plain yellow soap. . . . I found that most things that were good for me were nasty. But I was taught to put up with them, and made to put up with them. I'm used to it now: in fact I like the taste when the soap is really good.

> Crampton, in *You Never Can Tell*, act 1; *The Bodley Head Bernard Shaw: Collected Plays with their Prefaces*, vol. 1 (1970).
>
> First published in 1898.

She may be a good sort, but she's a bad lot.

> Frank, in *Mrs. Warren's Profession*, act 3; *The Bodley Head Bernard Shaw: Collected Plays with their Prefaces*, vol. 1 (1970).
>
> First published in 1898.

It is not enough to know what is good: you must be able to do it.

> Zoo, in *Back to Methuselah*, "Tragedy of an Elderly Gentleman," act 1; *The Bodley Head Bernard Shaw: Collected Plays with their Prefaces*, vol. 5 (1972).
>
> First published in 1921.

GOVERNMENT

The art of government is the organization of idolatry. The bureaucracy consists of functionaries; the aristocracy, of idols; the democracy, of idolaters.

> *Man and Superman, The Revolutionist's Handbook*, "Maxims for Revolutionists"; *The Bodley Head Bernard Shaw: Collected Plays with their Prefaces*, vol. 2 (1971).
>
> First published in 1903.

Let six hundred and seventy fools loose in the streets; and three policemen can scatter them. But huddle them together in a certain house in Westminster; and let them go through certain ceremonies and call themselves certain names until at last they get the courage to kill; and your six hundred and seventy fools become a government.

Andrew Undershaft, in *Major Barbara*, act 3; *The Bodley Head Bernard Shaw: Collected Plays with their Prefaces*, vol. 3 (1971).

First produced in 1905; the house in Westminster, a borough in London, is Parliament's House of Commons.

Governments must proceed on dogmatic assumptions, whether they call them dogmas or not; and they must clearly be assumptions common enough to stamp those who reject them as eccentrics or lunatics. And the greater and more heterogeneous the population the commoner the assumptions must be.

Androcles and the Lion, preface, "Christianity and the Empire"; *The Bodley Head Bernard Shaw: Collected Plays with their Prefaces*, vol. 4 (1972).

First published in 1916.

There is only one alternative to government by police, and that is government by massacre.

"International Government," *Complete Prefaces*, ed. Dan H. Laurence and Daniel J. Leary, vol. 2 (1995).

Introduction to two reports by Leonard S. Woolf prepared for the Fabian Research Department; first published in 1916.

If there was twenty ways of telling the truth and only one way of telling a lie, the Government would find it out. It's in the nature of governments to tell lies.

O'Flaherty, in *O'Flaherty, V.C.*; *The Bodley Head Bernard Shaw: Collected Plays with their Prefaces*, vol. 4 (1972).

First produced in 1917.

From the beginning [of World War I] the useless people set up a shriek for "practical businessmen." By this they meant men who had become rich by placing their personal interests before those of the country, and measuring the success of every activity by the pecuniary profit it brought to them and to those on whom they depended for their supplies of capital.

Heartbreak House, preface, "The Practical Businessmen"; *The Bodley Head Bernard Shaw: Collected Plays with their Prefaces*, vol. 5 (1972).

First published in 1919.

It is said that every people has the Government it deserves. It is more to the point that every Government has the electorate it deserves; for the orators of the front bench can edify or debauch an ignorant electorate at will.

> *Heartbreak House*, preface, "The Cherry Orchard"; *The Bodley Head Bernard Shaw: Collected Plays with their Prefaces*, vol. 5 (1972).
>
> First published in 1919.

The miseries of the world today are due in great part to our objection, not merely to bad government, but to being governed at all.

> *The Intelligent Woman's Guide to Socialism, Capitalism, Sovietism, and Fascism*, ch. 70; Constable (1949).
>
> First published in 1928 as *The Intelligent Woman's Guide to Socialism and Capitalism*.

Ninety-nine hundredths of it [government] is unknown to the people, and the remaining hundredth is resented by them as an invasion of their liberty or an increase in their taxation.

> King Magnus, in *The Apple Cart*, act 1; *The Bodley Head Bernard Shaw: Collected Plays with their Prefaces*, vol. 6 (1973).
>
> First produced in 1929.

Talent and genius live far more luxuriously in the service of the rich than we in the service of our country.

> King Magnus, in *The Apple Cart*, act 1; *The Bodley Head Bernard Shaw: Collected Plays with their Prefaces*, vol. 6 (1973).
>
> First produced in 1929.

The tremendous problem which confronts every Government as the very first condition of the existence of the country, that is to provide a satisfactory answer to the daily prayer, "Give us this day our daily bread."

> "Follies, Fallacies, and Facts," *Practical Politics*, ed. Lloyd J. Hubenka; U of Nebraska Press (1976).
>
> Extensively revised text of "A Cure for Democracy," lecture at the Fabian Society, November 27, 1930, first published in *The Clarion*, February 1931; the quotation, from *Matthew*, 6:11, is part of "The Lord's Prayer."

Democracy, then, cannot be government by the people: it can only be government by consent of the governed. Unfortunately, when democratic statesmen propose to govern us by our own consent, they find that we don't want to be governed at all, and that we regard rates and taxes and rents and death duties as intolerable burdens. What we want to know is how little government we can get along with without being murdered in our beds.

> *The Apple Cart*, preface; *The Bodley Head Bernard Shaw: Collected Plays with their Prefaces*, vol. 6 (1973).
>
> First published in 1930.

A government which robs Peter to pay Paul can always depend on the support of Paul.

> *Everybody's Political What's What?* ch. 30; Constable (1944).

GREATNESS

When I was foolish, I did what I liked. . . . Now that Caesar has made me wise, it is no use my liking or disliking: I do what must be done, and have no time to attend to myself. That is not happiness; but it is greatness.

> Cleopatra, in *Caesar and Cleopatra*, act 4; *The Bodley Head Bernard Shaw: Collected Plays with their Prefaces*, vol. 2 (1971).
>
> First published in 1901.

The strength of a chain is no greater than its weakest link; but the greatness of a poet is the greatness of his greatest moment. Shakespeare used to get drunk. Frederick the Great ran away from a battle. But it was what they could rise to, not what they could sink to, that made them great. They weren't good always; but they were good on their day.

> Gunner, in *Misalliance*; *The Bodley Head Bernard Shaw: Collected Plays with their Prefaces*, vol. 4 (1972).
>
> First produced in 1910.

The most effective way of shutting our minds against a great man's ideas is to take them for granted and admit he was great and have done with him.

> *The Quintessence of Ibsenism*, "preface to Second Edition," *The Drama Observed*, ed. Bernard F. Dukore, vol. 4; Penn State Press (1993).
>
> First published in revised edition, 1913.

The greatness of a dramatist is not a space dimension but a time dimension. How do you know where I shall stand as a dramatist when I have been as long dead as Euripides? Yet that is the only test.

> "The Drama, the Theatre, and the Films," *The Drama Observed*, ed. Bernard F. Dukore, vol. 4; Penn State Press (1993).
>
> First published in *Fortnightly Review*, September 1, 1924.

GRIEG, EDVARD

Grieg's *Peer Gynt* music, which consists of two or three catchpenny phrases served up with plenty of orchestral sugar.

"Music for the Theatre," *Shaw's Music*, vol. 2, ed. Dan H. Laurence (1981).

First published in *The World*, January 27, 1892.

GROWING UP

To be treated as a boy was to be taken on the old footing. I had become a new person; and those who knew the old person laughed at me. The only man who behaved sensibly was my tailor: he took my measure anew every time he saw me, whilst all the rest went on with their old measurements and expected them to fit me.

John Tanner, in *Man and Superman*, act 1; *The Bodley Head Bernard Shaw: Collected Plays with their Prefaces*, vol. 2 (1971).

First published in 1903.

GUESSES

As a rule I do not hazard guesses about artists until I have privately ascertained that my guesses are correct.

Quoted in Hesketh Pearson, *Bernard Shaw: His Life and Personality*, ch. 16; Atheneum (1963).

First published in 1942.

HAPPINESS

There is nothing so insufferable as happiness, except perhaps unhappiness.

"Gounod's Music," *Shaw's Music*, vol. 2, ed. Dan H. Laurence (1981).

First published in *The World*, February 22, 1893.

Man can climb to the highest summits; but he cannot dwell there long.

Morell, in *Candida*, act 3; *The Bodley Head Bernard Shaw: Collected Plays with their Prefaces*, vol. 1 (1970).

First produced in 1897.

He who desires a lifetime of happiness with a beautiful woman desires to enjoy the taste of wine by keeping his mouth always full of it.

> *Man and Superman*, *The Revolutionist's Handbook*, "Maxims for Revolutionists"; *The Bodley Head Bernard Shaw: Collected Plays with their Prefaces*, vol. 2 (1971).
>
> First published in 1903.

A lifetime of happiness. If it were only the first half hour's happiness, Tavy, I would buy it for you with my last penny. But a lifetime of happiness! No man alive could bear it: it would be hell on earth.

> *Man and Superman*, Epistle Dedicatory; *The Bodley Head Bernard Shaw: Collected Plays with their Prefaces*, vol. 2 (1971).
>
> First published in 1903.

The notion is that you can't have too much of a good thing; but you can: you can bear hardship much longer than you could bear heaven.

> Iddy, in *The Simpleton of the Unexpected Isles*, act 2; *The Bodley Head Bernard Shaw: Collected Plays with their Prefaces*, vol. 6 (1973).
>
> First produced in 1935.

$\mathcal{H}$ATRED

Hatred is the coward's revenge for being intimidated.

> Andrew Undershaft, in *Major Barbara*, act 3; *The Bodley Head Bernard Shaw: Collected Plays with their Prefaces*, vol. 3 (1971).
>
> First produced in 1905.

$\mathcal{H}$EARTBREAK

His heart is breaking: that is all. It is a curious sensation: the sort of pain that goes mercifully beyond our powers of feeling. When your heart is broken, your bridges are burned: nothing matters any more. It is the end of happiness and the beginning of peace.

> Ellie Dunn, in *Heartbreak House*, act 2; *The Bodley Head Bernard Shaw: Collected Plays with their Prefaces*, vol. 5 (1972).
>
> First published in 1919.

ℋEAVEN

In my dreams it is a country where the State is the Church and the Church the people: three in one and one in three. It is a commonwealth in which work is play and play is life: three in one and one in three. It is a temple in which the priest is the worshiper and the worshiper the worshipped: three in one and one in three. It is a godhead in which all life is human and all humanity divine: three in one and one in three.

Father Keegan, in *John Bull's Other Island*, act 4; *The Bodley Head Bernard Shaw: Collected Plays with their Prefaces*, vol. 2 (1971).

First produced in 1904.

The heavens are empty, child. The earth is fruitful.

Adam, in *Back to Methuselah*, "In the Beginning," act 2; *The Bodley Head Bernard Shaw: Collected Plays with their Prefaces*, vol. 5 (1972).

First published in 1921.

ℋEDDA GABLER

The tragedy of Hedda in real life is not that she commits suicide but that she continues to live.

Three Plays by Brieux, preface, "Zolaism as a Superstition," *The Drama Observed*, ed. Bernard F. Dukore, vol. 3; Penn State Press (1993).

First published in 1911; on *Hedda Gabler*.

ℋEGEMONY

A great Power guarantees the independence of a small nation only to acquire control of its foreign policy without responsibility.

"How to Settle the Irish Question," *Complete Prefaces*, ed. Dan H. Laurence and Daniel J. Leary, vol. 2 (1995).

First published as a series of articles in *Daily Express*, November 27-29, 1917; separately published as a pamphlet, *How to Settle the Irish Question*, preface, December 1917.

$\mathcal{H}$ELL

Hell, in short, is a place where you have nothing to do but amuse yourself.

The Statue, in *Man and Superman*, act 3; *The Bodley Head Bernard Shaw: Collected Plays with their Prefaces*, vol. 2 (1971).

First published in 1903.

Hell is the home of the unreal and of the seekers for happiness. It is the only refuge from heaven, which is, as I tell you, the home of the masters of reality, and from the earth, which is the home of the slaves of reality.

Don Juan, in *Man and Superman*, act 3; *The Bodley Head Bernard Shaw: Collected Plays with their Prefaces*, vol. 2 (1971).

First published in 1903.

$\mathcal{H}$ERESY

The heretic is always better dead. And mortal eyes cannot distinguish the saint from the heretic.

Bishop Cauchon, in *Saint Joan*, Epilogue; *The Bodley Head Bernard Shaw: Collected Plays with their Prefaces*, vol. 6 (1973).

First produced in 1923.

$\mathcal{H}$EROES AND HEROINES

The Victoria Cross has been won by men abjectly afraid of ghosts, dogs, and demons.

Everybody's Political What's What?, ch. 38; Constable (1944).

$\mathcal{H}$INDUISM

The apparent multiplicity of Gods is bewildering at the first glance; but you presently discover that they are all the same one God in different aspects and functions and even sexes. There is always one uttermost God who defies personification. This makes Hinduism the most tolerant religion in the world, because its one transcendent God includes all possible Gods . . . [and] makes room for the Virgin Mary and modern Feminism by making Shiva a woman as well as a man.

> Letter to the Rev. Ensor Walters, February 4, 1933, *Collected Letters*, ed. Dan H. Laurence, vol. 4 (1988).

*H*ISTORY

As to teaching history and economics, what we have found in the Fabian is that the man who learns them without also learning politics, trade, and the world, is ten times more unmanageable and obstructive than the ordinary rule-of-thumb Radical.

> Letter to William P. Johnson, January 30, 1893, vol. 1, *Collected Letters*, ed. Dan H. Laurence (1965).

SWINDON: What will History say?
BURGOYNE: History, sir, will tell lies, as usual.

> *The Devil's Disciple*, act 3; *The Bodley Head Bernard Shaw: Collected Plays with their Prefaces*, vol. 2 (1971).
>
> First produced in 1897.

History always repeats itself and yet never repeats itself.

> Letter to C.H. Norman, April 22, 1940, *Collected Letters*, ed. Dan H. Laurence, vol. 4 (1988).

All the Napoleons and Hitlers from Alexander and Attila to this day have been classed by their fellow countrymen not as the villains of historical melodrama, but as its heroes.

> *Everybody's Political What's What?*, ch. 17; Constable (1944).

*H*ITLER, ADOLF

He is the victim of bad biology and of a bogus ethnology. He seems to believe in the division of mankind into an Aryan race and a Latin race. That is all nonsense. We are an extraodinarily mixed lot, and not only is it impossible to divide the sheep from the goats, in that particular way, because they are not sheep and goats but a sort of animal that is half sheep and half goat, but I think the evidence is irresistible that, unless a stock is crossed and that pretty frequently, the stock degenerates.

"The Politics of Unpolitical Animals," *Practical Politics*, ed. Lloyd J. Hubenka, U of Nebraska Press (1976).

Lecture at the Fabian Society, November 23, 1933, published in the *Lecture Recorder,* December 1933.

Holidays

A perpetual holiday is a good working definition of hell.

Misalliance, preface, "Children's Happiness"; *The Bodley Head Bernard Shaw: Collected Plays with their Prefaces*, vol. 4 (1972).

First published in 1914.

Hollywood

It has no dramatic technique and no literary taste: it will stick a patch of slovenly speakeasy California dialect upon a fine passage of English prose without seeing any difference, like a color blind man sticking a patch of Highland tartan on his dress trousers.

Letter to Theresa Helburn, February 15, 1935, *Collected Letters*, ed. Dan H. Laurence, vol.4 (1988).

People expend tons of energy jumping in and out of automobiles, knocking at doors, running up and downstairs, opening and shutting bedroom doors, drawing automatics, being arrested and tried for inexplicable crimes, with intervals of passionate kissing . . . but of what it is all about neither I nor anyone else in the audience has the faintest idea.

Letter to Theresa Helburn, February 15, 1935, *Collected Letters*, ed. Dan H. Laurence, vol.4 (1988).

Home

The great advantage of a hotel is that it's a refuge from home life.

The Waiter, in *You Never Can Tell*, act 2; *The Bodley Head Bernard Shaw: Collected Plays with their Prefaces*, vol. 1 (1970).

First published in 1898.

Nobody has yet done justice to the modern clever Englishwoman's loathing of the very word Home.

> Plays Unpleasant, preface; *The Bodley Head Bernard Shaw: Collected Plays with their Prefaces*, vol. 1 (1970).
>
> First published in 1898.

Home is the girl's prison and the woman's workhouse.

> Man and Superman, *The Revolutionist's Handbook*, "Maxims for Revolutionists"; *The Bodley Head Bernard Shaw: Collected Plays with their Prefaces*, vol. 2 (1971).
>
> First published in 1903.

Home life as we understand it is no more natural to us than a cage is natural to a cockatoo.

> Getting Married, preface, "Hearth and Home"; *The Bodley Head Bernard Shaw: Collected Plays with their Prefaces*, vol. 3 (1971).
>
> First published in 1911.

*H*OMOSEXUALITY

I have all the normal repugnances to aberrations; but I have found that they are untrustworthy guides in estimating character. Normally sexed people are sometimes as devoid of conscience as it is humanly possible to be: homosexualists are sometimes conspicuously able and highminded.

> Letter to the Very Rev. Albert Victor Baillie, November 24, 1928, *Collected Letters*, ed. Dan H. Laurence, vol. 4 (1988).

My own experience of life has led me . . . to treat sexual life as outside the scope of the judgments we have to pass on one another for social, political, and business purposes. I have not found that even the most absurd aberrations are necessarily associated with any general depravity of character. . . . I should say that a dishonored cheque is a safer index to character for worldly purposes than inversion.

> Letter to the Very Rev. Albert Victor Baillie, November 24, 1928, *Collected Letters*, ed. Dan H. Laurence, vol. 4 (1988).

$\mathcal{H}$ONESTY

Absolute honesty is as absurd as absolute temperature or absolute value.

"The Case for the Critic-Dramatist," *The Drama Observed*, vol. 2, ed. Bernard F. Dukore; Penn State Press (1993).

First published in *Saturday Review*, November 16, 1895.

It is not true that men can be divided into absolutely honest persons and absolutely dishonest ones. Our honesty varies with the strain put on it.

Crude Criminology, "Imprisonment," *Doctors' Delusions, Crude Criminology, and Sham Education*; Constable (1950).

First published in seven parts in *New York American*, April 30–June 11, 1922.

$\mathcal{H}$ONOR

It is generally admitted that even good men have their weaknesses; what is less recognized is that rascals have their points of honor.

Everybody's Political What's What?, ch. 22; Constable (1944).

There are no perfectly honorable men; but every true man has one main point of honor and a few minor ones.

Man and Superman, The Revolutionist's Handbook, "Maxims for Revolutionists"; *The Bodley Head Bernard Shaw: Collected Plays with their Prefaces*, vol. 2 (1971).

First published in 1903.

$\mathcal{H}$OPE

He who has never hoped can never despair.

Caesar, in *Caesar and Cleopatra*, act 3; *The Bodley Head Bernard Shaw: Collected Plays with their Prefaces*, vol. 2 (1971).

First published in 1901.

Human Nature

Statements that are true to human nature always can be verified, if you take trouble enough.

Letter to Charles Dilke, October 18, 1900, *Collected Letters*, vol. 2, ed. Dan H. Laurence (1972).

It is said . . . you cannot change human nature. On the other hand, it is maintained that human nature is the easiest thing in the world to change if you catch it young enough.

"Freedom," *Platform and Pulpit*, ed. Dan H. Laurence; Hill & Wang (1961).

B.B.C. radio talk, June 18, 1935.

Humor

Anything that makes you laugh. But the finest sort draws a tear along with the laugh.

"Who I Am, and What I Think," *Sixteen Self Sketches*; Constable (1949).

First published in *The Candid Friend*, May 1901.

Why should humor and laughter be excommunicated? Suppose the world were only one of God's jokes, would you work any the less to make it a good joke instead of a bad one?

Letter to Count Leo Tolstoy, February 14, 1910, *Collected Letters*, vol. 2, ed. Dan H. Laurence (1972).

Hunger

Man may have his opinion as to the relative importance of feeding his body and nourishing his soul, but he is allowed by Nature to have no opinion whatever as to the need for feeding the body before the soul can think of anything but the body's hunger.

Letter, February 7, 1900, to R. Ellis Roberts, *Collected Letters*, vol. 2, ed. Dan H. Laurence (1972).

*H*USBANDS

A married man can do anything he likes if his wife don't mind. A widower
can't be too careful.

Tarleton, in *Misalliance*; *The Bodley Head Bernard Shaw: Collected Plays with their Prefaces*, vol. 4 (1972).

First produced in 1910.

*H*YGIENE

I will not here go into the vexed question of whether the peasant's way of
blowing his nose or the squire's is the more cleanly and hygienic, though
my experience as a municipal councillor of the way in which epidemics are
spread by laundries makes me incline to the side of the peasant.

Three Plays by Brieux, preface, "The Attitude of the People to the Literary Arts," *The Drama Observed*, ed. Bernard F. Dukore, vol. 3; Penn State Press (1993).

First published in 1911.

*H*YPOCRISY

May I ask what it is to you whether I am or am not a hypocrite. Are the
things I say true or not? If they are, what does it matter whether I believe
them or not, or with what feelings I utter them?

Letter to Alice Lockett, August 19, 1886, *Collected Letters*, ed. Dan H. Laurence, vol. 1 (1965).

*I*BSEN, HENRIK

Ibsen means all that most revolts his critic.

The Quintessence of Ibsenism, "The Two Pioneers," *The Drama Observed*, vol. 1, ed. Bernard F. Dukore, Penn State Press (1993).

First published in 1891.

M. Lugné-Poe and his dramatic company called L'Oeuvre came to us with the reputation of having made Ibsen cry by their performance of one of his works. There was not much in that: I have seen performances by English players which would have driven him to suicide.

"L'Oeuvre," *The Drama Observed*, vol. 1, ed. Bernard F. Dukore, ed. Bernard F. Dukore; Penn State Press (1993).

On Aurélien-Marie Lugné-Poe and his Théâtre de l'Oeuvre, first published in *Saturday Review*, March 30, 1895.

In Ibsen's works we find the old traditions and the new conditions struggling in the same play, like a gudgeon half swallowed by a pike. . . . He provides a final catastrophe of the approved fifth-act-blank-verse-type. Hedwig and Hedda shoot themselves; Rosmer and Rebecca throw themselves into the mill race; Solness and Rubek are dashed to pieces; Borkman dies of acute stage tragedy without discoverable lesions.

Three Plays by Brieux, preface, "Zolaism as a Superstition," *The Drama Observed*, ed. Bernard F. Dukore, vol. 3; Penn State Press (1993).

First published in 1911; the names are characters in Ibsen's plays: Hedwig in *The Wild Duck*, Hedda in *Hedda Gabler*, Rosmer and Rebecca in *Rosmersholm*, Solness in *The Master Builder*, Rubek in *When We Dead Awaken*, and Borkman in *John Gabriel Borkman*.

*I*DEALISM

There is even something fine in being duped by idealism; better be Don Quixote than Sancho Panza.

"A Socialism Program: The Gentle Art of Unpleasantness," *Practical Politics*, ed. Lloyd J. Hubenka, U of Nebraska Press (1976).

First published in *The Clarion*, August 9, 1907.

*I*DEAS

Pursue commonplace ideas with all the intensity of which you are capable, and you will reap instant and plentiful applause.

Quoted in Dan H. Laurence, "Katie Samuel: Shaw's Flameless 'Old Flame,'" *SHAW*, vol. 15 (1995).

Letter to Katie Samuel, June 4, 1884.

The history of the world shows that if you refuse to allow a man to express unusual and even shocking ideas there will never be any progress made. Ideas would never change, and a world where ideas never change means stagnation, decline, and decay.

"Censorship as a Police Duty," *Platform and Pulpit*, ed. Dan H. Laurence; Hill and Wang (1961).

Address at the Special General Conference of the Chief Constables' Association, June 8, 1928.

The prudent old precept "Don't throw out your dirty water until you get in your clean . . ." is the very devil unless completed by "This also I say unto you, that when you get your fresh water you must throw out the dirty, and be particuarly careful not to let the two get mixed." Now this is just what we never do. We persist in pouring the clean water into the dirty; and our minds are always muddled in consequence.

"The Black Girl in Search of God," preface, *The Black Girl in Search of God and Some Lesser Tales*; Constable (1948).

First published in 1932.

*I*DOLATRY

We are such an inverately idolatrous people that it would perhaps be well for us if we could go back frankly to the cultus of the graven image, and leave our great men unworshipped. It would take the conceit out of them and do the graven images no harm.

"Darwin Denounced," *Bernard Shaw's Book Reviews*, ed. Brian Tyson; Penn State Press (1991).

First published in *Pall Mall Gazette*, May 31, 1887.

*I*GNORANCE

I spend my life contemplating the ocean of my ignorance. I once boasted of having picked up a pebble on the endless beach of that ocean. I should have said a grain of sand.

Isaac Newton, in *"In Good King Charles's Golden Days,"* act 1; *The Bodley Head Bernard Shaw: Collected Plays with their Prefaces*, vol. 7 (1974).

First produced in 1939.

When I contemplate what I have known and have done (not that I ever do) I have a high opinion of myself, When I contemplate what I don't know and cannot do (which I am often forced to do) I feel as a worm might if it knew how big the world is.

Everybody's Political What's What?, ch. 6; Constable (1944).

*I*LLUSION, THEATRICAL

I am an advocate for stage illusion; stage realism is a contradiction in terms.

"Ten Minutes with Mr. Bernard Shaw," *The Drama Observed*, vol. 1, ed. Bernard F. Dukore; Penn State Press (1993).

Questionnaire-interview, first published in *Today*, April 28, 1894.

*I*MMORALITY

Immorality does not necessarily imply mischievous conduct: it implies conduct, mischievous or not, which does not conform to current ideals.

The Quintessence of Ibsenism, "The Moral of the Plays," *The Drama Observed*, vol. 1, ed. Bernard F. Dukore; Penn State Press (1993).

First published in 1891.

*I*MMORTALITY

I shall perhaps enjoy a few years of immortality.

Three Plays for Puritans, preface; *The Bodley Head Bernard Shaw: Collected Plays with their Prefaces*, vol. 2 (1971).

First published in 1901.

*I*MPORTANCE

There will be no difficulty about the important questions. There never is. It is the trifles that will wreck you at the harbor mouth.

Bohun, in *You Never Can Tell*, act 3; *The Bodley Head Bernard Shaw: Collected Plays with their Prefaces*, vol. 1 (1970).

First published in 1898.

*I*MPRESSIONISM

To proclaim nothing but the faults of men who are deliberately damning themselves from the dealer's point of view in order to paint sincerely, is to sin against the light. These impressionables render us the inestimable service of doing those things which the buyers do not want to be done, and leaving undone those things which the buyers want to be done: consequently there are no commissions in them.

"In the Picture Galleries," in *Bernard Shaw on the London Art Scene 1885-1950*, ed. Stanley Weintraub; Penn State Press (1989).

First published in *The World*, April 24, 1889; the second sentence parodies *The Book of Common Prayer*: "We have left undone those things which we ought to have done;/And we have done those things which we ought not to have done."

There are more people who laugh at Mr. Whistler's "impressions" and rage at M. Monet's; but when they go back to their pet pictures they find, to their dismay, that there is no art in the landscapes and no light—except studio light—on the figures.

"Is Mr. Buchanan a Critic with a Wooden Head?" *The Drama Observed*, vol. 1, ed. Bernard F. Dukore; Penn State Press (1993).

First published in *Pall Mall Gazette*, June 13, 1889.

*I*NCOME

A sufficient income is indispensable to the practice of virtue; and the man who will let any unselfish consideration stand between him and its attainment is a weakling, a dupe, and a predestined slave.

The Irrational Knot, preface; Constable (1950).

First published in 1905.

Already there is economic equality between captains, and economic equality between cabin boys. What is at issue still is whether there shall be economic equality between captains and cabin boys.

Androcles and the Lion, preface, "The Captain and the Cabin Boy"; *The Bodley Head Bernard Shaw: Collected Plays with their Prefaces*, vol. 4 (1972).

First published in 1916.

When I speak of The Case for Equality I mean human equality; and that, of course, can only mean one thing: it means equality of income.

The Case for Equality; The Shaw Society (London), Shavian Tract No. 6 (1958).

Speech at the Political and Economic Circle of the National Liberal Club, May 1, 1913.

The need for a drastic redistribution of income in all civilized countries is now as obvious and as generally admitted as the need for sanitation.

> *Androcles and the Lion*, preface, "Redistribution"; *The Bodley Head Bernard Shaw: Collected Plays with their Prefaces*, vol. 4 (1972).
>
> First published in 1916.

I am perfectly well aware that my income has no reference whatever to my merit.

> *The W.E.A. [Workers' Educational Association] Education Year Book*, preface to Part 1; *Complete Prefaces*, ed. Dan H. Laurence and Daniel J. Leary, vol. 2 (1995).
>
> First published in 1918.

Only where there is pecuniary equality can the distinction of merit stand out.

> *The Intelligent Woman's Guide to Socialism, Capitalism,Sovietism and Fascism*, ch. 22; Constable (1949).
>
> First published in 1928 as *The Intelligent Woman's Guide to Socialism and Capitalism.*

*I*NDECISION

I am free from the indecision which is called an open mind.

> Letter to Horace Plunkett, August 3, 1917, *Collected Letters*, ed. Dan H. Laurence, Vol. 3 (1985).

*I*NDEPENDENCE

I congratulate you especially on the fact that all your friends and relations regard you as a madman. That is an indispensable beginning to a respectable, independent life.

> Letter to R. Golding Bright, April 22, 1895, *Collected Letters*, ed. Dan H. Laurence, vol. 1 (1965).

*I*NEVITABILITY

The inevitable does not touch me; it is the non-avoidance of the evitable, the neglect of the possible, the falling short of attainable efficiency, clearness, accuracy, and beauty, that set me raging.

> Letter to Robert Buchanan, undated (late 1895), *Collected Letters*, vol. 1, ed. Dan H. Laurence (1965).

INFIDELITY

When a man gets tired of his wife and leaves her it is never because she has lost her good looks. The new love is often older and uglier than the old.

King Magnus, in *The Apple Cart*, interlude; *The Bodley Head Bernard Shaw: Collected Plays with their Prefaces*, vol. 6 (1973).

First produced in 1929.

INFLUENCE

I cannot change their minds; but I can increase their knowledge.

Geneva, preface, "Civilization's Will to Live Always Defeated by Democracy"; *The Bodley Head Bernard Shaw: Collected Plays with their Prefaces*, vol. 7 (1974).

First published in 1939.

INJURIES

If you injure your neighbor, better not do it by halves.

Man and Superman, The Revolutionist's Handbook, "Maxims for Revolutionists"; *The Bodley Head Bernard Shaw: Collected Plays with their Prefaces*, vol. 2 (1971).

First published in 1903.

INNOVATION

There are many people who have never admitted any merit in Wagner's music; but they cannot stand Donizetti's operas after it, for all that.

"Is Mr. Buchanan a Critic with a Wooden Head?" *The Drama Observed*, vol. 1, ed. Bernard F. Dukore; Penn State Press (1993).

First published in *Pall Mall Gazette*, June 13, 1889.

A modern manager need not produce *The Wild Duck*; but he must be very careful not to produce a play which will seem insipid and old-fashioned to playgoers who have seen *The Wild Duck*, even though they may have hissed it.

"Mr. Daly Fossilizes," *The Drama Observed*, vol. 2, ed. Bernard F. Dukore; Penn State Press (1993).

First published in *Saturday Review*, June 29, 1895.

INTELLECT

We still have a silly habit of talking and thinking as if intellect were a mechanical process and not a passion.

Misalliance, preface, "The Pursuit of Learning"; *The Bodley Head Bernard Shaw: Collected Plays with their Prefaces*, vol. 4 (1972).

First published in 1914.

Nobody in this country seems to know that intellect is a passion for solving problems, and that its exercise produces happiness, satisfaction, and a desirable quality of life.

The W.E.A. [Workers' Educational Association] Education Year Book, preface to Part 1; *Complete Prefaces*, ed. Dan H. Laurence and Daniel J. Leary, vol. 2 (1995).

First published in 1918.

INTELLIGENCE

We are intellectually still babies: this is perhaps why a baby's facial expression so strongly suggests the professional philosopher's.

"Who I Am, and What I Think," *Sixteen Self Sketches*; Constable (1949).

First published in *Candid Friend*, May 1901.

Men make more mistakes by being too clever than by being too good.

Ann, in *Man and Superman*, act 1; *The Bodley Head Bernard Shaw: Collected Plays with their Prefaces*, vol. 2 (1971).

First published in 1903.

What is the use of being bright, subtle, witty, genial, if these qualities lead to the subjection and poverty of India and Ireland, and to the political anarchy and corruption of the United States?

Letter to James Huneker, January 4, 1904; *Collected Letters*, ed. Dan H. Laurence, vol. 2 (1972).

It is useless to complain that the conventional masses are unintelligent. To begin with, they are not unintelligent except in the sense in which all men are unintelligent in matters in which they are not experts. I object to be called unintelligent merely because I do not know enough about mechanical construction to be able to judge whether a motor car of new

design is an improvement or not, and therefore prefer to buy one of the old
type to which I am accustomed.

> *Three Plays by Brieux*, preface, "The Dread of the Original Thinker," *The Drama Observed*, ed. Bernard
> F. Dukore, vol. 3; Penn State Press (1993).
>
> First published in 1911.

*I*NTENTIONS

All men mean well.

> *Man and Superman, The Revolutionist's Handbook*, "Maxims for Revolutionists"; *The Bodley Head
> Bernard Shaw: Collected Plays with their Prefaces*, vol. 2 (1971).
>
> First published in 1903.

*I*NTERESTS

A man's interest in the world is only the overflow from his interest in
himself. When you are a child your vessel is not yet full; so you care for
nothing but your own afairs. When you grow up, your vessel overflows;
and you are a politician, a philosopher, or an explorer and adventurer. In
old age the vessel dries up: there is no overflow: you are a child again.

> Captain Shotover, in *Heartbreak House*, act 2; *The Bodley Head Bernard Shaw: Collected Plays with their
> Prefaces*, vol. 5 (1972).
>
> First published in 1919.

*I*NTERVIEWS

Never let an interviewer put you on your guard: it is only his way of
putting you off it.

> Letter to Elizabeth Robins, February 5, 1893, *Collected Letters*, vol. 1, ed. Dan H. Laurence (1965)

Never let [an interviewer] know or see anything that is not for publication.

> Letter to Elizabeth Robins, February 5, 1893, *Collected Letters*, vol. 1, ed. Dan H. Laurence (1965)

IRELAND AND THE IRISH

In Ireland, nobody ever knows the words of anything; though a native who does not know the tune of everything may safely be put down as having no musical faculty whatever.

"Irish Patriotism and Italian Opera," *Shaw's Music*, vol. 3, ed. Dan H. Laurence (1981).

First published in *The World*, November 15, 1893.

I showed my own appreciation of my native land in the usual Irish way by getting out of it as soon as I possibly could; and I cannot say that I have the smallest intention of settling there again as long as the superior attractions of St. Helena (not to mention London) are equally available.

"Church and Stage," *The Drama Observed*, vol. 2, ed. Bernard F. Dukore; Penn State Press (1993).

First published in *Saturday Review*, January 25, 1896.

All an Irishman's hopes and ambitions turn on his opportunities of getting out of Ireland.

O'Flaherty, V.C., preface; *The Bodley Head Bernard Shaw: Collected Plays with their Prefaces*, vol. 4 (1972).

First published in 1919.

Incomprehensible as it may seem to an Englishman, Irish patriotism does not take the form of devotion to England and England's king.

O'Flaherty, V.C., preface; *The Bodley Head Bernard Shaw: Collected Plays with their Prefaces*, vol. 4 (1972).

First published in 1919.

ISLAM

Islam is . . . ferociously intolerant. . . . You accepted Allah or you had your throat cut by somebody who did accept him, and who went to Paradise for having sent you to Hell.

Letter to the Rev. Ensor Walters, February 4, 1933, *Collected Letters*, ed. Dan H. Laurence, vol. 4 (1988).

JAMES, HENRY

There is no reason why life as we find it in Mr. James's novels—life, that is, in which passion is subordinate to intellect and to fastidious artistic taste—

should not be represented on the stage. If it is real to Mr. James, it must be real to others; and why should not these others have their drama instead of being banished from the theatre . . . by the monotony and vulgarity of drama in which passion is everything, intellect nothing, and art only brought in by the incidental outrages upon it.

"Two New Plays," *The Drama Observed*, ed. Bernard F. Dukore, vol. 1; Penn State Press (1993).

First published in *Saturday Review*, January 12, 1895.

*J*EWS

No doubt Jews are most obnoxious creatures. Any competent historian or psychoanalyst can bring a mass of incontrovertible evidence to prove that it would have been better for the world if the Jews had never existed. But I, as an Irishman, can, with patriotic relish, demonstrate the same of the English. Also of the Irish.

The Millionairess, preface; *The Bodley Head Bernard Shaw: Collected Plays with their Prefaces*, vol. 6 (1973).

First published in 1936.

UNDERSHAFT: It is part of the tradition that they [the Undershafts] should take a partner with a Jewish name. It suggests financial ability; and he gets all the blame when our profits are considered exorbitant.

CUSINS: A scapegoat, then?

UNDERSHAFT: That is the role of the Jew in modern Capitalism.

Major Barbara, screen version; *Collected Screenplays*, ed. Bernard F. Dukore (1980).

Written in 1940, first published in 1946.

*J*OKES

The cap and bells are necessary. Without them people settle down into a comfortable solemn feeling that they have done something good, and in fact dispose of the whole matter creditably and sufficiently, when they have assented to the play and enjoy it. It is just at that point that a laugh in their face disconcerts them and leaves them without the fatal impression that *I* have solved the problem for them.

Letter to William Stead, December 13, 1905, *Collected Letters*, ed. Dan H. Laurence, vol. 2 (1972).

*J*OURNALISM

August has set me free to do what a journalist ought to do all the year round—that is, wander in search of something interesting to write about, instead of, as at the height of the season, cramming his column with records of thousands of insignificant things for no better reason than that they are happening, and that people are supposed to want to know everything that is going on, whether interesting or not.

"Ballet at the Alhambra," *Shaw's Music*, vol. 2, ed. Dan H. Laurence (1981).
First published in *The World*, August 27, 1890.

Contemporary journalism, like democracy, is always a better judge of second-rate than of first-rate.

"Ibsen," *The Drama Observed*, ed. Bernard F. Dukore, vol. 3; Penn State Press (1993).
Obituary, first published in *The Clarion*, June 1, 1906.

A man who is too inaccurate to be a clerk and too ignorant and untrained to be anything else can make his living as a journalist if he can string a few clichés together in newspaper English.

Letter to Alwyne Silby, August 30, 1918, *Collected Letters*, ed. Dan H. Laurence, Vol. 3 (1985).

If you want a problem stated, a practised journalist will do it with an air that is the next best thing to solving it. But he never solves it: he hasn't time, and wouldn't get paid any more for the solution if he had time. So he chalks up the statement, and runs away from the solution.

"Who I Am, and What I Think," *Sixteen Self Sketches*; Constable (1949).
First published in *Candid Friend*, May 1901.

*J*OY

This is the true joy in life, the being used for a purpose recognized by yourself as a mighty one; the being thoroughly worn out before you are thrown on the scrap heap; the being a force of Nature instead of a feverish selfish little clod of ailments and grievances complaining that the world will not devote itself to making you happy.

Man and Superman, Epistle Dedicatory; *The Bodley Head Bernard Shaw: Collected Plays with their Prefaces*, ed. Dan H. Laurence, vol. 2 (1971).
First published in 1903.

*J*UDGMENT DAY

In a living society every day is a day of judgment; and its recognition as such is not the end of all things but the beginning of a real civilization.

The Simpleton of the Unexpected Isles, preface; *The Bodley Head Bernard Shaw: Collected Plays with their Prefaces*, vol. 6 (1973).

First published in 1936.

*J*USTICE

Whatever can blow men up can blow society up. The history of the world is the history of those who had courage enough to embrace this truth.

Andrew Undershaft, in *Major Barbara*, act 3; *The Bodley Head Bernard Shaw: Collected Plays with their Prefaces*, vol. 3 (1971).

First produced in 1905.

Unless the highest court can be set in motion by the humblest individual justice is a mockery.

The Judge, in *Geneva*, act 2; *The Bodley Head Bernard Shaw: Collected Plays with their Prefaces*, vol. 7 (1974).

First produced in 1938.

*K*NOWLEDGE

A man's mouth may be shut and his mind closed much more effectually by his knowing all about a subject than by his knowing nothing about it.

"William Morris as Actor and Dramatist," *The Drama Observed*, vol. 2, ed. Bernard F. Dukore; Penn State Press (1993).

First published in *Saturday Review*, October 10, 1896.

I have always despised Adam because he had to be tempted by the woman, as she was by the serpent, before he could be induced to pluck the apple from the tree of knowledge. I should have swallowed every apple on the tree the moment the owner's back was turned.

The Doctor's Dilemma, preface, "The Higher Motive, the Tree of Knowledge"; *The Bodley Head Bernard Shaw: Collected Plays with their Prefaces*, vol. 3 (1971).

First published in 1911.

No knowledge is finally impossible of human attainment; for even though it may be beyond our present capacity, the needed capacity is not unattainable.

The Doctor's Dilemma, preface, "Cruelty for Its Own Sake"; *The Bodley Head Bernard Shaw: Collected Plays with their Prefaces*, vol. 3 (1971).

First published in 1911.

A little knowledge is a dangerous thing; but we must take that risk because a little is as much as our biggest heads can hold; and a citizen who knows that the earth is round and older than six thousand years is less dangerous than one of equal capacity who believes it is a flat ground floor between a first floor heaven and a basement hell.

Geneva, preface, "Civilization's Will to Live Always Defeated by Democracy"; *The Bodley Head Bernard Shaw: Collected Plays with their Prefaces*, vol. 7 (1974).

First published in 1939; perhaps purposely, the first phrase slightly misquotes Alexander Pope's *Essay on Criticism*: "A little learning is a dangerous thing."

To say that we know little is not to say that we know nothing; for that little may make all the difference between peaceful constitutional changes and civil wars that leave the country half ruined.

Everybody's Political What's What?, ch. 44; Constable (1944).

K*ORAN, THE*

We have a cheap and dainty edition of it which every traveler in the East ought to carry with him, if only to convince himself that the average Arab knows even less about it than the average Englishman knows about the Bible.

"The Critics of the White Prophet," *Complete Prefaces*, ed. Dan H. Laurence and Daniel J. Leary, vol. 1 (1993).

Preface to the second edition of *The Critics of the White Prophet* by Hall Caine, which was not issued; published instead as a pamphlet, 1909.

L*ABOR PARTY*

ARCHIBALD HENDERSON: You are a member of the Labor Party?
SHAW: Yes.

HENDERSON: Why?

SHAW: Why not? Would you have me support the Idleness parties?

Archibald Henderson, *Table-Talk of G.B.S.*, "The Great War and the Aftermath"; Harper & Brothers (1925).

LAISSER-FAIRE

What is laisser-faire but an orthodoxy? the most tyrannous and disastrous of all the orthodoxies, since it forbids you even to learn.

The Doctor's Dilemma, preface, "The Technical Problem"; *The Bodley Head Bernard Shaw: Collected Plays with their Prefaces*, vol. 3 (1971).

First published in 1911.

LANGUAGES

I cannot learn languages. I have tried hard, only to find that men of ordinary capacity can learn Sanscrit in less time than it takes me to buy a German dictionary.

"Duse and Bernhardt," *The Drama Observed*, vol. 2, ed. Bernard F. Dukore; Penn State Press (1993).

First published in *Saturday Review*, June 15, 1895.

Greek scholars are privileged men. Few of them know Greek; and none of them know anything else; but their position is unchallengeable. Other languages are the qualifications of waiters and commercial travellers; Greek is to a man of position what the hallmark is to silver.

Cusins, in *Major Barbara*, act 1; *The Bodley Head Bernard Shaw: Collected Plays with their Prefaces*, vol. 3 (1971).

First produced in 1905.

LAUGHTER

IMOGEN: Oh, do not make me laugh. Laughter dissolves too many just resentments, Pardons too many sins.

IACHIMO: And saves the world many thousand murders.

Cymbeline Refinished; The Bodley Head Bernard Shaw: Collected Plays with their Prefaces, vol 7 (1974) First produced in 1937.

LAW AND LAWYERS

A barrister in England gets an immense reputation as a criminals' advocate when a dozen of his clients have been hanged (the hanging being at once a proof and advertisement of the importance of the cases).

"Bassetto's Destructive Force," *Shaw's Music,* vol. 1, ed. Dan H. Laurence (1981). First published in *The Star,* March 7, 1890.

Laws, religions, creeds, and systems of ethics, instead of making society better than its best unit, make it worse than its average unit, because they are never up to date.

The Sanity of Art, Major Critical Essays; Constable (1948). First published as "A Degenerate's View of Nordau," *Liberty* (New York), July 27, 1895.

There is a bad side to the very convenience of law. It deadens the conscience of individuals by relieving them of the ethical responsibility of their own actions.

The Sanity of Art, Major Critical Essays; Constable (1949). First published as "A Degenerate's View of Nordau,"*Liberty* (New York), July 27, 1895.

The average lawyer is a nincompoop, who contradicts your perfectly sound impressions on notorious points of law, involves you in litigation when your case is hopeless, compromises when your success is certain, and cannot even make your will without securing the utter defeat of your intentions if anyone takes the trouble to dispute them.

"*Henry IV,*" *The Drama Observed,* vol. 2, ed. Bernard F. Dukore; Penn State Press (1993). First published in *Saturday Review,* May 16, 1896.

HAWKINS: The will is not exactly in proper legal phraseology.
RICHARD: No: my father died without the consolations of the law.

The Devil's Disciple, act 1; *The Bodley Head Bernard Shaw: Collected Plays with their Prefaces,* vol. 2 (1971).
First produced in 1897.

Our criminal law, based on a conception of crime and punishment which is nothing but our vindictiveness and cruelty in a virtuous disguise, is an unmitigated and abominable nuisance.

The Perfect Wagnerite, "Anarchism No Panacea," *Shaw's Music,* vol. 3, ed. Dan H. Laurence (1981).

First published in 1898.

Whenever you wish to do anything against the law, Cicely, always consult a good solicitor first.

Sir Howard, in *Captain Brassbound's Profession,* act 1; *The Bodley Head Bernard Shaw: Collected Plays with their Prefaces,* vol. 2 (1971).

First produced in 1900.

If you want to consult a man who not only has no legal knowledge but who has no conception of the nature of law, consult your solicitor.

"Life, Literature, and Political Economy"; *Practical Politics,* ed. Lloyd J. Hubenka, U of Nebraska Press (1976).

Speech to the Students' Union at the London School of Economics and Political Science, December 13, 1905, revised for publication in *Clare Market Review,* January 1906.

Most laws are, and all laws ought to be, stronger than the strongest individual.

Getting Married, preface, "Marriage Nevertheless Inevitable"; *The Bodley Head Bernard Shaw: Collected Plays with their Prefaces,* vol. 3 (1971).

First published in 1911.

When we are robbed we generally appeal to the criminal law, not considering that if the criminal law were effective we should not have been robbed. That convicts us of vengeance.

Androcles and the Lion, preface, "Limits to Free Will"; *The Bodley Head Bernard Shaw: Collected Plays with their Prefaces,* vol. 4 (1972).

First published in 1916.

It is much easier to write a good play than to make a good law. And there are not a hundred men in the world who can write a play good enough to stand daily wear and tear as long as a law must.

The Apple Cart, preface; *The Bodley Head Bernard Shaw: Collected Plays with their Prefaces,* vol. 6 (1973).

First published in 1930.

The law is equal before all of us; but we are not all equal before the law. Virtually there is one law for the rich and another for the poor, one law for the cunning and another for the simple, one law for the forceful and another for the feeble, one law for the ignorant and another for the learned, one law for the brave and another for the timid, and within family limits one law for the parent and no law at all for the child.

The Millionairess, preface; *The Bodley Head Bernard Shaw: Collected Plays with their Prefaces*, vol. 6 (1973).

First published in 1936.

*L*EARNING

You have learnt something. That always feels at first as if you had lost something.

Andrew Undershaft, in *Major Barbara*, act 3; *The Bodley Head Bernard Shaw: Collected Plays with their Prefaces*, vol. 3 (1971).

First produced in 1905.

When the Pursuit of Learning comes to mean the pursuit of learning by the child instead of the pursuit of the child by Learning, cane in hand, the danger will be precocity of the intellect, which is just as undesirable as precocity of the emotions.

Misalliance, preface, "The Pursuit of Learning"; *The Bodley Head Bernard Shaw: Collected Plays with their Prefaces*, vol. 4 (1972).

First published in 1914.

A man who has learned something new is not the man he was before he knew it.

"The Future of Western Civilization," *Practical Politics*, ed. Lloyd J. Hubenka; U of Nebraska Press (1976).

Lecture at the Fabian Society, November 22, 1928, first published as "Civilizations," *Newcastle Journaland North Star*, January 19, 1929.

*L*EISURE

We gain from machinery an enormous saving of time. Every new machine gives us daily a few years of leisure to "divide up" among the nation. We divide it exactly as we divide the material wealth. To him that hath, much more is given; and from him that hath little, we take that which he already hath.

"Art and Society," *Bernard Shaw on the London Art Scene 1885-1950*, ed. Stanley Weintraub; Penn State Press (1989).

Lecture to the Bedford Debating Society, December 10, 1885; the phrase in the last sentence plays on Matthew 25:29: "Unto every one that hath shall be given, and he shall have abundance: but from him that hath not shall be taken away even that which he hath."

*L*IBERTY

We all profess the deepest regard for liberty; but no sooner does anyone claim to exercise it than we declare with horror that we are in favor of liberty but not of licence, and demand indignantly whether true freedom can ever mean freedom to do wrong, to preach sedition and immorality, to utter blasphemy. Yet this is exactly what liberty does mean.

The W.E.A. [Workers' Educational Association] Education Year Book, preface to Part 1; *Complete Prefaces*, ed. Dan H. Laurence and Daniel J. Leary, vol. 2 (1995).

First published in 1918.

The cry of Liberty is always on the lips of the propertied classes who own the lion's share of land and capital and have nothing to fear but nationalization of these resources, because it implies that the less government activity there is the more free the people are, and because it helps to elect the thoughtless who always support the status quo because anything unusual shocks them.

The Intelligent Woman's Guide to Socialism, Capitalism, Sovietism, and Fascism, ch. 85; Constable (1949).

First published in 1937.

How much liberty have men—even independent British yeomen who call themselves "their own masters"—when they have to work sixteen hours a day to pay their rents and mortagage interests and keep alive?

"How to Talk Ingelligently About the War," *SHAW: The Annual of Bernard Shaw Studies*, vol. 16, ed. Dan H. Laurence and Margot Peters; Penn State Press (1996).

Written in July 1940.

*L*IES

EDITH: Does anybody want me to flatter and be untruthful?
HOTCHKISS: Well, since you ask me, I do. Surely it's the very first qualification for tolerable social intercourse.

The Bishop, in *Getting Married*; *The Bodley Head Bernard Shaw: Collected Plays with their Prefaces*, vol. 3 (1971).

First produced in 1908.

*L*IFE

To endure the pain of living, we all drug ourselves more or less with gin, with literature, with superstitions, with romance, with idealism, political, sentimental, and moral, with every possible preparation of that universal hashish: imagination.

"Ibsen's New Play," *The Drama Observed*, vol. 2, ed. Bernard F. Dukore; Penn State Press (1993).

Review of translation of *John Gabriel Borkman*, first published in *The Academy*, January 16, 1897.

To me the tragedy and comedy of life lie in the consequences, sometimes terrible, sometimes ludicrous, of our persistent attempts to found our institutions on the ideals suggested to our imaginations by our half-satisfied passions, instead of on a genuinely scientific natural history.

Preface, *Plays Pleasant*; *The Bodley Head Bernard Shaw: Collected Plays with their Prefaces*, vol. 1 (1970).

First published in 1898.

Happiness is not the object of life: life has no object: it is an end in itself; and courage consists in the readiness to sacrifice happiness for an intenser quality of life.

Letter to Eva Christy, undated: December 1900, *Collected Letters*, vol. 2, ed. Dan H. Laurence (1972).

As long as I can conceive something better than myself I cannot be easy unless I am striving to bring it into existence or clearing the way for it. That is the law of my life.

Don Juan, in *Man and Superman*, act 3, *The Bodley Head Bernard Shaw: Collected Plays with their Prefaces*, vol. 2 (1971).

First published in 1903.

The ice of life is slippery.

Fanny O'Dowda, in *Fanny's First Play*, Induction; *The Bodley Head Bernard Shaw: Collected Plays with their Prefaces*, vol. 4 (1972).

First produced in 1911; Fanny calls this the motto of the Cambridge Fabian Society.

If any man wants a better life, he should not seek for that life for himself alone, but should attain it by raising the general level of life.

The Case for Equality; The Shaw Society (London), Shavian Tract No. 6 (1958).

Speech at the Political and Economic Circle of the National Liberal Club, May 1, 1913.

Life is an adventure, not the compounding of a prescription.

Letter to V.O. Plenazár, July 15, 1929, *Collected Letters*, ed. Dan H. Laurence, vol. 4 (1988).

I believe in life everlasting; but not for the individual.

Statement to Judy Musters, October 25, 1950; quoted in *Collected Letters*, ed. Dan H. Laurence, vol. 4 (1988).

LITERATURE

Literature is the recorded expression of the former consciousness of the race; and in contributing anything new to literature you are adding to that consciousness.

"Life, Literature, and Political Economy"; *Practical Politics*, ed. Lloyd J. Hubenka, U of Nebraska Press (1976).

Speech to the Students' Union at the London School of Economics and Political Science, December 13, 1905, revised for publication in *Clare Market Review*, January 1906.

All great Art and Literature is propaganda.

On the Rocks, preface, "The Case of Galileo"; *The Bodley Head Bernard Shaw: Collected Plays with their Prefaces*, vol. 6 (1973).

First published in 1934.

LOGIC

The irresistibility of a chain of logic lies, not in the logic, but in the acceptability of the conclusion to the person addressed. For instance,

corporal punishment is an abominable practice to my mind; but the
reasons for it are "irresistible" to those who approve of it.

> Letter to E.C. Chapman, July 29, 1891, *Collected Letters*, ed. Dan H. Laurence, vol. 1 (1965).

Long runs

The actor who knows one part, and consequently one play thoroughly, is
superior to the actor who can scramble with assistance through a dozen.
The one gets into the skin of one character: the other only puts on the
clothes of twelve. One impersonation is worth more than many
impostures. Long runs mean impersonations: palminess means imposture.

> "Palmy Days at the Opera," *Shaw's Music*, vol. 1, ed. Dan H. Laurence (1981).
>
> First published in *Magazine of Music*, January 1886; "palminess" alludes to the title, which
> refers to repertory theatre.

Love

Love loses its charm when it is not free; and whether the compulsion is that
of custom and law, or of infatuation, the effect is the same: it becomes
valueless. The desire to give inspires no affection unless there is also the
power to withhold.

> *The Quintessence of Ibsenism*, "The Womanly Woman," *The Drama Observed*, vol. 1, ed. Bernard F.
> Dukore; Penn State Press (1993).
>
> First published in 1891.

A man's power of love and admiration is like any other of his powers: he
has to throw it away many times before he learns what is really worthy of it.

> Valentine, in *You Never Can Tell*, act 3; *The Bodley Head Bernard Shaw: Collected Plays with their
> Prefaces*, vol. 1 (1970).
>
> First published in 1898.

GLORIA: You have tried to make me love you.
VALENTINE: I have.
GLORIA: Well, you have succeeded in making me hate you: passionately.
VALENTINE: It's surprising how little difference there is between the two.

> *You Never Can Tell*, act 3; *The Bodley Head Bernard Shaw: Collected Plays with their Prefaces*, vol. 1
> (1970).
>
> First published in 1898.

When we want to read of the deeds that are done for love, whither do we turn? To the murder column; and there we are rarely disappointed.

Three Plays for Puritans, preface; *The Bodley Head Bernard Shaw: Collected Plays with their Prefaces*, vol. 2 (1971).

First published in 1901.

First love is only a little foolishness and a lot of curiosity.

Broadbent, in *John Bull's Other Island*, act 4; *The Bodley Head Bernard Shaw: Collected Plays with their Prefaces*, vol. 2 (1971).

First produced in 1904.

Love is an infinite mystery, like everything else, until you have been through it, when it becomes as finite to you as anything else.

Letter to Erica Cotterill, September 28, 1905, *Collected Letters*, vol. 2, ed. Dan H. Laurence (1972).

There are larger loves and diviner dreams than the fireside ones.

Barbara Undershaft, in *Major Barbara*, act 3, *The Bodley Head Bernard Shaw: Collected Plays with their Prefaces*, vol. 3 (1971).

First produced in 1905.

A love affair should always be a honeymoon. And the only way to make sure of that is to keep changing the man; for the same man can never keep it up.

The Countess, in *Too True To Be Good*, act 2; *The Bodley Head Bernard Shaw: Collected Plays with their Prefaces*, vol. 6 (1973).

First produced in 1932.

Love gets people into difficulties, not out of them.

The Patient, in *Too True to be Good*, act 3; *The Bodley Head Bernard Shaw: Collected Plays with their Prefaces*, vol. 6 (1973).

First produced in 1932.

You're only a beginner; and what you think is love, and interest, and all that, is not real love at all: three quarters of it is only unsatisfied curiosity.

The Countess, in *Too True to be Good*, act 2; *The Bodley Head Bernard Shaw: Collected Plays with their Prefaces*, vol. 6 (1973).

First produced in 1932.

I was taught when I was young that if people would only love one another, all would be well with the world. This seemed simple and very nice; but I found when I tried to put it in practice not only that other people were seldom lovable, but that I was not very lovable myself.

"School," *Platform and Pulpit*, ed. Dan H. Laurence; Hill & Wang (1961).
B.B.C. radio talk, June 11, 1937.

Such a command as "Love one another," as I see it, is a stupid refusal to accept the facts of human nature. Are we lovable animals? Do you love the rate collector? Do you love Mr. Lloyd George, and, if you do, do you love Mr. Winston Churchill? Have you an all-embracing affection for Messrs. Mussolini, Hitler, Franco, Atatürk, and the Mikado? I do not like all these gentlemen, and even if I did how could I offer myself to them as a delightfully lovable person?

"This Danger of War," *Platform and Pulpit*, ed. Dan H. Laurence; Hill & Wang (1961).
B.B.C. broadcast, November 2, 1937.

$\mathcal{M}$ADNESS

When all the world goes mad, one must accept madness as sanity, since sanity is, in the last analysis, nothing but the madness on which the whole world happens to agree.

Letter to Maxim Gorky, December 28, 1915, *Collected Letters*, ed. Dan H. Laurence, vol. 3 (1985).
On World War I.

We want a few mad people now. See where the sane ones have landed us!

Poulengey, in *Saint Joan*, scene 1; *The Bodley Head Bernard Shaw: Collected Plays with their Prefaces*, vol. 6 (1973).
First produced in 1923.

$\mathcal{M}$ANKIND

When you have said that Charlie has "*so much* in him—depths unfathomable," you have said nothing at all: any mother will plead the same for her ugly duckling, and plead it truthfully too; for we all have "depths unfathomable" in us, since it must have taken millions of ages to evolve even a human idiot.

> Letter to Janet Achurch, May 24, 1895, *Collected Letters*, vol. 1, ed. Dan H. Laurence (1965).
>
> "Charlie" (Charles Charrington) was Janet Achurch's husband.

No man manages his own affairs as well as a tree does.

> "Life, Literature, and Political Economy"; *Practical Politics*, ed. Lloyd J. Hubenka, U of Nebraska Press (1976).
>
> Speech to the Students' Union at the London School of Economics and Political Science, December 13, 1905, revised for publication in *Clare Market Review*, January 1906.

Man is your real king of beasts.

> "Androcles and the Lion," *Complete Prefaces*, ed. Dan H. Laurence and Daniel J. Leary, vol. 2 (1995).
>
> Program of *Androcles and the Lion*, St. James's Theatre, London, September 1, 1913.

History records very little in the way of mental activity on the part of the mass of mankind except a series of stampedes from affirmative errors into negative ones and back again.

> *Back to Methuselah*, preface, "The Danger of Reaction"; *The Bodley Head Bernard Shaw: Collected Plays with their Prefaces*, vol. 5 (1972).
>
> First published in 1921.

Mankind, though pugnacious, yet has an instinct which checks it on the brink of self-destruction.

> *Geneva*, preface, "Civilization's Will to Live Always Defeated by Democracy"; *The Bodley Head Bernard Shaw: Collected Plays with their Prefaces*, vol. 7 (1974).
>
> First published in 1939.

*M*ANNERS

The great secret, Eliza, is not having bad manners or good manners or any other particular sort of manners, but having the same manner for all human souls: in short, behaving as if you were in Heaven, where there are no third-class carriages, and one soul is as good as another.

> Henry Higgins, in *Pygmalion*, act 5; *The Bodley Head Bernard Shaw: Collected Plays with their Prefaces*, vol. 4 (1972).
>
> First produced (in German) in 1913.

Bourgeois manners may be snobbish manners: there may be no pleasure in them, as you say; but they are better than no manners.

> Franklyn Barnabas, in *Back to Methuselah*, "The Gospel of the Brothers Barnabas"; *The Bodley Head Bernard Shaw: Collected Plays with their Prefaces*, vol. 5 (1972).
>
> First published in 1921.

Manners will never be universally good until every person is every other person's customer.

> A, in *Village Wooing*, scene 3; *The Bodley Head Bernard Shaw: Collected Plays with their Prefaces*, vol. 6 (1973).
>
> First published in 1934.

MARRIAGE

Unmarried couples cohabit without incurring any legal penalty. More than that, the woman's legal standing is better every way than that of a wife; and the man, whilst he escapes heavy responsibilities, forfeits nothing but his control over his children: a disability which, judging from the average solicitude of men for their illegitimate children, he can endure with considerable fortitude.

> Review of *The Future of Marriage*, SHAW: *The Annual of Bernard Shaw Studies*, vol. 16, ed. Dan H. Laurence and Margot Peters; Penn State Press (1996).
>
> Written on March 9, 1885 for *The Commonweal*, which rejected it.

Wedlock is a heavy chain for a man to rivet upon himself; but the woman is born with the chain on: to her, wedlock only means riveting the other end of it upon a man. Abolish wedlock, and the man is free; but the woman is left to bear the whole weight of her servitude alone.

> Review of *The Future of Marriage*, SHAW: *The Annual of Bernard Shaw Studies*, vol. 16, ed. Dan H. Laurence and Margot Peters; Penn State Press (1996).
>
> Written on March 9, 1885 for *The Commonweal*, which rejected it.

What is any respectable girl brought up to do but to catch some rich man's fancy and get the benefit of his money by marrying him?—as if a marriage ceremony could make any difference in the right or wrong of the thing!

> Mrs. Warren, in *Mrs. Warren's Profession*, act 2; *The Bodley Head Bernard Shaw: Collected Plays with their Prefaces*, vol. 1 (1970).
>
> First published in 1898.

If you are in favor of marriage in its present English form as compared to the greater freedom of the French system or many of the American ones, then say why; but do not absurdly assume that there is no middle course between our system and general prostitution and promiscuity.

Letter to the Evacustus Phipson, Jr., March 8, 1892; *Bernard Shaw on the London Art Scene 1885-1950*, ed. Stanley Weintraub; Penn State Press (1989).

First published in *Cat's Paw Utopia* by Ray Reynolds (1972).

Marriage is a mantrap baited with simulated accomplishments and delusive idealizations.

Don Juan, in *Man and Superman*, act 3; *The Bodley Head Bernard Shaw: Collected Plays with their Prefaces*, vol. 2 (1971).

First published in 1903.

Marriage is the most licentious of human institutions . . . that is the secret of its popularity.

Don Juan, in *Man and Superman*, act 3; *The Bodley Head Bernard Shaw: Collected Plays with their Prefaces*, vol. 2 (1971).

First published in 1903.

Marriage is popular because it combines the maximum of temptation with the maximum of opportunity.

Man and Superman, The Revolutionist's Handbook, "Maxims for Revolutionists"; *The Bodley Head Bernard Shaw: Collected Plays with their Prefaces*, vol. 2 (1971).

First published in 1903.

Those who talk most about the blessings of marriage and the constancy of its vows are the very people who declare that if the chain were broken and the prisoners left free to choose, the whole social fabric would fly asunder. You cannot have the argument both ways. If the prisoner is happy, why lock him in? If he is not, why pretend that he is?

Don Juan, in *Man and Superman*, act 3; *The Bodley Head Bernard Shaw: Collected Plays with their Prefaces*, vol. 2 (1971).

First published in 1903.

What is Virtue but the Trade Unionism of the married?

Don Juan, in *Man and Superman*, act 3; *The Bodley Head Bernard Shaw: Collected Plays with their Prefaces*, vol. 2 (1971).

First published in 1903.

If you will only make marriage reasonable and decent, you can do as you like about divorce.

> Lesbia, in *Getting Married*; *The Bodley Head Bernard Shaw: Collected Plays with their Prefaces*, vol. 3 (1971).
>
> First produced in 1908.

Marriage is good enough for the lower classes: they have facilities for desertion that are denied to us.

> Hotchkiss, in *Getting Married*; *The Bodley Head Bernard Shaw: Collected Plays with their Prefaces*, vol. 3 (1971).
>
> First produced in 1908.

Unless the law of marriage were first made human, it could never become divine.

> The Bishop, in *Getting Married*; *The Bodley Head Bernard Shaw: Collected Plays with their Prefaces*, vol. 3 (1971).
>
> First produced in 1908.

If marriages were made by putting all the men's names into one sack and the women's names into another, and having them taken out by a blindfolded child like lottery numbers, there would be just as high a percentage of happy marriages as we have here in England. . . . If you can tell me of any trustworthy method of selecting a wife, I shall be happy to make use of it.

> Joey Percival, in *Misalliance*; *The Bodley Head Bernard Shaw: Collected Plays with their Prefaces*, vol. 4 (1972).
>
> First produced in 1910.

When two people are under the influence of the most violent, most insane, most delusive, and most transient of passions, they are required to swear that they will remain in that excited, abnormal, and exhausting condition continuously until death do them part.

> *Getting Married*, preface, "For Better For Worse"; *The Bodley Head Bernard Shaw: Collected Plays with their Prefaces*, vol. 3 (1971).
>
> First published in 1911.

You made a business convenience of my father. Well, a woman's business is marriage. Why shouldn't I make a domestic convenience of you?

> Ellie Dunn, in *Heartbreak House*, act 2; *The Bodley Head Bernard Shaw: Collected Plays with their Prefaces*, vol. 5 (1972).
>
> First published in 1919.

I found sex hopeless as a basis for permanent relations, and never dreamt of marriage in connection with it.

Letter to Frank Harris, June 24, 1930, *Collected Letters*, ed. Dan H. Laurence, vol. 4 (1988).

All young women begin by believing they can change and reform the men they marry. They can't.

Sir Arthur Chavender, in *On the Rocks*, act 2; *The Bodley Head Bernard Shaw: Collected Plays with their Prefaces*, vol. 6 (1973).

First produced in 1933.

$\mathcal{M}$ARTYRDOM

Martyrdom . . . is the only way in which a man can become famous without ability.

General Burgoyne, in *The Devil's Disciple*, act 3; *The Bodley Head Bernard Shaw: Collected Plays with their Prefaces*, vol. 2 (1971).

First produced in 1897.

$\mathcal{M}$ARX, KARL

Marx's Capital is not a treatise on Socialism: it is a jeremiad against the bourgoisie.

"Who I Am, and What I Think," *Sixteen Self Sketches*; Constable (1949).

First published in *Candid Friend*, May 1901.

Old Dr. Marx . . . thought that when he'd explained the Capitalist System to the working classes of Europe they'd unite and overthrow it. Fifty years after he founded his Red International the working classes of Europe rose up and shot one another down and blew one another to bits, and turned millions and millions of their infant children out to starve in the snow or steal and beg in the sunshine, as if Dr. Marx had never been born.

Hipney, in *On the Rocks*, act 1; *The Bodley Head Bernard Shaw: Collected Plays with their Prefaces*, vol. 6 (1973).

First produced in 1933; in 1864, Karl Marx founded the First International Workingmen's Association in London and New York; in 1914, World War I broke out.

The first volume of *Capital* (all I ever read of it) changed the mind of Europe.

Letter to H.G. Wells, December 7, 1939, *Selected Correspondence of Bernard Shaw: Bernard Shaw and H.G. Wells*, ed. J. Percy Smith; U of Toronto Press (1995).

*M*EN AND WOMEN

It is not surprising that our society, being directly dominated by men, comes to regard Woman, not as an end in herself like Man, but solely as a means of ministering to his appetite. The ideal wife is one who does everything that the ideal husband likes, and nothing else. Now to treat a person as a means instead of an end is to deny that person's right to live.

The Quintessence of Ibsenism, "The Womanly Woman," *The Drama Observed*, vol. 1, ed. Bernard F. Dukore; Penn State Press (1993).

First published in 1891.

A woman is something more than a piece of sweetstuff to fatten a man's emotions.

"King Arthur," *The Drama Observed*, vol. 1, ed. Bernard F. Dukore; Penn State Press (1993).

First published in *Saturday Review*, January 19, 1895.

Treat her as a human being like himself, fully recognizing that he is not a creature of one superior species, Man, living with a creature of another and inferior species, Woman, but that Mankind is male and female, like other kinds, and that the inequality of the sexes is literally a cock and bull story.

"*A Doll's House* Again," *The Drama Observed*, vol. 3, ed. Bernard F. Dukore; Penn State Press (1993).

First published in *Saturday Review*, May 15, 1897.

I find that the moment I let a woman make friends with me, she becomes jealous, exacting, suspicious, and a damned nuisance. I find that the moment I let myself make friends with a woman, I become selfish and tyrannical.

Henry Higgins, in *Pygmalion*, act 2, *The Bodley Head Bernard Shaw: Collected Plays with their Prefaces*, vol. 4 (1972).

First produced (in German) in 1913.

I am a woman; and you are a man, with a slight difference that doesn't matter except on special occasions.

A, in *Village Wooing*, scene 1; *The Bodley Head Bernard Shaw: Collected Plays with their Prefaces*, vol. 6 (1973).

First published in 1934.

*M*EN

In debating with women, men brazen out all the ridiculous conclusions of which they are convicted, and then they say that there is no use in arguing with a woman. Neither is there, because the woman is always right.

Marian, in *The Irrational Knot*, ch. 14; London: Constable (1950).

First published in 1885.

Man's one gift is that at his best he *can* love—not constantly, nor faithfully, nor often, nor for long, but for a moment—a few minutes perhaps out of years.

Letter to Ellen Terry, April 6, 1896, *Collected Letters*, vol. 1, ed. Dan H. Laurence (1965).

When men hold forth about Woman, they invariably make fools of themselves.

"Ibsen and Things," *The Drama Observed*, vol. 2, ed. Bernard F. Dukore; Penn State Press (1993).

First published in *The Clarion*, February 20, 1897.

*M*IDDLE *AGE*

I stand midway between youth and age like a man who has missed his train: too late for the last and too early for the next.

Aubrey, in *Too True to be Good*, act 3; *The Bodley Head Bernard Shaw: Collected Plays with their Prefaces*, vol. 6 (1973).

First produced in 1932.

Every man over forty is a scoundrel.

Man and Superman, *The Revolutionist's Handbook*, "Maxims for Revolutionists"; *The Bodley Head Bernard Shaw: Collected Plays with their Prefaces*, vol. 2 (1971).

First published in 1903.

MIDDLE CLASS

I have to live for others and not for myself: that's middle class morality.

Doolittle, in *Pygmalion*, act 5; *The Bodley Head Bernard Shaw: Collected Plays with their Prefaces*, vol. 4 (1972).

First produced (in German) in 1913.

MILITARY, THE

Compulsory military service is the most complete slavery known to civilized mankind.

Everybody's Political What's What?, ch. 17; Constable (1944).

MINISTERS

The banished Duke in *As You Like It*, who found sermons in stones, has probably often been envied on Saturday afternoons by ecclesiastics at a loss for the morrow's discourse.

"Folk Lore, English and Scotch," *Bernard Shaw's Book Reviews*, ed. Brian Tyson; Penn State Press (1991).

First published in *Pall Mall Gazette*, August 25, 1885.

MIRACLES

A miracle, my friend, is an event which creates faith. That is the purpose and nature of miracles. They may seem very wonderful to the people who witness them, and very simple to those who perform them. That does not matter: if they confirm or create faith they are true miracles.

The Archbishop, in *Saint Joan*, scene 2; *The Bodley Head Bernard Shaw: Collected Plays with their Prefaces*, vol. 6 (1973).

First produced in 1923.

If it could be proved today that not one of the miracles of Jesus actually occurred, that proof would not invalidate a single one of his didactic utterances; and conversely, if it could be proved that not only did the miracles actually occur, but that he had wrought a thousand other miracles a thousand times more wonderful, not a jot of weight would be added to his doctrine.

> *Androcles and the Lion*, Preface, "The Miracles"; *The Bodley Head Bernard Shaw: Collected Plays with their Prefaces*, vol. 4 (1972).
>
> First published in 1916.

The world is full of miracles. Consciousness, for instance, is a complete miracle. Birth is a miracle; life is a miracle. . . . There are lots of miracles about; and the man who denies their existence is always a man who is simply wrong in his definition of a miracle. By a miracle he means only something that he is not accustomed to and did not expect.

> "A Retort on Mr. Chesterton," *Shaw on Religion*, ed. Warren Sylvester Smith; Dodd, Mead (1967).
>
> First published in *New Age* as "On Miracles—A Retort," December 10, 1908.

$\mathcal{M}$ISERY

The secret of being miserable is to have leisure to bother about whether you are happy or not. The cure for it is occupation, and the preoccupied person is neither happy nor unhappy, but simply active and alive.

> Quoted in Hesketh Pearson, *Bernard Shaw: His Life and Personality*, ch. 17; Atheneum (1963).
>
> First published in 1942.

$\mathcal{M}$ISUNDERSTANDING

I have said enough to make myself thoroughly misunderstood.

> "Acting, by One Who Does not Believe In It," *The Drama Observed*, vol. 1, ed. Bernard F. Dukore; Penn State Press (1993).
>
> Paper read at a meeting of the Church and Stage Guild, February 5, 1889.

Modesty

I really cannot respond to this demand for mock-modesty. I am ashamed neither of my work nor of the way it is done. I like explaining its merits to the huge majority who don't know good work from bad. It does them good.

Three Plays for Puritans, preface; *The Bodley Head Bernard Shaw: Collected Plays with their Prefaces*, vol. 2 (1971).
First published in 1901.

Money

You can be as romantic as you please about love, Hector; but you mustn't be romantic about money.

Violet, in *Man and Superman*, act 2; *The Bodley Head Bernard Shaw: Collected Plays with their Prefaces*, vol. 2 (1971).
First published in 1903.

Money is indeed the most important thing in the world; and all sound and successful personal and national morality should have this fact for its basis. Every teacher or twaddler who denies it or suppresses it, is an enemy of life.

The Irrational Knot, preface; Constable (1950).
First published in 1905.

The crying need of the nation is not for better morals, cheaper bread, temperance, liberty, culture, redemption of fallen sisters and erring brothers, nor the grace, love and fellowship of the Trinity, but simply for enough money. And the evil to be attacked is not sin, suffering, greed, priestcraft, kingcraft, demagogy, monopoly, ignorance, drink, war, pestilence, nor any of the scapegoats which reformers sacrifice, but simply poverty.

Major Barbara, preface, "The Gospel of St. Andrew Undershaft"; *The Bodley Head Bernard Shaw: Collected Plays with their Prefaces*, vol. 3 (1971).
First published in 1907.

The universal regard for money is the one hopeful fact in our civilization, the one sound spot in our social conscience. Money is the most important thing in the world. It represents health, strength, honor, generosity and beauty as conspicuously and undeniably as the want of it represents illness, weakness, disgrace, meanness and ugliness.

Major Barbara, preface, "The Gospel of St. Andrew Undershaft"; *The Bodley Head Bernard Shaw: Collected Plays with their Prefaces*, vol. 3 (1971).

First published in 1907.

To . . . teach children that it is sinful to desire money, is to strain towards the extreme possible limit of impudence in lying and corruption in hypocrisy.

Major Barbara, preface, "The Gospel of St. Andrew Undershaft"; *The Bodley Head Bernard Shaw: Collected Plays with their Prefaces*, vol. 3 (1971).

First published in 1907.

The surest way to ruin a man who doesn't know how to handle money is to give him some.

Boss Mangan, in *Heartbreak House*, act 2; *The Bodley Head Bernard Shaw: Collected Plays with their Prefaces*, vol. 5 (1972).

First published in 1919.

Money talks: money prints: money broadcasts: money reigns; and kings and labor leaders alike have to register its decrees, and even, by a staggering paradox, to finance its enterprises and guarantee its profits. Democracy is no longer bought: it is bilked.

The Apple Cart, preface; *The Bodley Head Bernard Shaw: Collected Plays with their Prefaces*, vol. 6 (1973).

First published in 1930.

MORALITY

The low people and the high people are alike in one thing: they have no scruples, no morality. The low are beneath morality, the high above it.

Napoleon, in *The Man of Destiny*; *The Bodley Head Bernard Shaw: Collected Plays with their Prefaces*, vol. 1 (1970).

First produced in 1897.

My dear: you are the incarnation of morality. Your conscience is clear and your duty done when you have called everybody names.

Andrew Undershaft, in *Major Barbara*, act 3; *The Bodley Head Bernard Shaw: Collected Plays with their Prefaces*, vol. 3 (1971).

First produced in 1905.

Morality consists in suspecting other people of not being legally married.

Dubedat, in *The Doctor's Dilemma*, act 3; *The Bodley Head Bernard Shaw: Collected Plays with their Prefaces*, vol. 3 (1971).

First produced in 1906.

I claim to be a conscientiously immoral writer.

"Testimony on the Censorship of Plays," *The Drama Observed*, ed. Bernard F. Dukore, vol. 3; Penn State Press (1993).

Verbatim report from the minutes of evidence before the Joint Select Committee of the House of Lords and the House of Commons on the Stage Plays, July 30, 1909.

From one end of the Bible to the other the words "moral" and "immoral" are not used.

"Testimony on the Censorship of Plays," *The Drama Observed*, ed. Bernard F. Dukore, vol. 3; Penn State Press (1993).

Verbatim report from the minutes of evidence before the Joint Select Committee of the House of Lords and the House of Commons on the Stage Plays, July 30, 1909.

Mere morality, or the substitution of custom for conscience.

Fanny's First Play, preface; *The Bodley Head Bernard Shaw: Collected Plays with their Prefaces*, vol. 4 (1972).

First published in 1914.

Morality demands, not that we should behave morally (an impossibility to our sinful nature) but that we shall not attempt to defend our immorality.

Overruled, preface, "Farcical Comedy Shirking Its Subject"; *The Bodley Head Bernard Shaw: Collected Plays with their Prefaces*, vol. 4 (1972).

First published in 1916.

$\mathcal{M}$ORALS

There is only one true morality for every man; but every man has not the same true morality.

Andrew Undershaft, in *Major Barbara*, act 1; *The Bodley Head Bernard Shaw: Collected Plays with their Prefaces*, vol. 3 (1971).

First produced in 1905.

The nation's morals are like its teeth: the more decayed they are the more it hurts to touch them.

The Shewing-up of Blanco Posnet, preface, "Star Chamber Sentimentality"; *The Bodley Head Bernard Shaw: Collected Plays with their Prefaces*, vol. 3 (1971).

First published in 1911.

Whatever is contrary to established manners and customs is immoral. An immoral act or doctrine is not necessarily a sinful one: on the contrary, every advance in thought and conduct is by definition immoral until it has converted the majority.

The Shewing-up of Blanco Posnet, preface, "The Definition of Immorality"; *The Bodley Head Bernard Shaw: Collected Plays with their Prefaces*, vol. 3 (1971).

First published in 1911.

*M*OTHERS

I ought to have children. I should be a good mother to children. I believe it would pay the country very well to pay ME very well to have children. But the country tells me that I can't have a child in my house without a man in it too; so I tell the country that it will have to do without my children.

Lesbia, in *Getting Married*; *The Bodley Head Bernard Shaw: Collected Plays with their Prefaces*, vol. 3 (1971).

First produced in 1908.

The one point on which all women are in furious secret rebellion against the existing law is the saddling of the right to a child with the obligation to become the servant of a man.

Getting Married, preface, "The Right to Motherhood"; *The Bodley Head Bernard Shaw: Collected Plays with their Prefaces*, vol. 3 (1971).

First published in 1911.

No woman can shake off her mother.

The Patient, in *Too True to be Good*, act 3; *The Bodley Head Bernard Shaw: Collected Plays with their Prefaces*, vol. 6 (1973).

First produced in 1932.

*M*OVIES

The cinema is going to form the mind of England. The national conscience, the national ideals and tests of conduct, will be those of the film.

"The Cinema as a Moral Leveler," *The Drama Observed*, ed. Bernard F. Dukore; Penn State Press (1993). First published in *New Statesman*, June 27, 1914.

The cinema tells its story to the illiterate as well as the literate; and it keeps its victim (if you like to call him so) not only awake but fascinated as if by a serpent's eye.

"The Cinema as a Moral Leveler," *The Drama Observed*, ed. Bernard F. Dukore, vol. 4; Penn State Press (1993). First published in *New Statesman*, June 27, 1914.

I shall not be surprised if the cinematograph and phonograph turn out to be the most revolutionary inventions since writing and printing, and, indeed, far more revolutionary than either; for the number of people who can read is small, the number of those who can read to any purpose much smaller, and the number of those who are too tired after a day's work to read without falling asleep enormous.

"What the Films May Do to the Drama," *The Drama Observed*, ed. Bernard F. Dukore, vol. 4; Penn State Press (1993). First published in *Metropolitan Magazine* (New York), May 1915.

The colossal proportions make mediocrity compulsory.

"The Drama, the Theatre, and the Films," *The Drama Observed*, ed. Bernard F. Dukore, vol. 4; Penn State Press (1993). First published in *Fortnightly Review*, September 1, 1924.

The theatre may survive as a place where people are taught to act, but apart from that there will be nothing but "talkies" soon.

"Shaw Asserts Theatre Is Lost, Signs for Films," *The Drama Observed*, ed. Bernard F. Dukore, vol. 4; Penn State Press (1993). First published in *New York Herald Tribune*, August 8, 1930.

The talkie does not ape the theatre any more than a Rolls Royce apes a Victorian four-wheeled cab. It just plays it off the stage when it is well handled.

"Relationship of the Cinema to the Theatre," *The Drama Observed*, ed. Bernard F. Dukore, vol. 4; Penn State Press (1993). Answers to typed questions by Huntly Carter, May 9, 1932.

The invention of the movie (film muet [silent]) was enormously profitable because the audience was the whole world. The invention of the talkie (film parlant) involves the nationalization of the film and the end of the world audience.

Letter to Augustin Hamon, February 13, 1935, *Collected Letters*, ed. Dan H. Laurence, vol. 4 (1988).

There is no such thing as the average movie. In fine art there is always trash, mediocrity, and treasure.

"What I Think About the Film Industry," *Daily Film Renter*, January 1, 1946.

*M*OZART, *WOLFGANG AMADEUS*

Here was a master compared to whom Berlioz was a musical pastry cook.

"The *Don Giovanni* Centenary," *Shaw's Music*, vol. 1, ed. Dan H. Laurence (1981).

First published in *Pall Mall Gazette*, October 31, 1887.

The Mozart mania of the first quarter of the century . . . was followed, like other manias, by a reaction, through which we have been living, and which will be succeeded next century by a reaction against Wagner. This sort of thing happens to all great men.

"A Mozart Controversy," *Shaw's Music*, vol. 2, ed. Dan H. Laurence (1981).

First published in *The World*, June 11, 1890.

Mozart never follows his inspiration . . . he leads it, makes its course for it, removes obstacles, holds it in from gadding erratically after this or that passing fancy, thinks for it, and finally produces with it an admirable whole, the full appreciation of which keeps every faculty on the alert from beginning to end.

"Brahms: Music Without Mind," *Shaw's Music*, vol. 3, ed. Dan H. Laurence (1981).

First published in *The World*, February 7, 1894.

*M*USIC HALLS

The other evening, feeling rather in want of a headache, I bethought me that I had not been to a music hall for a long time.

"Ballet at the Alhambra," *Shaw's Music*, vol. 3, ed. Dan H. Laurence (1981).

First published in *The World*, January 24, 1894.

Music

The theory that music has a depraving effect on morals has now been abandoned to the old women of both sexes.

"Unconscionable Abuses," *SHAW: The Annual of Bernard Shaw Studies*, vol. 16, ed. Dan H. Laurence and Margot Peters; Penn State Press (1996).

Written on October 31, 1879.

Bad music may be better for the workman than gin; but from an artistic point of view it is better to have no music at all than bad music. If no music at all happens to mean gin under present arangements, that is not an argument in favor of bad music, but an additional argument—if any were needed—in favor of fresh arrangements.

"Art and Society," *Bernard Shaw on the London Art Scene 1885-1950*, ed. Stanley Weintraub; Penn State Press (1989).

Lecture to the Bedford Debating Society, December 10, 1885.

Gounod does not express his ideas worse than Handel; but then he has fewer ideas to express.

"*The Redemption* at the Crystal Palace," *Shaw's Music*, vol. 1, ed. Dan H. Laurence (1981).

First published in *Dramatic Review*, May 8, 1886.

The chorus did everything to perfection except sing.

"The Masterly Richter," *Shaw's Music*, vol. 1, ed. Dan H. Laurence (1981).

First published in *The Star*, July 9, 1889.

Just as cheap literature is restoring Shakespeare to the stage and banishing gag, Garrick, and Cibber, so cheap music will banish cuts, interpolations, alterations, and perversions from the opera house. It will not teach the people to sing; but it will teach them to miss the qualities which are never forthcoming with bad singers and to value those which are always forthcoming with good ones.

"How Not to Teach Singing," *Shaw's Music*, vol. 1, ed. Dan H. Laurence (1981).

First published in *The Star*, July 12, 1889.

The weather was warm enough to make anybody play wrong notes—almost warm enough to make me play right ones.

"The Farewell of Henry Lazarus," *Shaw's Music*, vol. 2, ed. Dan H. Laurence (1981).

First published in *The World*, June 8, 1892.

If I despised the musical farces, it was because they never had the courage of their vices.

> *Three Plays for Puritans*, preface; *The Bodley Head Bernard Shaw: Collected Plays with their Prefaces*, vol. 2 (1971).
>
> First published in 1901.

Is the devil to have all the passions as well as all the good tunes?

> John Tanner, in *Man and Superman*, act 1; *The Bodley Head Bernard Shaw: Collected Plays with their Prefaces*, vol. 2 (1971).
>
> First published in 1903; parody of the nineteenth-century Reverend Rowland Hill's statement that he saw no reason why the devil should have all the good tunes.

NAKEDNESS

Would you insist on cages being put round the Trafalgar Square lions? If not, why do you not apply the same argument to the figleaf of Hermes?

> Letter to Evacustus Phipson, Jr., March 8, 1892; *Bernard Shaw on the London Art Scene 1885-1950*, ed. Stanley Weintraub; Penn State Press (1989).
>
> First published in *Cat's Paw Utopia* by Ray Reynolds (1972).

The camera can represent flesh so superbly that, if I dared, I would never photograph a figure without asking that figure to take its clothes off. I delight in mankind as nature makes it.

> "Some Criticisms of the Exhibitions," *Shaw on Photography*, ed. Bill Jan and Margaret Moore; Peregrine Smith Books (1989).
>
> First published in *Amateur Photographer*, October 16, 1902.

NEED

As long as I have a want, I have a reason for living. Satisfaction is death.

> Gregory Lunn, in *Overruled*; *The Bodley Head Bernard Shaw: Collected Plays with their Prefaces*, vol. 4 (1972).
>
> First produced in 1912.

NEUTRALITY

No state will value another's neutrality more highly than its own national existence.

Letter to William R. Paton, September 21, 1916, *Collected Letters*, ed. Dan H. Laurence, vol. 3 (1985).

NEWSPAPERS, ENGLISH

When a tornado devastates an American province it is chronicled in a quarter of a column. Yet were a gust of wind to blow off our Sovereign's headgear tomorrow, "The Queen's bonnet" would crowd Bulgaria out of the papers. Clearly, the ideal of Royalty is still with us; and it is as the impersonatrix of that ideal that the Queen is worshipped by us.

"The Year of Jubilee," *Bernard Shaw's Book Reviews*, ed. Brian Tyson; Penn State Press (1991).

First published in *Pall Mall Gazette*, November 16, 1886.

NINETEENTH CENTURY

This wickedest of all the centuries.

"Children in Theatres," *Shaw's Music*, vol. 1, ed. Dan H. Laurence (1981).

First published in *The Star*, January 24, 1890.

On the whole, perhaps the most villainous page of recorded human history.

Three Plays by Brieux, preface, "How the Nineteenth Century Found Itself Out," *The Drama Observed*, ed. Bernard F. Dukore, vol. 3; Penn State Press (1993).

First published in 1911.

NORMALITY

As for your normal and universal, there are no such real categories. You get your normal simply by ignoring the abnormalities. Thus you can identify chalk with cheese by abstracting everything except what is common to the

two, as weight and bulk, for instance; and I admit the necessity of
performing such abstraction for the purpose of fixing parcels post tariff.
But when you go on to spread chalk on my bread, and tell me that my
refusal to eat it means moral chaos, then I laugh at you.

Letter to E.G. Girdlestone, October 13, 1890, *Collected Letters*, ed. Dan H. Laurence, vol. 1 (1965).

*N*OVELS

They say that man in embryo is successively a fish, a bird, a mammal, and
so on, before he develops into a man. Well, popular novel-writing is the
fish stage of your Jonathan Swift.

Letter, no date given, quoted in Frank Harris, *Bernard Shaw*, ch. 8; Garden City Publishing Co (1931).

*N*OVELTY

The novelties of one generation are only the resuscitated fashions of the
generation before last.

Three Plays for Puritans, preface; *The Bodley Head Bernard Shaw: Collected Plays with their Prefaces*, vol.
2 (1971).

First published in 1901.

*N*UDITY

Though you cannot walk through Paris without coming at every corner
upon some fountain or trophy or monument for which the only possible
remedy is dynamite, you can always count upon the design including a
female figure free from the defect known to photographers as
underexposure.

"Samson et Dalila," *Shaw's Music*, vol 2, ed Dan H. Laurence (1981).

First published in *The World*, October 4, 1893.

In India, nudity, which we ridiculous westerners still think the climax of
S.A. [sex appeal] (in spite of our everyday experience of sunbathing)

means simply poverty. The Indian enchantress is dressed in wonderful silks right up to the wrists and ankles, finishing off with circlets of gold.

Letter to the Theatre Guild, April 7, 1935, *Collected Letters*, ed. Dan H. Laurence, vol. 4 (1988).

OBEDIENCE

Obedience simulates subordination as fear of the police simulates honesty.

Man and Superman, The Revolutionist's Handbook, "Maxims for Revolutionists"; *The Bodley Head Bernard Shaw: Collected Plays with their Prefaces*, vol. 2 (1971).

First published in 1903.

A bishop will defer to and obey a king; but let a curate venture to give him an order, however necessary and sensible, and the bishop will forget his cloth and damn the curate's impudence. The more obedient a man is to accredited authority, the more jealous he is of allowing any unauthorized person to order him about.

Saint Joan, preface, "The Conflict Between Genius and Discipline"; *The Bodley Head Bernard Shaw: Collected Plays with their Prefaces*, vol. 6 (1973).

First published in 1924.

OBSOLESCENCE

There is a disease to which plays as well as men become liable with advancing years. In men it is called doting, in plays dating. The more topical the play the more it dates.

Preface, *The Philanderer; The Bodley Head Bernard Shaw: Collected Plays with their Prefaces*, vol. 1 (1970).

First published in 1898.

OFFENBACH, JACQUES

Offenbach's music is wicked. It is abandoned stuff: every accent in it is a snap of the fingers in the face of moral responsibility: every ripple and sparkle on its surface twits me for my teetotalism, and mocks at the early rising of which I fully intend to make a habit some day.

"All About the Brigands," *Shaw's Music*, vol. 1, ed. Dan H. Laurence (1981).

First published in *The Star*, September 20, 1889.

OLD AGE

Old men are dangerous: it doesn't matter to them what is going to happen to the world.

Captain Shotover, in *Heartbreak House*, act 2; *The Bodley Head Bernard Shaw: Collected Plays with their Prefaces*, vol. 5 (1972).

First published in 1919.

Age has the effect of destroying one's historical perspective, so that everything that ever happened to me seems to have happened within the last fortnight.

Letter to the Very Rev. H.R.L. Sheppard, August 5, 1930, *Collected Letters*, ed. Dan H. Laurence, vol. 4 (1988).

I have another trick for imposing on the young. I am old: over eighty, in fact. Also I have a white beard; and these two facts are somehow associated in people's mind with wisdom. That is a mistake. If a person is a born fool, the folly will get worse, not better, by long life's practice.

"School," *Platform and Pulpit*, ed. Dan H. Laurence; Hill & Wang (1961).

B.B.C. radio talk, June 11, 1937.

Age doesn't bring wisdom but it brings experience that young people can't have. Even the stupidest person when he's ninety has seen things that none of you can have seen.

"Goodbye, Goodbye," *Platform and Pulpit*, ed. Dan H. Laurence; Hill & Wang (1961).

Recorded and filmed for televison by the B.B.C. on July 26, 1946, Shaw's 90th birthday.

OPERA

Those persons who object to English versions on the score of their literary demerits are presumably unacquainted with the Italian language.

"An Opera in Translation," *Shaw's Music*, vol. 1 (1981), ed. Dan H. Laurence.

First published in *The Hornet*, August 8, 1877.

We have at our opera houses a system of gesticulation so unmeaning, so impotent to excite even derisive mirth, that the ghastliest and most ludicrous traditions of the old melodramatic stage would, if revived, be more tolerable to us.

"Opera in Italian," *Shaw's Music*, vol. 1 (1981), ed. Dan H. Laurence.

First published in *The Saturday Musical Review*, February 22, 1879.

I have long since learnt to leave my common sense at the door when I go to the Opera.

"*Hamlet*: A Foolish Opera," *Shaw's Music*, vol. 2, ed. Dan H. Laurence (1981).

First published in *The World*, July 30, 1890.

OPERATION

Whenever I see the word Operation, especially Trifling Operation, I at once write off the patient as dead.

The Correspondence of Bernard Shaw: Bernard Shaw and Gabriel Pascal, ed. Bernard F. Dukore; U of Toronto Press (1996).

Letter, July 27, 1949, to Gabriel Pascal.

ORATORY

Nine-tenths of the art of popular oratory lies in sympathizing with the grievances of your hearers.

"What About the Middle Class? A Lay Sermon," *Practical Politics*, ed. Lloyd J. Hubenka; U of Nebraska Press (1976).

First published in *Daily Citizen*, October 18, 1912.

ORCHESTRAS

A good orchestra is every whit as important to a town as a good hospital.

"Culture for the Provinces," *Shaw's Music*, vol. 2, ed. Dan H. Laurence (1981).

First published in *The World*, August 9, 1893.

*O*RDINARINESS

What is wrong with the prosaic Englishman is what is wrong with the prosaic men of all countries: stupidity.

Man and Superman, Epistle Dedicatory; *The Bodley Head Bernard Shaw: Collected Plays with their Prefaces*, vol. 2 (1971).

First published in 1903.

*O*RIGINALITY

What the world calls originality is only an unaccustomed method of tickling it.

Three Plays for Puritans, preface; *The Bodley Head Bernard Shaw: Collected Plays with their Prefaces*, vol. 2 (1971).

First published in 1901.

This is the real secret of the terror inspired by an original thinker. In repudiating convention he is repudiating that on which his neighbors are relying for their sense of security.

Three Plays by Brieux, preface, "The Dread of the Original Thinker," *The Drama Observed*, ed. Bernard F. Dukore, vol. 3; Penn State Press (1993).

First published in 1911.

I am myself what is called an original thinker, my business being to question and test all the established creeds and codes to see how far they are still valid and how far worn out or superseded, and even to draft new creeds and codes.

The Intelligent Woman's Guide to Socialism, Capitalism, Sovietism, and Fascism, ch. 70; Constable (1949).

First published in 1928 as *The Intelligent Woman's Guide to Socialism and Capitalism*.

*O*VERSTATEMENT

It is always necessary to overstate a cast startlingly to make people sit up and listen to it, and to frighten them into acting on it.

Everybody's Political What's What?, ch. 6; Constable (1944).

$\mathcal{P}$AIN

The most intolerable pain is produced by prolonging the keenest pleasure.

Man and Superman, The Revolutionist's Handbook, "Maxims for Revolutionists"; *The Bodley Head Bernard Shaw: Collected Plays with their Prefaces*, vol. 2 (1971).

First published in 1903.

$\mathcal{P}$AINTING

I paint pictures to make me feel sane. Dealing with men and women makes me feel mad. Humanity always fails me: Nature never.

Colonel Tallboys, in *Too True to be Good*, act 2; *The Bodley Head Bernard Shaw: Collected Plays with their Prefaces*, vol. 6 (1973).

First produced in 1932.

$\mathcal{P}$ARADOXES

Paradoxes are the only truths.

Tarleton, in *Misalliance*; *The Bodley Head Bernard Shaw: Collected Plays with their Prefaces*, vol. 4 (1972).

First produced 1910.

$\mathcal{P}$ARENTS AND PARENTHOOD

It is of course quite true that the majority of women are kind to children and prefer their own to other people's. But exactly the same thing is true of the majority of men, who nevertheless do not consider that their proper sphere is the nursery.

The Quintessence of Ibsenism, "The Womanly Woman," 1891 (*The Drama Observed*, ed. Bernard F. Dukore, vol. 1, Penn State Press (1993).

First published in 1891.

The vilest abortionist is he who attempts to mould a child's character.

Man and Superman, The Revolutionist's Handbook, "Maxims for Revolutionists"; *The Bodley Head Bernard Shaw: Collected Plays with their Prefaces*, vol. 2 (1971).

First published in 1903.

The best brought-up children, other things being equal, are those who have been brought up in a large family, where the parents have had no time to study individual children much, and where the children themselves have knocked one another into some sort of communal conscience without the least sense of duty or the least desire to impose a moral program.

Letter to Cliff Keane, April 2, 1904; *Collected Letters*, ed. Dan H. Laurence, vol. 2 (1972).

It is amazing how parents forget their experiences as children. Women treat their grown-up daughters as if they were still infants.

Letter to E. Margaret Wheeler, January 6, 1948, *Collected Letters*, ed. Dan H. Laurence, vol. 4 (1988).

$\mathcal{P}$ARIS

Though Paris is easily the most prejudiced, old-fashioned, obsolete-minded city in the west of Europe, yet when she produces great men she certainly does not do it by halves.

Three Plays by Brieux, preface, "Parisian Stupidity," *The Drama Observed*, ed. Bernard F. Dukore, vol. 3; Penn State Press (1993).
First published in 1911.

$\mathcal{P}$ARLIAMENT

Parliamentary constitutionalism holds good up to a certain point: the point at which the people who are outvoted in Parliament will accept their defeat.

The Intelligent Woman's Guide to Socialism, Capitalism, Sovietism, and Fascism, ch. 75; Constable (1949).
First published in 1928 as *The Intelligent Woman's Guide to Socialism and Capitalism*.

The only difference between the parliamentary locomotive and the engineers' locomotive is that the safety valve in the parliamentary locomotive is made so extremely weak that it blows off in hot air before there is the slightest possibility of the train moving at all.

"In Praise of Guy Fawkes," *Platform and Pulpit*, ed. Dan H. Laurence; Hill and Wang (1961).
Lecture under the auspices of the Fabian Society, November 25, 1932.

What is the historical function of Parliament in this country? It is to prevent the Government from governing.

"In Praise of Guy Fawkes," *Platform and Pulpit*, ed. Dan H. Laurence; Hill and Wang (1961).

Lecture under the auspices of the Fabian Society, November 25, 1932.

Our old parliamentary hands . . . react to the shocks and surprises of social evolution as unintelligently as a cricket ball reacts to the stroke of a bat.

Everybody's Political What's What?, ch. 44; Constable (1944).

*P*ASSION

Passion is the steam engine of all religious and moral systems.

The Sanity of Art, Major Critical Essays; Constable (1949).

First published as "A Degenerate's View of Nordau," *Liberty* (New York), July 27, 1895.

Moral passion is the only real passion.

John Tanner, in *Man and Superman*, act 1; *The Bodley Head Bernard Shaw: Collected Plays with their Prefaces*, vol. 2 (1971).

First published in 1903.

*P*ATRIOTISM

Patriotism is, fundamentally, a conviction that a particular country is the best in the world because you were born in it.

"Irish Patriotism and Italian Opera," *Shaw's Music*, vol. 3, ed. Dan H. Laurence (1981).

First published in *The World*, November 15, 1893.

Does not patriotism consist mainly in covering your own country with fictitious whitewash, and the enemy with fictitious pitch?

"Is Britain Blameless?" *Complete Prefaces*, ed. Dan H. Laurence and Daniel J. Leary, vol. 2 (1995).

First published as "Is England Blameless?" *Labour Leader*, February 4, 1915.

*P*EACE

Peace shall not prevail save with a sword in her hand.

Andrew Undershaft, in *Major Barbara*, Act 3; *The Bodley Head Bernard Shaw: Collected Plays with their Prefaces*, vol. 3 (1971).

First produced in 1905.

It turns out that we do not and cannot love one another—that the problem before us is how to establish peace among people who heartily dislike one another, and have very good reasons for doing so.

The Secretary, in *Geneva*, act 4; *The Bodley Head Bernard Shaw: Collected Plays with their Prefaces*, vol. 7 (1974).

First produced in 1938.

*P*ENSIONS

There is no difference between the Liberals and Conservatives on the question of old age pensions. The conservatives say, if you would only let them in, and allow them to have a tariff, they would give you bigger old age pensions. So the thing goes on. But, I ask you now, where does the middle class come in, in all this? The middle class has to pay for it; for, politically, it is the most helplessly foolish and absurd class that ever existed on the face of the earth.

"Socialist Politics," *Practical Politics*, ed. Lloyd J. Hubenka; U of Nebraska Press (1976).

Lecture delivered before the Liverpool Fabian Society, October 28, 1908.

*P*EOPLE

The employment of a generic term, such as "the people," to denote one section of the community is not wholly defensible, but the sanction of custom must be an excuse for its use in the present instance; and, after all, it is a more complimentary expression than the "proletariat," or the "lower orders," and not more open to question than the "working classes."

"Music for the People," *Shaw's Music*, vol. 1 (1981), ed. Dan H. Laurence.

First published in *Musical Review*, March 10 and 17, 1883.

It is not true that it takes all sorts to make a world; for there are some sorts that would destroy any world very soon if they were suffered to live and have their way.

> *On the Rocks*, preface, "Importance of Laziness for Fallowing"; *The Bodley Head Bernard Shaw: Collected Plays with their Prefaces*, vol. 6 (1973).
>
> First published in 1934.

There are two sorts of people in the world: the people anyone can live with and the people that no one can live with.

> Patricia, in *The Millionairess*, act 1; *The Bodley Head Bernard Shaw: Collected Plays with their Prefaces*, vol. 6 (1973).
>
> First produced (in German) in 1936.

*P*ERCEPTION

Better see rightly on a pound a week than squint on a million.

> Preface, *Plays Unpleasant*; *The Bodley Head Bernard Shaw: Collected Plays with their Prefaces*, vol. 1 (1970).
>
> First published in 1898.

*P*ERSECUTION

Persecution is not a term applicable to the acts of the Emperor. The Emperor is the Defender of the Faith. In throwing you to the lions he will be upholding the interests of religion in Rome. If you were to throw him to the lions, that would no doubt be persecution.

> The Captain, in *Androcles and the Lion*, act 1; *The Bodley Head Bernard Shaw: Collected Plays with their Prefaces*, vol. 4 (1972).
>
> First produced in 1913.

When you prevent me from doing anything I want to do, that is persecution; but when I prevent you from doing anything you want to do, that is law, order, and morals.

> "On Ritual, Religion, and the Intolerableness of Tolerance," *Shaw on Religion*, ed. Warren S. Smith; Dodd, Mead (1967).
>
> Written c. 1922.

⟊*P*ESSIMISM

From the pessimist's point of view there is something to be said for the implied opinion that our family affection, honesty, disinterested love, and chivalry are for the most parts shams; but no acute pessimist believes that they are hypocritical shams; we are ourselves imposed on no less than we impose on others.

"Two Novels of Modern Society," *Bernard Shaw's Book Reviews*, ed. Brian Tyson; Penn State Press (1991).

First published in *Pall Mall Gazette*, July 15, 1885.

Pessimists are, after all, wonderfully pleasant fellows in their way of putting unpleasant things.

"A Handbook of Human Error," *Bernard Shaw's Book Reviews*, ed. Brian Tyson; Penn State Press (1991).

First published in *Pall Mall Gazette*, July 28, 1886.

*P*ETS

If the instinct to have something to pet is uncontrollable, have (or hire) a baby, not a dog.

Letter to Charlotte Payne-Townshend, January 11, 1897, *Collected Letters*, vol. 1, ed. Dan H. Laurence (1965).

To take a dog from a country house and pen it up at the top of a house in London, thereby condemning it to disease and everybody else to a life of preoccupation about taking the beast out, is positive imbecility, monstrosity, idiocy, wanton perversion and waste of life and feeling.

Letter to Charlotte Payne-Townshend, January 11, 1897, *Collected Letters*, vol. 1, ed. Dan H. Laurence (1965).

*P*HILISTINISM

A Philistine is a prosaic person whose artistic conscience is unawakened, and who has no ideals.

"The Two Latest Comedies," *The Drama Observed*, vol. 2, ed. Bernard F. Dukore; Penn State Press (1993).

First published in *Saturday Review*, May 18, 1895.

𝓟HILOSOPHERS

I sing, not arms and the hero, but the philosophic man: he who seeks in contemplation to discover the inner will of the world, in invention to discover the means of fulfilling that will, and in action to do that will by the so-discovered means.

Don Juan, in *Man and Superman*, act 3; *The Bodley Head Bernard Shaw: Collected Plays with their Prefaces*, vol. 2 (1971).

First published in 1903; the first phrase parodies the first line of Virgil's *Aeneid,* "Arms and the man I sing"; the quotation also supplied the title of Shaw's fourth play, *Arms and the Man.*

If you can find, at a University, a man who is by nature utterly incapable of abstract thought, you will generally find him going in for philosophy and metaphysics.

"Life, Literature, and Political Economy"; *Practical Politics*, ed. Lloyd J. Hubenka, U of Nebraska Press (1976).

Speech to the Students' Union at the London School of Economics and Political Science, December 13, 1905, revised for publication in *Clare Market Review*, January 1906.

𝓟LAYS

I offer it as my own criticism of the author of *Widowers' Houses* that the disillusion which makes all great dramatic poets tragic has here made him only derisive; and derision is by common consent a baser atmosphere than that of tragedy. I had better have written a beautiful play, like *Twelfth Night*, or a grand play, like the tragic masterpieces; but, frankly, I was not able to: modern commercialism is a bad art school, and cannot, with all its robberies, murders, and prostitutions, move us in the grand manner to pity and terror.

Author's Preface to the 1893 edition of *Widowers' Houses; The Bodley Head Bernard Shaw: Collected Plays with their Prefaces*, vol. 1 (1970).

First published in 1893.

You will at once detect an enormous assumption on my part that I am a man of genius. But what can I do—on what other assumption am I to proceed if I am to write plays at all?

Letter to Henry Arthur Jones, 2 December 1894, *Collected Letters*, vol. 1, ed. Dan H. Laurence (1965).

Only in the problem play is there any real drama, because drama is no mere setting up of the camera to nature: it is the presentation in parable of the conflict between Man's will and his environment: in a word, of problem.

The Author's Apology to *Mrs. Warren's Profession*; *The Bodley Head Bernard Shaw: Collected Plays with their Prefaces*, vol. 1 (1970).

First published in 1902.

On the chance occasions when I descend from the opera house to the theatre I am often made to feel acutely that the play would be much more enjoyable if the dialogue were omitted.

"*L'Enfant Prodigue*," *Shaw's Music*, vol. 2, ed. Dan H. Laurence (1981).

First published in *The World*, April 8, 1891.

*P*LEASURE

Life on board a pleasure steamer violates every moral and physical condition of healthy life except fresh air. . . . It is a guzzling, lounging, gambling, dog's life. The only alternative to excitement is irritability.

Letter to Sydney C. Cockerell, October 17, 1899. *Collected Letters*, vol. 2, ed. Dan H. Laurence (1972).

*P*OETRY AND POETS

There is another difference between Elizabethan and Victorian audiences which tends to make Shakespeare appear dull to the latter. In his time, books and readers were scarce. There was a a demand for poetry, and the people expected to find it at the playhouse. The demand still exists; but the supply comes from the library and the magazine.

"*The Merchant of Venice* at the Lyceum," *The Drama Observed*, vol. 1, ed. Bernard F. Dukore; Penn State Press (1993).

Review of Henry Irving's performance of Shylock, written April 7, 1880.

It must not be supposed that the poets and artists are the romantic people, and their readers and audiences the matter-of-fact people. On the contrary, it is the poets and artists who spend their lives in trying to make the unreal real; whereas the ordinary man's life struggle is to escape from reality, to avoid all avoidable facts and deceive himself as to the real nature of those which he cannot avoid.

"Ballet at the Alhambra," *Shaw's Music*, vol. 3, ed. Dan H. Laurence (1981).

First published in *The World,* January 24, 1894.

*P*OLITENESS

You must always be polite, particularly to those whom you dislike; because politeness is a mark of superiority; and in order to make unpleasant people respect you, you should endeavor to appear as superior to them as possible.

My Dear Dorothea; Phoenix House (1956).

To a six-year old girl; written in 1878.

*P*OLITICAL PARTIES

With the exception of the Party system of government, I know of no business establishment, in which one man is sent in to do a job and another man is sent in to prevent him doing it.

"The Politics of Unpolitical Animals," *Practical Politics*; ed. Lloyd J. Hubenka, U of Nebraska Press (1976).

Lecture at the Fabian Society, November 23, 1933, published in the *Lecture Recorder,* December 1933.

*P*OLITICAL SCIENCE

Political science has been as recklessly neglected by Governments and electorates during my lifetime as sanitary science was in the days of Charles the Second.

Heartbreak House, preface, "Nature's Long Credits"; *The Bodley Head Bernard Shaw: Collected Plays with their Prefaces*, vol. 5 (1972).

First published in 1919.

$\mathcal{P}$OLITICIANS

He knows nothing and thinks he knows everything. That points clearly to a political career.

> Andrew Undershaft, in *Major Barbara*, act 3; *The Bodley Head Bernard Shaw: Collected Plays with their Prefaces*, vol. 3 (1971).
>
> First produced in 1905.

Any sort of plain speaking is better than the nauseous sham good fellowship our democratic public men get up for shop use.

> Franklyn Barnabas, in *Back to Methuselah*, "The Gospel of the Brothers Barnabas"; *The Bodley Head Bernard Shaw: Collected Plays with their Prefaces*, vol. 5 (1972).
>
> First published in 1921.

Practical politicians are people who have mastered the art of using parliament to prevent anything being done.

> Conrad Barnabas, in *Back to Methuselah*, "The Gospel of the Brothers Barnabas"; *The Bodley Head Bernard Shaw: Collected Plays with their Prefaces*, vol. 5 (1972).
>
> First published in 1921.

$\mathcal{P}$OLITICS

Political party speeches, like leading articles, are essentially nothing but party advertisements; and people do not trust advertisements.

> "Criticism on the Hustings," *The Drama Observed*, vol. 2, ed. Bernard F. Dukore; Penn State Press (1993).
>
> First published in *Saturday Review*, July 20, 1895.

Mankind, being for the most part incapable of politics, accepts vituperation as an easy and congenial substitute.

> *Three Plays for Puritans*, "Notes" to *The Devil's Disciple*; *The Bodley Head Bernard Shaw: Collected Plays with their Prefaces*, vol. 2 (1971).
>
> First published in 1901.

A political scheme that cannot be carried out except by soldiers will not be a permanent one.

> *John Bull's Other Island*, preface, "Down with the Soldier!"; *The Bodley Head Bernard Shaw: Collected Plays with their Prefaces*, vol. 3 (1971).
> First published in 1907.

The art of manipulating public opinion, which is a necessary art for the democratic politician, and, like other arts, is sometimes practised with greater virtuosity by knaves than by honest men (who are apt to disdain it), has a different technique in different countries. For instance, in England we excel in whitewashing: in America they excel in tarring and feathering. We strain our nerves and stretch our consciences to avoid a scandal: Americans do the same to make one.

> "Our Morals and Our Police," *Independent Shavian*, Fall 1974.
> First published in *New Statesman*, May 10, 1913.

In politics, all facts are selected facts.

> "Why a Labor Year Book?" *Complete Prefaces*, ed. Dan H. Laurence and Daniel J. Leary, vol. 2 (1995).
> Preface to *The Labour Year Book*, 1916.

$\mathcal{P}$ORNOGRAPHY

A pornographic novelist is one who exploits the sexual instinct as a prostitute does. A legitimate sex novel elucidates it or brings out its poetry, tragedy, or comedy.

> Archibald Henderson, *Table-Talk of G.B.S.*, "Literature and Science"; Harper & Brothers (1925).

$\mathcal{P}$OVERTY

We hardly realize what excessive work and squalor really means, because the standard of comfort for the working classes is so atrociously low; and we have become so hardened by the contemplation of misery in comparison to which mere squalor is luxury, that we think a working man pretty well off when he is half as well housed and not quite twice as hard worked as a prosperous country doctor's cob [horse].

"Art and Society," *Bernard Shaw on the London Art Scene 1885-1950*, ed. Stanley Weintraub; Penn State Press (1989).

Lecture to the Bedford Debating Society, December 10, 1885.

What is the matter with the poor? It is not vice, or idleness, or want of thrift. These are consequences rather than causes, though, like all secondary maladies, they help to aggravate the evil from which they spring.

"The Gospel According to St. Jude's," *Bernard Shaw's Book Reviews*, ed. Brian Tyson; Penn State Press (1991).

First published in *Pall Mall Gazette*, December 26, 1888.

What is the matter with the poor is Poverty: what is the matter with the rich is Uselessness.

Man and Superman, *The Revolutionist's Handbook*, "Maxims for Revolutionists"; *The Bodley Head Bernard Shaw: Collected Plays with their Prefaces*, vol. 2 (1971).

First published in 1903.

Leave it to the poor to pretend that poverty is a blessing: leave it to the coward to make a religion of his cowardice by preaching humility.

Andrew Undershaft, in *Major Barbara*, act 2; *The Bodley Head Bernard Shaw: Collected Plays with their Prefaces*, vol. 3 (1971).

First produced in 1905.

The worst of crimes. All the other crimes are virtues beside it: all the other dishonors are chivalry itself by comparison. Poverty blights whole cities; spreads horrible pestilences; strikes dead the very souls of all who come within sight, sound, or smell of it.

Andrew Undershaft, in *Major Barbara*, act 3; *The Bodley Head Bernard Shaw: Collected Plays with their Prefaces*, vol. 3 (1971).

First produced in 1905.

If a man is indolent, let him be poor. If he is drunken, let him be poor. . . . Also—somewhat inconsistently—blessed are the poor!

Major Barbara, preface, "The Gospel of St. Andrew Undershaft"; *The Bodley Head Bernard Shaw: Collected Plays with their Prefaces*, vol. 3 (1971).

First published in 1907.

The greatest of our evils, and the worst of our crimes is poverty.

Major Barbara, preface, "The Gospel of St. Andrew Undershaft"; *The Bodley Head Bernard Shaw: Collected Plays with their Prefaces*, vol. 3 (1971).

First published in 1907.

Such poverty as we have today in all our great cities degrades the poor, and infects with its degradation the whole neighborhood in which they live. And whatever can degrade a neighborhood can degrade a country and a continent and finally the whole civilized world, which is only a large neighborhood.

The Intelligent Woman's Guide to Socialism, Capitalism, Sovietism and Fascism, ch. 14; Constable (1949).
First published in 1928 as The Intelligent Woman's Guide to Socialism and Capitalism.

POWER

You cannot have power for good without having power for evil too. Even mother's milk nourishes murderers as well as heroes.

Cusins, in Major Barbara, act 3; The Bodley Head Bernard Shaw: Collected Plays with their Prefaces, vol. 3 (1971).
First produced in 1905.

PRACTICALITY

My method of examining any proposition is to take its two extremes, both of them impracticable; make a scale between them; and try to determine at what point on the scale it can best be put in practice. A mother who has to determine the temperature of her baby's bath has two fixed limits to work between. The baby must not be boiled and must not be frozen.

Everybody's Political What's What?, ch. 20; Constable (1944).

PRAYER

The bitterest of prayers is the prayer that our prayers may not be granted; but it has been prayed ever since we discovered that the meanest trick our gods can play on us is to take us at our word.

"The Comedy of Calf Love," The Drama Observed, vol. 3, ed. Bernard F. Dukore; Penn State Press (1993).
First published in Saturday Review, January 15, 1898.

Common people do not pray, my lord: they only beg.

Lina, in *Misalliance*; *The Bodley Head Bernard Shaw: Collected Plays with their Prefaces*, vol. 4 (1972).

First produced in 1910.

If the truth were known, I suspect we all want our prayers to be answered only by halves: the agreeable halves.

Margaret, in *Fanny's First Play*, act 2; *The Bodley Head Bernard Shaw: Collected Plays with their Prefaces*, vol. 4 (1972).

First produced in 1911.

*P*REACHING

St. Anthony preached to the fishes, who probably understood at least as much of his sermon as a modern fashionable congregation would have done.

"Androcles and the Lion," *Complete Prefaces*, ed. Dan H. Laurence and Daniel J. Leary, vol. 2 (1995).

Program of *Androcles and the Lion*, St. James's Theatre, London, September 1, 1913.

*P*RINCIPLES

Abstract principles of conduct break down in practice because kindness and truth and justice are not duties founded on abstract principles external to man, but human passions, which have, in their time, conflicted with higher passions as well as with lower ones.

The Sanity of Art, Major Critical Essays; Constable (1949).

First published as "A Degenerate's View of Nordau," *Liberty* (New York), July 27, 1895.

If you're going to pick and choose your acquaintances on moral principles, you'd better clear out of this country, unless you want to cut yourself out of all decent society.

Sir George Crofts, in *Mrs. Warren's Profession*, act 3; *The Bodley Head Bernard Shaw: Collected Plays with their Prefaces*, vol. 1 (1970).

First published in 1898.

PRISONS

Imprisonment does not spare the life of the criminal: it takes it and wastes it in the most cruel way.

Imprisonment, "The Sacredness of Human Life from the Warder's Side," *Doctors' Delusions, Crude Criminology, and Sham Socialism*; Constable (1950).

First published in 1922.

PROBLEMS

My business tonight will be very largely to raise difficulties. That is all the use I am really in this world.

"Cultural Internationalism," *Practical Politics*, ed. Lloyd J. Hubenka; U of Nebraska Press (1976).

Lecture at the Fabian Society, November 24, 1926, first published as "Shaw Expounds Socialism as World Panacea," *The New York Times*, December 12, 1926.

PROFESSIONS

All professions are conspiracies against the laity.

Sir Patrick Cullen, in *The Doctor's Dilemma*, act 1; *The Bodley Head Bernard Shaw: Collected Plays with their Prefaces*, vol. 3 (1971).

First produced in 1906.

PROFESSORS

When a man is mentally incapable of abstract thought he takes to metaphysics; and they make him a professor. When he is incapable of conceiving quantity in the abstract he takes to mathematics; and they make him a professor. When he is incapable of distinguishing between a clockwork mouse and a real one he takes to biology; and they make him a professor. And so on. The fact is, these chaps are clockwork mice themselves. By tutoring them and coaching them and stuffing them with textbooks you wind them up, and they go.

> Franklyn Barnabas, in "A Glimpse of the Domesticity of Franklyn Barnabas"; *The Bodley Head Bernard Shaw: Collected Plays with their Prefaces*, vol. 5 (1972).

> Originally intended to be act 2 of *The Gospel of the Brothers Barnabas*, first published in *Short Stories, Scraps and Shavings*, 1930.

*P*ROGRESS

Social progress takes effect through the replacement of old institutions by new ones; and since every institution involves the recognition of the duty of conforming to it, progress must involve the repudiation of an established duty at every step.

> *The Quintessence of Ibsenism*, "The Two Pioneers," *The Drama Observed*, vol. 1, ed. Bernard F. Dukore; Penn State Press (1993).

> First published in 1891.

If we count the generations of Progressive elderly gentlemen since, say, Plato, and add together the sucessive enormous improvements to which each of them has testified, it will strike us at once as an unaccountable fact that the world, instead of having been improved in 67 generations out of all recognition, presents, on the whole, a rather less dignified appearance in Ibsen's *Enemy of the People* than in Plato's *Republic*.

> *Caesar and Cleopatra*, "Notes"; *The Bodley Head Bernard Shaw: Collected Plays with their Prefaces*, vol. 2 (1971).

> First published in 1901.

All progress is initiated by challenging current conceptions, and executed by supplanting existing institutions.

> The Author's Apology to *Mrs. Warren's Profession*; *The Bodley Head Bernard Shaw: Collected Plays with their Prefaces*, vol. 1 (1970).

> First published in 1902.

An epoch is but a swing of the pendulum, and each generation thinks the world is progressing because it is always moving.

> The Devil, in *Man and Superman*, act 3; *The Bodley Head Bernard Shaw: Collected Plays with their Prefaces*, vol. 2 (1971).

> First published in 1903.

The reasonable man adapts himself to the world: the unreasonable one persists in trying to adapt the world to himself. Therefore all progress depends on the unreasonable man.

Man and Superman, The Revolutionist's Handbook, "Maxims for Revolutionists"; *The Bodley Head Bernard Shaw: Collected Plays with their Prefaces*, vol. 2 (1971).

First published in 1903.

All progress means war with Society.

The Bishop, in *Getting Married*; *The Bodley Head Bernard Shaw: Collected Plays with their Prefaces*, vol. 3 (1971).

First produced in 1908.

PROPAGANDA

Fine art is the subtlest, the most seductive, the most effective instrument of moral propaganda in the world, excepting only the example of personal conduct; and I waive even this exception in favor of the art of the stage, because it works by exhibiting examples of personal conduct made intelligible and moving to crowds of unobservant unreflecting people to whom real life means nothing.

The Author's Apology to *Mrs. Warren's Profession*; *The Bodley Head Bernard Shaw: Collected Plays with their Prefaces*, vol. 1 (1970).

First published in 1902.

PROPHECY

My usual plan [is] prophesying nothing that has not already arrived and is at work (and therefore sure to be discovered by the English Press generally in from ten to fifty years).

"Romance In Its Last Ditch," *The Drama Observed*, vol. 3, ed. Bernard F. Dukore; Penn State Press (1993).

First published in *Saturday Review,* October 23, 1897.

It is more dangerous to be a great prophet or poet than to promote twenty companies for swindling simple folk out of their savings.

Misalliance, preface, "Art Teaching"; *The Bodley Head Bernard Shaw: Collected Plays with their Prefaces,* vol. 4 (1972).

First published in 1914.

The prophet is without honor in his own family.

> Conrad Barnabas, in *Back to Methuselah*, "The Gospel of the Brothers Barnabas"; *The Bodley Head Bernard Shaw: Collected Plays with their Prefaces*, vol. 5 (1972).
>
> First published in 1921; parody of *Matthew*, 13:57: "A prophet is without honor, save in his own country."

*P*SYCHOANALYSIS

As I write, there is a craze for what is called psychoanalysis, or the cure of diseases by explaining to the patient what is the matter with him: an excellent plan if you happen to know what is the matter with him, especially when the explanation is that there is nothing the matter with him.

> *Immaturity*, preface; Constable (1950).
>
> First published in 1921.

Modern psychoanalysis has taught us that prayer is a first-rate prescription for despairing pessimism, and that the therapeutic value of confession is enormous.

> "Shaw on Prayers," *Agitations*, ed. Dan H. Laurence and James Rambeau; Frederick Ungar (1985).
>
> Letter to *The Freethinker*, February 5, 1950.

*P*UBLIC LIFE

Public life is the paradise of voluble windbags.

> *Back to Methuselah*, preface, "The Miracle of Condensed Recapitulation"; *The Bodley Head Bernard Shaw: Collected Plays with their Prefaces*, vol. 5 (1972).
>
> First published in 1921.

*P*UBLIC OPINION

Public opinion cannot for a moment be relied upon as a force which operates uniformly as a compulsion upon men to act morally. Its operation is for all practical purposes quite arbitrary, and is as often immoral as moral. It is just as hostile to the reformer as to the criminal.

> *The Impossibilities of Anarchism*, "Communist Anarchism," *Essays in Fabian Socialism*; Constable (1949).
>
> Paper read to the Fabian Society, October 16, 1891.

Public opinion is a great power so long as you take good care that the public has no opportunity of expressing it.

"Follies, Fallacies, and Facts," *Practical Politics*, ed. Lloyd J. Hubenka; U of Nebraska Press (1976).

Extensively revised text of "A Cure for Democracy," lecture at the Fabian Society, November 27, 1930, first published in *The Clarion*, February 1931.

*P*UERILITY

I thought it puerile to the uttermost publishable extreme of jejuniority.

"*The Red Robe*," *The Drama Observed*, vol. 2, ed. Bernard F. Dukore; Penn State Press (1993).

On the novel *The Red Robe* by (John) Stanley Weyman; first published in *Saturday Review*, October 24, 1896.

*P*UNISHMENT

Forcing children to learn by beating them is unskilled labor of an unedifying and repulsive character.

The W.E.A. [Workers' Educational Association] Education Year Book, preface to Part 1; *Complete Prefaces*, ed. Dan H. Laurence and Daniel J. Leary, vol. 2 (1995).

First published in 1918.

If you are to punish a man retributively, you must injure him. If you are to reform him, you must improve him. And men are not improved by injuries. To propose to punish and reform people by the same operation is exactly as if you were to take a man suffering from pneumonia, and attempt to combine punitive and curative treatment.

Imprisonment, "The Retribution Muddle," *Doctors' Delusions, Crude Criminology, and Sham Socialism*; Constable (1950).

First published in 1922.

Increased severity of punishment, which the uninstructed public always clamors for in a panic, is quite useless without inceased certainty of detection, which is the only really effective deterrent.

"Insanity and the Law," *Agitations*, ed. Dan H. Laurence and James Rambeau; Ungar (1985).

Letter to *The Times*, written September 15, 1932, declined by the editor.

Puritanism

A Puritan is no doubt often at the same disadvantage as the Philistine in respect of his insensibility to Art; but he is a fanatical idealist, to whom all stimulations of the sense of beauty are abhorrent because he is only conscious of them insofar as they appeal to his sex instinct, which he regards as his enemy.

"The Two Latest Comedies," *The Drama Observed*, vol. 2, ed. Bernard F. Dukore; Penn State Press (1993).

First published in *Saturday Review*, May 18, 1895.

Purpose

Give a man health and a course to steer; and he'll never stop to trouble about whether he's happy or not.

Brassbound, in *Captain Brassbound's Profession*, act 3, *The Bodley Head Bernard Shaw: Collected Plays with their Prefaces*, vol. 2 (1971).

First produced in 1900.

One man that has a mind and knows it can always beat ten men who haven't and don't.

Proteus, in *The Apple Cart*, act 1; *The Bodley Head Bernard Shaw: Collected Plays with their Prefaces*, vol. 6 (1973).

First produced in 1929.

Questions

No question is so difficult to answer as that to which the answer is obvious.

"The Independent Theatre," *The Drama Observed*, vol. 1, ed. Bernard F. Dukore; Penn State Press (1993).

First published in *Saturday Review*, January 26, 1895.

RACISM

We laugh at the haughty American nation because it makes the Negro clean its boots and then proves the moral and physical inferiority of the Negro by the fact that he is a shoeblack.

> *Man and Superman*, Epistle Dedicatory; *The Bodley Head Bernard Shaw: Collected Plays with their Prefaces*, vol. 2 (1971).
>
> First published in 1903.

There is nothing new in this resentment of the virtues of a competitor, and nothing unnatural in it; for the virtues of your competitor screw up the standard you are expected to reach. The agitation to exclude Chinamen, which has been successful in America and Australia, was an agitation against their virtues, not against their vices.

> "The Play and Its Author," *The Drama Observed*, ed. Bernard F. Dukore, vol. 4; Penn State Press (1993).
>
> Souvenir Program, *Woman on Her Own* by Eugène Brieux, November 15, 1913.

READING

It's the end of education. How can you dare teach a man to read until you've taught him everything else first?

> Lord Summerhays, in *Misalliance*; *The Bodley Head Bernard Shaw: Collected Plays with their Prefaces*, vol. 4 (1972).
>
> First produced in 1910.

Everybody knows how to read and nobody knows what to read.

> *The W.E.A. [Workers' Educational Association] Education Year Book*, preface to Part 1; *Complete Prefaces*, ed. Dan H. Laurence and Daniel J. Leary, vol. 2 (1995).
>
> First published in 1918.

REALISM

They do not seem to have got much further than an opinion that the romance of the drawing room is less real than the romance of the kitchen, the romance of the kitchen than that of the slum, that of the slum than that of the sewer, and, generally, that reality is always in inverse proportion to self-control, education, health, and decency.

"Realism, Real and Unreal," *Bernard Shaw's Book Reviews*, ed. Brian Tyson; Penn State Press (1991).

On realistic novelists, first published in *Pall Mall Gazette*, September 29, 1887.

The question at issue just now is not whether Zola hits the truth or misses it, but whether it is permissible to aim at the truth at all.

"Asides," *SHAW: The Annual of Bernard Shaw Studies*, vol. 16, ed. Dan H. Laurence and Margot Peters; Penn State Press (1996).

Written on June 9, 1889; Zola's British publisher, Henry Vizetelly, was prosecuted for publishing Zola's novel *Soil* (*La terre*), which the crown called "an obscene libel"; in May, on his solicitor's advice, he pleaded guilty and paid a fine of £100.

REALITY

Men are for the most part so constituted that realities repel, and illusions attract them.

"The Illusions of Socialism," *Shavian Tract* No. 4 (1956) .

First published in September 1896.

The Real has always been a hard bird to catch. Plato did not succeed in getting it under his hat until he had divested it of everything that is real to the realists of noveldom today.

"Realism, Real and Unreal," *Bernard Shaw's Book Reviews*, ed. Brian Tyson; Penn State Press (1991).

First published in *Pall Mall Gazette*, September 29, 1887.

A Philosopher opposes the reality of a thing to its mere appearance; but to the Matter-of-Fact Man the appearance *is* the reality, and things that have no appearance are less real to him than tangible, ponderable, visible things. There is something convincing to him in a brick, which he misses in, for instance, a number.

"That Realism Is the Goal of Fiction," *SHAW: The Annual of Bernard Shaw Studies*, vol. 16, ed. Dan H. Laurence and Margot Peters; Penn State Press (1996).

Address to the Blackheath Essay and Debating Society, January 18, 1888.

REASON

Faith in reason as a prime motor is no longer the criterion of the sound mind, any more than faith in the Bible is the criterion of righteous intention.

The Quintessence of Ibsenism, "The Two Pioneers," *The Drama Observed*, vol. 1, ed. Bernard F. Dukore, Penn State Press (1993).

First published in 1891.

REBELLION

All movements which attack the existing state of society attract both the people who are not good enough for the world and the people for whom the world is not good enough.

"Androcles and the Lion," *Complete Prefaces*, ed. Dan H. Laurence and Daniel J. Leary, vol. 2 (1995).

Program of *Androcles and the Lion*, St. James's Theatre, London, September 1, 1913.

REFORM

Nothing is ever done until a startling catastrophe wakens up the people to the need of social reform. It was the cholera that forced us to adopt sanitation. It was the Crimean War that forced us to reform the Civil Service.

"The Dynamitards of Science," *Platform and Pulpit*; Hill & Wang (1961).

Speech before the London Anti-Vivisection Society, May 30, 1900.

It is doubtless wise, when a reform is introduced, to try to persuade the British public that it is not a reform at all; but appearances must be kept up to some extent at least.

"The Simplified Spelling Proposals," *On Language*, ed. Abraham Tauber; Philosophical Library (1963).

Letter to *The Times* (London), September 25, 1906.

Hard words, even when uttered by eloquent essayists and lecturers, or carried unanimously at enthusiastic public meetings on the motion of eminent reformers, break no bones.

Major Barbara, preface, "Barbara's Return to the Colors"; *The Bodley Head Bernard Shaw: Collected Plays with their Prefaces*, vol. 3 (1971).

First published in 1907.

We must reform society before we can reform ourselves.

Misalliance, preface, "We Must Reform Society Before We Can Reform Ourselves"; *The Bodley Head Bernard Shaw: Collected Plays with their Prefaces*, vol. 4 (1972).

First published in 1914.

As a professional reformer you had better be content to preach one form of unconventionality at a time. For instance, if you rebel against high-heeled shoes, take care to do it in a very smart hat.

The Intelligent Woman's Guide to Socialism, Capitalism, Sovietism, and Fascism, ch. 79; Constable (1949).

First published in 1928 as *The Intelligent Woman's Guide to Socialism and Capitalism*.

ℛELATIVES

When our relatives are at home, we have to think of all their good points or it would be impossible to endure them. But when they are away, we console ourselves for their absence by dwelling on their vices.

Captain Shotover, in *Heartbreak House*, act 1; *The Bodley Head Bernard Shaw: Collected Plays with their Prefaces*, vol. 5 (1972).

First published in 1919.

ℛELIGION

The real religion of today was made possible only by the materialistic-physicists and atheist-critics who performed for us the indispensable preliminary operation of purging us thoroughly of the ignorant and vicious superstitions which were thrust down our throats as religion in our helpless childhood.

"On Going to Church," *Shaw on Religion*, ed. Warren S. Smith; Dodd Mead (1967).

First published in *The Savoy*, January 1896.

There is only one religion, though there are a hundred versions of it.

Plays Pleasant, preface; *The Bodley Head Bernard Shaw: Collected Plays with their Prefaces*, vol. 1 (1970).

First published in 1898.

Religion [was] for me a mere excuse for laziness, since it had set up a God who looked at the world and saw it was good, against the instinct in me that looked through my eyes at the world and saw that it could be improved.

> Don Juan, in *Man and Superman*, act 3, *The Bodley Head Bernard Shaw: Collected Plays with their Prefaces*, vol. 2 (1971).
>
> First published in 1903.

I am a Millionaire. That is my religion.

> Andrew Undershaft, in *Major Barbara*, act 2; *The Bodley Head Bernard Shaw: Collected Plays with their Prefaces*, vol. 3 (1971).
>
> First produced in 1905.

You have made for yourself something that you call a morality or a religion or what not. It doesn't fit the facts. Well, scrap it. Scrap it and get one that does fit. That is what is wrong with the world at present. It scraps its obsolete steam engines and dynamos; but it won't scrap its old prejudices and its old moralities and its old religions and its old political constitutions.

> Andrew Undershaft, in *Major Barbara*, act 3; *The Bodley Head Bernard Shaw: Collected Plays with their Prefaces*, vol. 3 (1971).
>
> First produced in 1905.

Religion is a great force: the only real motive force in the world; but what you fellows don't understand is that you must get at a man through his own religion and not through yours.

> Hotchkiss, *Getting Married*; *The Bodley Head Bernard Shaw: Collected Plays with their Prefaces*, vol. 3 (1971).
>
> First produced in 1908.

The fact that a believer is happier than a skeptic is no more to the point than the fact that a drunken man is happier than a sober one. The happiness of credulity is a cheap and dangerous quality of happiness, and by no means a necessity of life.

> *Androcles and the Lion*, preface, "The Importance of Hell in the Salvation Scheme"; *The Bodley Head Bernard Shaw: Collected Plays with their Prefaces*, vol. 4 (1972).
>
> First published in 1916.

Very few people are really religious. Most people think that a harmonium is sacred, but not quite so sacred as an organ; and their notion of blasphemy is to play ragtime on a harmonium. I love playing ragtime on harmoniums, just to show them that one can do it without being struck dead, and that religion is something quite different.

Letter to Rosina Filippi, September 16, 1913, *Collected Letters*, ed. Dan H. Laurence, vol. 3 (1985).

There is a voluptuous side to religious ecstasy and a religious side to voluptuous ecstasy; and the notion that one is less sacred than the other is the opportunity of the psychiatrist who seeks to discredit the saints by showing that the passion which exalted them was in its abuse capable also of degrading sinners.

"Mr. Shaw on Morals," *The Drama Observed*, ed. Bernard F. Dukore, vol. 4; Penn State Press (1993).

Letter to the Editor, *The Times*, November 8, 1913.

It is the adulteration of religion by the romance of miracles and paradises and torture chambers that makes it reel at the impact of every advance in science, instead of being clarified by it.

Back to Methuselah, preface, "Religion and Romance"; *The Bodley Head Bernard Shaw: Collected Plays with their Prefaces*, vol. 5 (1972).

First published in 1921.

Surely religion is one thing, and the British marriage law another.

Sir Ferdinand Flopper, *Buoyant Billions*, act 3; *The Bodley Head Bernard Shaw: Collected Plays with their Prefaces*, vol. 7 (1974).

First produced (in German) in 1948.

It is also evident from the hanging law and from the general consensus of opinion that death is the greatest of evils, that the doctrine of the immortality of the soul, like that of returning good for evil, is only formally professed and not really believed in.

Letter to the editor of *The Star*, written September 20, 1888, *Collected Letters*, vol. 1, ed. Dan H. Laurence (1965).

Written above the pseudonym Shendar Brwa, an anagram; first published November 20, 1957 in *The Flying Dutchman*, Hofstra College student newspaper.

ℛESPECTABILITY

If I swerve by a hair's breadth from the straight line of the most rigid respectability, I'm done for.

Valentine, in *You Never Can Tell*, act 1; *The Bodley Head Bernard Shaw: Collected Plays with their Prefaces*, vol. 1 (1970).

First published in 1898.

The more things a man is ashamed of, the more respectable he is.

John Tanner, in *Man and Superman*, act 1; *The Bodley Head Bernard Shaw: Collected Plays with their Prefaces*, vol. 2 (1971).

First published in 1903.

We don't really know what's right and what's wrong. We're all right as long as things go on the way they always did. We bring our children up just as we were brought up; and we go to church or chapel just as our parents did; and we say what everybody says; and it goes on all right until something out of the way happens. . . . We find out then that with our respectability and piety, we've no real religion and no way of telling right from wrong. We've nothing but our habits.

Mrs. Knox, in *Fanny's First Play*, act 3; *The Bodley Head Bernard Shaw: Collected Plays with their Prefaces*, vol. 4 (1972).

First produced in 1911.

All biological necessities have to be made respectable whether we like it or not.

Conrad Barnabas, in *Back to Methuselah*, "The Gospel of the Brothers Barnabas"; *The Bodley Head Bernard Shaw: Collected Plays with their Prefaces*, vol. 5 (1972).

First published in 1921.

What was unmentionable yesterday is a common topic of polite conversation today.

"Censorship as a Police Duty," *Platform and Pulpit*, ed. Dan H. Laurence; Hill and Wang (1961).

Address at the Special General Conference of the Chief Constables' Association, June 8, 1928.

ℛEVENGE

The Sermon on the Mount . . . is a very moving exhortation, and it gives you one first-rate tip, which is to do good to those who despitefully use you and persecute you. I, who am a much hated man, have been doing that all my life, and I can assure you that there is no better fun, whereas revenge and resentment make life miserable and the avenger hateful.

"This Danger of War," *Platform and Pulpit*, ed. Dan H. Laurence; Hill & Wang (1961).

B.B.C. broadcast, November 2, 1937.

ℛEVOLUTION

The professional and penniless younger son classes are the revolutionary element in society: the proletariat is the Conserative element.

"Who I Am, and What I Think," *Sixteen Self Sketches*; Constable (1949).

First published in *Candid Friend,* May 1901.

Hot water is the revolutionist's element. You clean men as you clean milk-pails, by scalding them.

Tanner, in *Man and Superman,* act 4; *The Bodley Head Bernard Shaw: Collected Plays with their Prefaces,* vol. 2 (1971).

First published in 1903.

I am, and always have been, and shall now always be, a revolutionary writer, because our laws make law impossible; our liberties destroy all freedom; our property is organized robbery; our morality is an impudent hypocrisy; our wisdom is administered by inexperienced or malexperienced dupes, our power wielded by cowards and weaklings, and our honor false in all its points. I am an enemy of the existing order for good reasons.

Major Barbara, preface, "Sane Conclusions"; *The Bodley Head Bernard Shaw: Collected Plays with their Prefaces,* vol. 3 (1971).

First published in 1907.

It has been said that the French Revolution was the work of Voltaire, Rousseau and the Encyclopedists. It seems to me to have been the work of men who had observed that virtuous indignation, caustic criticism, conclusive argument and instructive pamphleteering, even when done by the most earnest and witty literary geniuses, were as useless as praying.

Major Barbara, preface, "Barbara's Return to the Colors"; *The Bodley Head Bernard Shaw: Collected Plays with their Prefaces,* vol. 3 (1971).

First published in 1907.

Revolutionary movements attract those who are not good enough for established institutions as well as those who are too good for them.

Androcles and the Lion, epilogue; *The Bodley Head Bernard Shaw: Collected Plays with their Prefaces,* vol. 4 (1972).

First published in 1916.

If you don't begin to be a revolutionist at the age of twenty, then at fifty you will be a most impossible old fossil. If you are a red revolutionary at the age of twenty, you have some chance of being up-to-date when you are forty!

"Universities and Education," *Platform and Pulpit*, ed. Dan H. Laurence; Hill and Wang (1961). Speech at University of Hong Kong, February 12, 1933.

Rich, the

The more I see of the moneyed classes, the more I understand the guillotine.

Letter to Edward Pope, September 25, 1899, *Collected Letters 1898–1910*, ed. Dan H. Laurence, vol. 2 (1972).

Richard III

It is not enough to see *Richard III*: you should be able to *whistle* it.

"Richard Orchestrated," *Shaw's Music*, vol. 1, ed. Dan H. Laurence (1891). First published in *The Star*, March 23, 1889.

Righteousness

Personal righteousness is impossible in an unrighteous environment.

Letter to H.G. Wells, May 17, 1917, *Selected Correspondence of Bernard Shaw: Bernard Shaw and H.G. Wells*, ed. J. Percy Smith; U of Toronto Press (1995).

I came not to call sinners, but the righteous, to repentance.

The Archbishop, in *Back to Methuselah*, "The Thing Happens"; *The Bodley Head Bernard Shaw: Collected Plays with their Prefaces*, vol. 5 (1972). First published in 1921; reversal of *Matthew*, 9:13.

Risk

You can't live without running risks.

Lina, in *Misalliance*; *The Bodley Head Bernard Shaw: Collected Plays with their Prefaces*, vol. 4 (1972). First produced in 1910.

ROMANCE

People are seduced by romance because they are ignorant of reality.

Cashel Byron's Profession, preface; Constable (1950).

Preface written in 1901.

ROYALTY

What private man in England is worse off than the constitutional monarch? We deny him all privacy; he may not marry whom he chooses, consort with whom he prefers, dress according to his taste, or live where he pleases. I don't believe he may even eat or drink what he likes best; a taste for tripe and onions on his part would provoke a remonstrance from the Privy Council.

Trefusis, in *An Unsocial Socialist*, ch. 12; Constable (1950).

First published in 1887.

RULES

The fact is, there are no rules, and there never were any rules, and there never will be any rules of musical composition except rules of thumb; and thumbs vary in length, like ears.

"No Rules," *Shaw's Music*, vol. 3, ed. Dan H. Laurence (1981).

First published in *The World*, February 28, 1894.

The social rule must be "Live; and let live," and people who break this rule persistently must be liquidated.

"This Danger of War," *Platform and Pulpit*, ed. Dan H. Laurence; Hill & Wang (1961).

B.B.C. broadcast, November 2, 1937.

SAINTS

Those who are called saints are not saintly all the time and in everything.

Immaturity, preface; Constable (1950).

First published in 1921.

It is far more dangerous to be a saint than to be a conqueror.

> *Saint Joan*, preface, "Contrast with Napoleon"; *The Bodley Head Bernard Shaw: Collected Plays with their Prefaces*, vol. 6 (1973).
>
> First published in 1924.

SALVATION

There are two things necessary to Salvation. . . . Money and gunpowder.

> Andrew Undershaft, in *Major Barbara*, act 2; *The Bodley Head Bernard Shaw: Collected Plays with their Prefaces*, vol. 3 (1971).
>
> First produced in 1905.

The salvation of the world depends on the men who will not take evil good-humoredly, and whose laughter destroys the fool instead of encouraging him.

> *The Quintessence of Ibsenism*, "What Is the New Element in the Norwegian School?" *The Drama Observed*, ed. Bernard F. Dukore, vol. 4; Penn State Press (1993).
>
> First published in revised edition, 1913.

The notion that those who reject the Christian (or any other) scheme of salvation by atonement must reject also belief in personal immortality and in miracles is as baseless as the notion that if a man is an atheist he will steal your watch.

> *Androcles and the Lion*, preface, "Belief in Personal Immortality No Criterion"; *The Bodley Head Bernard Shaw: Collected Plays with their Prefaces*, vol. 4 (1972).
>
> First published in 1916.

SALVATION ARMY

All religious organizations exist by selling themselves to the rich.

> Andrew Undershaft, in *Major Barbara*, act 2; *The Bodley Head Bernard Shaw: Collected Plays with their Prefaces*, vol. 3 (1971).
>
> First produced in 1905.

It is a very significant thing, this instinctive choice of the military form of organization, this substitution of the drum for the organ, by the Salvation Army. Does it not suggest that the Salvationists divine that they must actually fight the devil, instead of merely praying at him? At present, it is true, they have not quite ascertained his correct address.

Major Barbara, preface, "Barbara's Return to the Colors"; *The Bodley Head Bernard Shaw: Collected Plays with their Prefaces*, vol. 3 (1971).

First published in 1907.

SCENERY

It is one thing to banish vulgarity and monstrosity from the stage and replace them by conventional refinement and scrupulous verisimilitude. It is quite another to surround a real drama with its appropriate atmosphere, and provide a poetic background or an ironically prosaic setting for a tragic scene. There are some rooms in which no reasonable person could possibly commit suicide.

"Mr John Hare," *The Drama Observed*, vol. 2, ed. Bernard F. Dukore; Penn State Press (1993).

First published in *Saturday Review*, December 21, 1895.

The more scenery you have the less illusion you produce.

Overruled, preface, "Our Disillusive Scenery"; *The Bodley Head Bernard Shaw: Collected Plays with their Prefaces*, vol. 4 (1972).

First published in 1916.

SCHOOL

The school remains what it was in my boyhood, because its real object remains what it was. And that object, I repeat, is to keep the children out of mischief: mischief meaning for the most part worrying the grown-ups.

Misalliance, preface, "Alleged Novelties in Modern Schools"; *The Bodley Head Bernard Shaw: Collected Plays with their Prefaces*, vol. 4 (1972).

First published in 1914.

SCIENCE

You have only to search an emancipated man's mind long enough to come upon an abyss of superstition somewhere—nowadays generally "scientific."

Letter to Charles Charrington, November 6, 1895, *Collected Letters*, vol. 1, ed. Dan H. Laurence (1965).

I have actually known a man to die of a disease from which he was, scientifically speaking, immune. But that does not affect the fundamental truth of science.

B.B., in *The Doctor's Dilemma*, act 3; *The Bodley Head Bernard Shaw: Collected Plays with their Prefaces*, vol. 3 (1971).

First produced in 1906.

If you had been scientifically trained, Mr. Dubedat, you would know how very seldom an actual case bears out a principle.

B.B., in *The Doctor's Dilemma*, act 3; *The Bodley Head Bernard Shaw: Collected Plays with their Prefaces*, vol. 3 (1971).

First produced in 1906.

SIR PATRICK: Modern science is a wonderful thing. Look at your great discovery! Look at all the great discoveries! Where are they leading to? Why, right back to my poor dear old father's ideas and discoveries. He's been dead now over forty years. Oh, it's very interesting.

RIDGEON: Well, there's nothing like progress, is there?

The Doctor's Dilemma, act 1; *The Bodley Head Bernard Shaw: Collected Plays with their Prefaces*, vol. 3 (1971).

First produced in 1906.

SCRUPLES

No man is scrupulous all round. He has, according to his faculties and interests, certain points of honor, whilst in matters that do not interest him he is careless and unscrupulous.

"Biographers' Blunders Corrected," *Sixteen Self Sketches*; Constable (1949).

Letter to Charles Henry Duffin, 1947-48.

SEDITION

"Sedition". . . in 1810 was as useful for the muzzling of inconveniently progressive editors as "blasphemy" and "obscenity" are at present.

"Cobbett's Rural Rides," *Bernard Shaw's Book Reviews*, ed. Brian Tyson; Penn State Press (1991).

First published in *Pall Mall Gazette*, July 27, 1885.

SERIOUSNESS

Your reader, I fear, thought the book was not serious—perhaps because it was not dull.

Letter to Macmillan & Co., January 14, 1885, *Collected Letters*, ed. Dan H. Laurence, vol. 1 (1965).

Macmillan & Co. had rejected Shaw's novel *An Unsocial Socialist.*

SERVANTS

I have to get your room ready for you: to sweep and dust, to fetch and carry. How could that degrade me if it did not degrade you to have it done for you?

Louka, in *Arms and the Man*, act 3, *The Bodley Head Bernard Shaw: Collected Plays with their Prefaces*, vol. 1 (1970).

First produced in 1894.

Masters and servants are both tyrannical; but the masters are the more dependent of the two.

Man and Superman, *The Revolutionist's Handbook*, "Maxims for Revolutionists"; *The Bodley Head Bernard Shaw: Collected Plays with their Prefaces*, vol. 2 (1971).

First published in 1903.

SEX

I have a technical objection to making sexual infatuation a tragic theme. Experience proves that it is only effective in the comic spirit.

Three Plays for Puritans, preface; *The Bodley Head Bernard Shaw: Collected Plays with their Prefaces*, vol. 2 (1971).

First published in 1901.

Sexually, Man is Woman's contrivance for fulfilling Nature's behest in the most economical way.

Don Juan, in *Man and Superman*, act 3; *The Bodley Head Bernard Shaw: Collected Plays with their Prefaces*, vol. 2 (1971).

First published in 1903.

We shall never attain to a reasonably healthy public opinion on sex questions until we offer, as the data for that opinion, our actual conduct and our real thoughts intead of a moral fiction which we agree to call virtuous conduct, and which we then—and here comes in the mischief—pretend is our conduct and our thoughts.

> *Overruled*, preface, "The Missing Data of a Scientific Natural History of Marriage"; *The Bodley Head Bernard Shaw: Collected Plays with their Prefaces*, vol. 4 (1972).
> First published in 1916.

We have two tyrannous physical passions: concupiscence and chastity. We become mad in pursuit of sex: we become equally mad in the persecution of that pursuit. Unless we gratify our desire the race is lost: unless we restrain it we destroy ourselves. We are thus led to devise marriage institutions which will at the same time secure opportunities for the gratification of sex and raise up innumerable obstacles to it.

> *Androcles and the Lion*, preface, "Inconsistency of the Sex Instinct"; *The Bodley Head Bernard Shaw: Collected Plays with their Prefaces*, vol. 4 (1972).
> First published in 1916.

I am afraid the authors of Genesis and St. Paul and the rest of them tangled up the original sin of disobedience with the loss of sexual innocence too thoroughly for you to hope to unravel them.

> Letter to W.E. Stafford, December 13, 1922. *Collected Letters*, ed. Dan H. Laurence, vol. 3 (1985).

The relation between the parties in copulation is not a personal relation. It can be irresistibly desired and rapturously executed between persons who could not endure one another for a day in any other relation.

> Letter to Frank Harris, June 24, 1930, *Collected Letters*, ed. Dan H. Laurence, vol. 4 (1988).

We all have—to put it as nicely as I can—our lower centres and our higher centres. Our lower centres act: they act with terrible power that sometimes destroys us; but they don't talk. . . . Since the war the lower centres have become vocal. And the effect is that of an earthquake. For they speak truths that have never been spoken before—truths that the makers of our domestic institutions have tried to ignore.

> Aubrey, in *Too True to be Good*, act 2; *The Bodley Head Bernard Shaw: Collected Plays with their Prefaces*, vol. 6 (1973).
> First produced in 1932.

Instruction in sex is as important as instruction in food; yet not only are our adolescents not taught the phsyiology of sex, but never warned that the stongest sexual attraction may exist between persons so incompatible in tastes and capacities that they could not endure living together for a week much less a lifetime.

> *Everybody's Political What's What?*, ch. 21; Constable (1944).

The sex illusion is not a fixed quantity: not what mathematicians call a constant. It varies from zero in my wife's case to madness in that of our stepsister.

> Secondborn, in *Buoyant Billions*, act 3; *The Bodley Head Bernard Shaw: Collected Plays with their Prefaces*, vol. 7 (1974).
> First produced (in German) in 1948.

*S*HAKESPEARE, WILLIAM

Mr. Irving calls his arrangement of the *Merchant* an "acting version." What does he call the original?

> "*The Merchant of Venice* at the Lyceum," *The Drama Observed*, vol. 1, ed. Bernard F. Dukore; Penn State Press (1993).
> Review of Henry Irving's performance of Shylock, written April 7, 1880.

I myself, born of profane stock, and with a quarter-century of playgoing, juvenile and manly, behind me, have not seen as many as a full half of Shakespeare's plays acted; and if my impressions of his genius were based solely on these representations, I should be in darkness indeed.

> "The Religion of the Pianoforte," *Shaw's Music*, vol. 3, ed. Dan H. Laurence (1981).
> First published in *Fortnightly Review*, February 1894.

Shakespeare, whose many-sidedness included a remarkable power of writing badly.

> "*Troilus and Cressida*," *The Drama Observed*, vol. 1, ed. Bernard F. Dukore; Penn State Press (1993).
> Speech for the New Shakespeare Society, read in Shaw's absence, February 29, 1884.

The practice of Shakespeare enthusiasts to dwell fondly on such of his ideas as happen to reflect their own, and to deny the existence of the rest unconditionally.

> "*Troilus and Cressida*," *The Drama Observed*, vol. 1, ed. Bernard F. Dukore; Penn State Press (1993).
> Speech for the New Shakespeare Society, read in Shaw's absence, February 29, 1884.

Shakespeare is for an afternoon, but not for all time.

"The Immortal William," *The Drama Observed*, vol. 2, ed. Bernard F. Dukore; Penn State Press (1993).

Parody of Ben Jonson's "He was not of an age, but for all time!" ("To the Memory of My Beloved . . . Shakespeare"; first published in *Saturday Review*, May 2, 1896.

With the single exception of Homer, there is no eminent writer, not even Sir Walter Scott, whom I can despise so entirely as I despise Shakespeare when I measure my mind against his. . . . But I am bound to add that I pity the man who cannot enjoy Shakespeare. He has outlasted thousands of abler thinkers, and will outlast a thousand more.

"Blaming the Bard," *The Drama Observed*, vol. 2, ed. Bernard F. Dukore; Penn State Press (1993).

First published in the *Saturday Review*, September 26, 1896.

Bardolatry!

Three Plays for Puritans, preface; *The Bodley Head Bernard Shaw: Collected Plays with their Prefaces*, vol. 2 (1971).

Neologism, meaning blind or indiscriminate idolatry of the bard (Shakespeare); first published in 1901.

Shakespeare's power lies in his enormous command of word-music, which gives fascination to his most blackguardly repartees and sublimity to his hollowest platitudes.

"Bernard Shaw Abashed," *The Drama Observed*, ed. Bernard F. Dukore, vol. 3; Penn State Press (1993).

Letter to the *Daily News*, April 17, 1905.

S*HAW, BERNARD*

My method is to take the utmost trouble to find the right thing to say, and then to say it with the utmost levity.

Quoted in Eric Bentley, *Bernard Shaw* (1947).

"George Bernard Shaw," Questionnaire-Interview by Clarence Rook, first published in *Candid Friend*, November 1, 1896.

The real joke is that I am in earnest.

Quoted in Eric Bentley, *Bernard Shaw* (1947).

"George Bernard Shaw," Questionnaire-Interview by Clarence Rook, first published in *Candid Friend*, November 1, 1896.

I am nothing if not explanatory.

Three Plays for Puritans, preface; *The Bodley Head Bernard Shaw: Collected Plays with their Prefaces* (1971), vol. 2.

First published in 1901.

I did not throw myself into the struggle for life: I threw my mother into it. I was not a staff to my father's old age: I hung on to his coat tails.

The Irrational Knot, preface; Constable (1950).

First published in 1905.

My mission is not to deal with obvious horrors, but to open the eyes of normal respectable men to evils which are escaping their consideration.

Getting Married, preface, "The Pathology of Marriage"; *The Bodley Head Bernard Shaw: Collected Plays with their Prefaces*, vol. 3 (1971).

First published in 1911.

I have "risen" by sheer gravitation.

Sixteen Self Sketches, "Biographers' Blunders Corrected"; Constable (1949).

Letter to Thomas Demetrius O'Bolger, August 7, 1919.

*S*HELLEY, PERCY BYSSHE

Shelley, although he rushed into print before he was ripe for it, and often disgraced himself by doing very ordinary literary jobs in an unworkmanlike way, is yet, with the exception—under certain limitations—of Shakespeare, the greatest of English poets.

"[*The Cenci*]," *The Drama Observed*, ed. Bernard F. Dukore, vol. 1; Penn State Press (1993) ,

First published in *Our Corner*, June 1886 .

SHOCK

The plain working truth is that it is not only good for people to be shocked occasionally, but absolutely necessary to the progress of society that they should be shocked pretty often.

> *The Quintessence of Ibsenism*, "The Lesson of the Plays," *The Drama Observed*, ed. Bernard F. Dukore, vol. 1; Penn State Press (1913).
>
> First published in revised edition, 1913.

SHYNESS

All the love in the world is longing to speak; only it dare not, because it is shy! shy! shy! That is the world's tragedy.

> Marchbanks, in *Candida*, act 2; *The Bodley Head Bernard Shaw: Collected Plays with their Prefaces*, vol. 1 (1970).
>
> First produced in 1897.

SILENCE

Silence is the most perfect expression of scorn.

> Ecrasia, in *Back to Methuselah*, "As Far as Thought Can Reach"; *The Bodley Head Bernard Shaw: Collected Plays with their Prefaces*, vol. 5 (1972).
>
> First published in 1921.

SIN

The seven deadly sins. . . . Food, clothing, firing, rent, taxes, respectability and children. Nothing can lift these seven millstones from man's neck but money; and the spirit cannot soar until the millstones are lifted.

> Andrew Undershaft, in *Major Barbara*, act 3; *The Bodley Head Bernard Shaw: Collected Plays with their Prefaces*, vol. 3 (1971).
>
> First produced in 1905.

The worst sin towards our fellow creatures is not to hate them, but to be indifferent to them; that's the essence of inhumanity.

> Anderson, in *The Devil's Disciple*, act 2; *The Bodley Head Bernard Shaw: Collected Plays with their Prefaces*, vol. 2 (1971).
>
> First produced in 1897.

I suppose we're all sinners, in a manner of speaking; but I don't like to have it thrown at me as if I'd really done anything.

> Gilbey, in *Fanny's First Play*, act 3; *The Bodley Head Bernard Shaw: Collected Plays with their Prefaces*, vol. 4 (1972).
>
> First produced in 1911.

SIN, ORIGINAL

"Original sin" is the will doing mischief. "Divine grace" is the will doing good.

> *The Quintessence of Ibsenism*, "The Two Pioneers"; *The Drama Observed*, vol. 1, ed. Bernard F. Dukore; Penn State Press (1993).
>
> First published in 1891.

SINGING

At present a great deal of audacity, a little affectation, some judicious puffing, and sufficient lung power to make a noise at brief intervals for three hours or so complete the list of acquirements necessary for a *primo tenore*.

> "Vocalists of the Season," *Shaw's Music*, vol. 1 (1981), ed. Dan H. Laurence.
>
> First published in *The Hornet*, June 27, 1877.

SIX CHARACTERS IN SEARCH OF AN AUTHOR

I rank P[irandello] as first-rate among playwrights, and have never come across a play so *original* as *Six Characters*.

> Letter to Frederick May, probably August 8, 1950, *Collected Letters*, ed. Dan H. Laurence, vol. 4 (1988).

SLAVERY

The slave ... sees nothing ahead of him but his freedom. He may be a moth flying towards a candle; but he has the moth's power of making it impossible for us to attend to our own business if we undertake the task of keeping him out of the candle by any other means than killing him.

"A Crib for Home Rulers," *Bernard Shaw's Book Reviews*, ed. Brian Tyson; Penn State Press (1991).

First published in *Pall Mall Gazette*, September 25, 1888.

SMOKING

Have you ever taken a country walk to a railway station, and then stepped into a smoking carriage? If you can do so without at least a momentary disgust, you must be lost to all sense of smell.

"Biographers' Blunders Corrected," *Sixteen Self Sketches*; Constable (1949).

Letter to Charles Henry Duffin, 1947 or 1948.

SNOBBERY

The enormous majority of the English people are snobs.

Hotchkiss, in *Getting Married*; *The Bodley Head Bernard Shaw: Collected Plays with their Prefaces*, vol. 3 (1971).

First produced in 1908.

SOCIAL QUESTIONS

Social questions are produced by the conflict of human institutions with human feeling.

"The Problem Play," *The Drama Observed*, vol. 1, ed. Bernard F. Dukore; Penn State Press (1993).

First published in *The Humanitarian*, May 1895.

*S*OCIALISM

The line of cleavage between the people who are socialists in England, and those who are not, does not coincide with or even lie in the same direction as that between those who call themselves socialists and those who do not.

Letter to Walter Crane, December 15, 1895, *Collected Letters*, vol. 1, ed. Dan H. Laurence (1965).

Many people look forward to Socialism as a system where everybody will get what they want without having to pay for it. One cannot do that now (except when the shopkeeper is not looking), but our present system of society does it under the names of Rent and Interest, by means of which an idle rich man gets his goods for nothing.

"What Socialism Will Be Like," *Platform and Pulpit*, ed. Dan H. Laurence; Hill & Wang (1961).
Lecture before the Hammersmith Socialist Society, July 12, 1896.

The first thing that strikes one in discussing the matter with a Socialist—if you have a critical habit of mind, as I have, professionally—is the superstitious resemblance of the notion your ordinary Socialist has of what Socialism will be like to the good old idea of what heaven will be like!

"What Socialism Will Be Like," *Platform and Pulpit*, ed. Dan H. Laurence; Hill & Wang (1961).
Lecture before the Hammersmith Socialist Society, July 12, 1896.

The dramatic illusion of Socialism is that which presents the working class as a virtuous hero and heroine in the toils of a villain called "the capitalist," suffering terribly and struggling nobly, but with a happy ending for them, and a fearful retribution for the villain, in full view before the fall of the curtain on a future of undisturbed bliss.

"The Illusions of Socialism," *Shavian Tract* No. 4 (1956).
First published in September 1896.

The cherished illusion that all Socialists are agreed in principle though they may differ as to tactics . . . is perhaps the most laughable of all the illusions of Socialism, so outrageously is it contradicted by the facts. It is quite true that the Socialists are in perfect agreement with one another except on those points on which they happen to differ.

"The Illusions of Socialism," *Shavian Tract* No. 4 (1956).
First published in September 1896.

There are certain questions on which I am, like most Socialists, an extreme Individualist.

> *Plays Unpleasant*, preface; *The Bodley Head Bernard Shaw: Collected Plays with their Prefaces*, vol. 1 (1970).
> First published in 1898.

Socialism is full of seductive cul-de-sacs and mirror-made halls of a million pillars.

> Letter to Edward Rose, March 14, 1900, *Collected Letters*, vol. 2, ed. Dan H. Laurence (1972).

LUBIN: I am glad you agree with me that Socialism and Votes for Women are signs of decay.

FRANKLYN BARNABAS: Not at all: they are only the difficulties that overtax your capacity.

> *Back to Methuselah*, "The Gospel of the Brothers Barnabas"; *The Bodley Head Bernard Shaw: Collected Plays with their Prefaces*, vol. 5 (1972).
> First published in 1921.

Socialists usually begin with no experience and great expectations. They mature with great experience and no expectations.

> Quoted in introduction, *Selected Correspondence of Bernard Shaw: Bernard Shaw and H.G. Wells*, ed. J. Percy Smith, U of Toronto Press (1995).
> Draft notes for a speech at Kingsway Hall, September 1924.

Precisely the same realism that confirms my Socialism as I grow older dispels my democratic illusions as to the power of mere idealists to establish it.

> Letter to Augustin Hamon, April 9, 1927, *Collected Letters*, ed. Dan H. Laurence, vol. 4 (1988).

Socialism means equality of income and nothing else.

> *The Intelligent Woman's Guide to Socialism, Capitalism, Sovietism, and Fascism*, ch. 26; Constable (1949).
> First published in 1928 as *The Intelligent Woman's Guide to Socialism and Capitalism*.

Much of my life as a propagandist has been spent on curing converts to Socialism of the notion that the program will be capitalism in full blast on Saturday, revolution on Sunday, and Socialism complete on Monday.

> Letter to I.J. Pitman, September 16, 1941, *Collected Letters*, ed. Dan H. Laurence, vol. 4 (1988).

*S*OCIETY

As society becomes more honest and intelligent, it becomes apparently more cynical. It perceives that the formulation of a code of honor applicable to all possible circumstances is neither possible nor desirable.

"Two Plays," *The Drama Observed*, vol. 2, ed. Bernard F. Dukore; Penn State Press (1993).
First published in *Saturday Review*, October 17, 1896.

As long as you don't fly openly in the face of society, society doesn't ask any inconvenient questions; and it makes precious short work of the cads who do. There are no secrets better kept than the secrets everybody guesses.

Sir George Crofts, in *Mrs. Warren's Profession*, act 3; *The Bodley Head Bernard Shaw: Collected Plays with their Prefaces*, vol. 1 (1970).
First published in 1898.

*S*OLDIERS

I never expect a soldier to think, sir.

Richard Dudgeon, in *The Devil's Disciple*, act 3; *The Bodley Head Bernard Shaw: Collected Plays with their Prefaces*, vol. 2 (1971).
First produced in 1897.

NAPOLEON: What shall we do with this officer, Giuseppe? Everything he says is wrong.
GIUSEPPE: Make him a general, excellency; and then everything he says will be right.

The Man of Destiny; *The Bodley Head Bernard Shaw: Collected Plays with their Prefaces*, vol. 1 (1970).
First produced in 1897.

What is an Englishman? A man who has extorted from his rulers Magna Carta, the Habeas Corpus Act, the Bill of Rights, the franchise for everyone, with a free press, a free platform, and the championship of the world's liberty. What is a soldier? A man stripped of every one of these rights.

Letter to J.T. Wootton, May 15, 1919, *Collected Letters*, ed. Dan H. Laurence, vol. 3 (1985).

SOUL, THE

It is not the sale of my soul that troubles me: I have sold it too often to care about that. I have sold it for a professorship. I have sold it for an income. I have sold it to escape being imprisoned for refusing to pay taxes for hangmen's ropes and unjust wars and things that I abhor. What is all human conduct but the daily and hourly sale of our souls for trifles?

Cusins, in *Major Barbara*, act 3; *The Bodley Head Bernard Shaw: Collected Plays with their Prefaces*, vol. 3 (1971).

First produced in 1905.

I've got a soul: don't tell me I haven't. Cut me up and you can't find it. Cut up a steam engine and you can't find the steam. But, by George, it makes the engine go.

Tarleton, in *Misalliance*; *The Bodley Head Bernard Shaw: Collected Plays with their Prefaces*, vol. 4 (1972).

First produced in 1910.

SPECIALIZATION

No man can be a pure specialist without being in the strict sense an idiot.

Man and Superman, *The Revolutionist's Handbook*, "Maxims for Revolutionists"; *The Bodley Head Bernard Shaw: Collected Plays with their Prefaces*, vol. 2 (1971).

First published in 1903.

SPEECH

It is impossible for an Englishman to open his mouth without making some other Englishman despise him.

Pygmalion, preface; *The Bodley Head Bernard Shaw: Collected Plays with their Prefaces*, vol. 4 (1972).

First published in 1916.

If I were to speak to you as carelessly as I speak to my wife at home, this record would be useless; and if I were to speak to my wife at home as carefully as I am speaking to you, she would think I was going mad.

"Spoken English and Broken English," *On Language*, ed. Abraham Tauber; Philosophical Library (1963).

Recording, Linguaphone Institute, 1928.

The old differences in speech and dress and manners are much less than
they were, partly because the working class is picking up middle class
manners, but much more because they are forcing their own manners and
speech on the middle class as standards.

The Intelligent Woman's Guide to Socialism, Capitalism, Sovietism, and Fascism, ch. 44; Constable (1949).
First published in 1928 as *The Intelligent Woman's Guide to Socialism and Capitalism.*

Can you show me any English woman who speaks English as it should be
spoken? Only foreigners who have been taught to speak it speak it well.

Nepommuck, in screenplay of *Pygmalion; The Bodley Head Bernard Shaw: Collected Plays with their
Prefaces*, vol. 4 (1972).
Written and filmed in 1938, first published in Penguin Books in 1941.

SPORTS

The sportsman: the man so primitive and uncritical in his tastes that the
destruction of life is an amusement to him, the man whose outlook is as
narrow as that of his dog.

Killing for Sport, preface, ed. Henry S. Salt; *Complete Prefaces*, ed. Dan H. Laurence and Daniel J. Leary,
vol. 2 (1995).
First published in 1914.

STATISTICS

Even trained statisticians often fail to appreciate the extent to which
statistics are vitiated by the unrecorded assumptions of their interpreters.

The Doctor's Dilemma, preface, "Statistical Illusions"; *The Bodley Head Bernard Shaw: Collected Plays
with their Prefaces*, vol. 3 (1971).
First published in 1911.

STRENGTH

I have noticed a widespread opinion among Britons lately that the
way to become strong is to lift heavy weights. Personally I incline

rather to the opinion that the way to lift heavy weights is to become strong.

Fabianism and the Fiscal Question, preface; *Complete Prefaces*, ed. Dan H. Laurence and Daniel J. Leary, vol. 1 (1993).

First published in 1904.

*S*TUDENTS

Once in ten thousand times it happens that the schoolboy is a born master of what they try to teach him.

Cusins, in *Major Barbara*, act 3; *The Bodley Head Bernard Shaw: Collected Plays with their Prefaces*, vol. 3 (1971).

First produced in 1905.

*S*TUPIDITY

Stupidity has all the knowledge, and Imagination all the intelligence.

Don Juan, in *Man and Superman*, act 3, *The Bodley Head Bernard Shaw: Collected Plays with their Prefaces*, vol. 2 (1971).

First published in 1903.

*S*TYLE

Effectiveness of assertion is the Alpha and Omega of style. He who has nothing to assert has no style and can have none: he who has something to assert will go as far in power of style as its momentousness and his conviction carry him. Disprove his assertion after it is made, yet its style remains.

Man and Superman, Epistle Dedicatory; *The Bodley Head Bernard Shaw: Collected Plays with their Prefaces*, vol. 2 (1971).

First published in 1903.

In literature the ambition of the novice is to acquire the literary language: the struggle of the adept is to get rid of it.

Quoted in Hesketh Pearson, *Bernard Shaw: His Life and Personality*, ch. 16; Atheneum (1963).

First published in 1942.

SUCCESS

Success in a fine art is a trifle that is to be picked up by the way as you go in search of your real self. It is never found by those who make it their sole object. Like happiness, it eludes direct search and drops into the hands of the careless passerby.

Quoted in Dan H. Laurence, "Katie Samuel: Shaw's Flameless 'Old Flame,'" *SHAW*, vol. 15; Penn State Press (1995).

Letter to Katie Samuel, June 4, 1884

I dread success. To have succeeded is to have finished one's business on earth, like the male spider, who is killed by the female the moment he has succeeded in his courtship. I like a state of continual becoming, with a goal in front and not behind.

Letter to Ellen Terry, August 28, 1896, *Collected Letters*, vol. 1, ed. Dan H. Laurence (1965).

Success in literature depends on what you have to say as well as on how you say it.

Letter to Mabel Shaw, January 30, 1928, *Collected Letters*, ed. Dan H. Laurence, vol. 4 (1988).

SUICIDE

Killing yourself is a matter for your own judgment. Nobody can prevent you; and if you are convinced that you are not worth your salt, and an intolerable nuisance to yourself and everyone else, it is a solution to be considered. But you can always put it off to tomorrow on the chance of something interesting turning up that evening.

Letter to William Rowbottom, January 5, 1946, *Collected Letters*, ed. Dan H. Laurence, vol. 4 (1988).

SUPERIORITY

We have in England a curious belief in first-rate people, meaning all the people we do not know; and this consoles us for the undeniable second-rateness of the people we do know.

The Irrational Knot, preface; Constable (1950).

First published in 1905.

SURGERY

A surgeon will get a reputation as the only possible man to consult in cancer cases simply because he has cut off more breasts than anyone else.

"Socialism and Superior Brains," *Essays in Fabian Socialism*; Constable (1949).
First published in 1894.

A surgeon who has mastered a dangerous operation can say to his patient, in effect, "Your money or your life."

The Intelligent Woman's Guide to Socialism, Capitalism, Sovietism, and Fascism, ch. 70; Constable (1949).
First published in 1928 as *The Intelligent Woman's Guide to Socialism and Capitalism*.

TALKING

As long as men can talk politics they will never do anything else except work for their daily bread.

Andrew Undershaft, in *Major Barbara*, screen version; *Collected Screenplays*, ed. Bernard F. Dukore (1980).
Written in 1940, first published in 1946.

TASTE

Conditions discreditable to civilization make up the greater part of our national life. Nor is there any form of toleration of evil more contemptible than the "good taste" which pretends not to know this, and strives to boycott those who refuse to join the conspiracy of silence.

"Realism, Real and Unreal," *Bernard Shaw's Book Reviews*, ed. Brian Tyson; Penn State Press (1991).
First published in *Pall Mall Gazette*, September 29, 1887.

If we could only make up our minds on both sides that there is a Yipiaddy public and a Beethoven public; that they must agree to live and let live; and that if the same men are to criticize for both they must be capable of both and must make an end of ignorant complaints that Beethoven is not Yipiaddy and uppish complaints that Yipiaddy is not Beethoven, then we shoud begin to get along.

"On Our Stage and Its Critics," *The Drama Observed*, ed. Bernard F. Dukore, vol. 3; Penn State Press (1993).

Written in 1910-11.

*T*AXES

An income tax is an exceedingly Socialistic institution. In fact, that is one of the objections of the upper class to it.

"What Socialism Will Be Like," *Platform and Pulpit*, ed. Dan H. Laurence; Hill & Wang (1961).

Lecture before the Hammersmith Socialist Society, July 12, 1896.

Taxes are the chief business of a conqueror of the world.

Caesar, in *Caesar and Cleopatra*, act 2; *The Bodley Head Bernard Shaw: Collected Plays with their Prefaces*, vol. 2 (1971).

First published 1901.

That citizens get better value for the rates and taxes they pay than for most other items in their expenditure never occurs to them. They will pay a third of their weekly earnings or more to an idle landlord as if that were a law of nature; but a collection from them by the rate collector they resent as sheer robbery: the truth being precisely the reverse.

Geneva, preface, "Civilization's Will to Live Always Defeated by Democracy"; *The Bodley Head Bernard Shaw: Collected Plays with their Prefaces*, vol. 7 (1974).

First published in 1939.

What happens when you make your financiers statesmen? Their first duty is to find out how much taxation you can bear.

"The Political Madhouse in America and Nearer Home," *The Political Madhouse in America and Nearer Home*; Constable (1933).

Speech broadcast on NBC from the Metropolitan Opera House, New York, April 11, 1933.

TEACHING

He who can, does. He who cannot, teaches.

Man and Superman, The Revolutionist's Handbook, "Maxims for Revolutionists"; *The Bodley Head Bernard Shaw: Collected Plays with their Prefaces*, ed. Dan H. Laurence, vol. 2 (1971).
First published in 1903.

You can't teach people anything they don't want to know.

Hipney, in *On the Rocks*, act 1; *The Bodley Head Bernard Shaw: Collected Plays with their Prefaces*, vol. 6 (1973).
First produced in 1933.

TELEVISION

For well-to-do people the theatre is less comfortable than home; and the trouble and expense of getting there, and the cost of stalls and boxes, are all against it. But proletarian homes are mostly uncomfortable, overcrowded, and dull. "Going to the play" is a treat for their inhabitants. When (if ever) all homes are comfortable audiences of millions will have their fill of drama and music without leaving their firesides, at a negligible cost.

"G.B.S. on Television," *The Drama Observed*, ed. Bernard F. Dukore, vol. 4; Penn State Press (1993).
First published in *Television Magazine*, January 1947.

Nobody who can see an adequate performance for nothing in comfort at home with his family will dress up, leave his fireside, and pay guineas for theatre stalls and taxis.

Letter to Val Gielgud, May 5, 1950, *The Correspondence of Bernard Shaw: Theatrics*, ed. Dan H. Laurence; U of Toronto Press (1995).

TELLING

When a man has anything to tell in this world, the difficulty is not to make him tell it, but to prevent him from telling it too often.

Caesar, in *Caesar and Cleopatra*, act 4; *The Bodley Head Bernard Shaw: Collected Plays with their Prefaces*, vol. 2 (1971).
First published in 1901.

*T*EMPTATION

I never resist temptation, because I have found that things that are bad for me do not tempt me.

King Magnus, in *The Apple Cart*, interlude; *The Bodley Head Bernard Shaw: Collected Plays with their Prefaces*, vol. 6 (1973).

First produced in 1929.

*T*EXTBOOKS

A school book is, by definition, one which no human being would read except under compulsion.

"Life, Literature, and Political Economy"; *Practical Politics*, ed. Lloyd J. Hubenka, U of Nebraska Press (1976).

Speech to the Students' Union at the London School of Economics and Political Science, December 13, 1905, revised for publication in the *Clare Market Review*, January 1906.

Nobody, except under the threat of torture, can read a school book.

Misalliance, preface, "Art Teaching"; *The Bodley Head Bernard Shaw: Collected Plays with their Prefaces*, vol. 4 (1972).

First published in 1914.

I lay my eternal curse on whomsoever shall now or at any time hereafter make schoolbooks of my works, and make me hated, as Shakespeare is hated. My plays were not designed as instruments of torture.

Letter to Otto Kyllmann, November 24, 1927, *Collected Letters*, ed. Dan H. Laurence, vol. 4 (1988).

*T*HEATRE, THE

The theatre is as holy a place as the church and the function of the actor no less sacred than that of the priest.

"The Second *Parsifal*," *Shaw's Music*, vol. 1, ed. Dan H. Laurence (1981).

First published in *The Star*, August 7, 1889.

A man who has read a play no more knows it than a musician knows a symphony when he has turned over the leaves of the score. He knows something about it: that is all.

"Wagner in Bayreuth," *Shaw's Music*, vol. 1, ed. Dan H. Laurence (1981).

First published in *English Illustrated Magazine,* October 1889.

The theatre of today, with its literature, its criticism, and its audiences, though a self-contained, consistent, and useful institution, ignores and is ignored by the class which is only interested in realities, and which enjoys thinking as others enjoy eating.

"Wagner in Bayreuth," *Shaw's Music*, vol. 1, ed. Dan H. Laurence (1981).

First published in *English Illustrated Magazine,* October 1889.

The theatre is really the weekday church; and a good play is essentially identical with a church service as a combination of artistic ritual, profession of faith, and sermon.

"Told You So," *The Drama Observed*, vol. 2, ed. Bernard F. Dukore; Penn State Press (1993).

First published in *Saturday Review,* December 7, 1895.

Theatrical management in this country is one of the most desperate commercial forms of gambling.

Preface to *The Theatrical "World" of 1894* by William Archer, *The Drama Observed*, vol. 1, ed. Bernard F. Dukore; Penn State Press (1993).

First published in 1895.

A theatre is a potent engine for working up the passions and the imagination of mankind; and like all such engines it is capable of the noblest recreations or the basest debauchery according to the spirit of its direction. So is a church.

Letter to W.T. Stead, undated: c. July 1904; *Collected Letters*, ed. Dan H. Laurence, vol. 2 (1972).

[The] Christian Church . . . has become the Church where you must not laugh; and so it is giving way to that older and greater Church to which I belong: the Church where the oftener you laugh the better, because by laughter only can you destroy evil without malice, and affirm good fellowship without mawkishness.

"The Author's Apology," *The Drama Observed*, ed. Bernard F. Dukore, vol. 3; Penn State Press (1993).

Preface to *Dramatic Opinions and Essays* (October 1906).

This would be a very good thing if the theatre took itself seriously as a factory of thought, a prompter of conscience, an elucidator of social conduct, an armory against despair and dullness, and a temple of the Ascent of Man.

"The Author's Apology," *The Drama Observed*, ed. Bernard F. Dukore, vol. 3; Penn State Press (1993).
Preface to *Dramatic Opinions and Essays* (October 1906).

A Bishop who goes into a theatre and declares that the performances there must not suggest sexual emotion is in the position of a playwright going into a church and declaring that the service there must not suggest religious emotion.

"Mr. Shaw on Morals," *The Drama Observed*, ed. Bernard F. Dukore, vol. 4; Penn State Press (1993).
Letter to the Editor, *The Times*, November 8, 1913.

*T*HEFT

MENDOZA: I am a brigand: I live by robbing the rich.
TANNER: I am a gentleman: I live by robbing the poor.

Man and Superman, act 3; *The Bodley Head Bernard Shaw: Collected Plays with their Prefaces*, vol. 2 (1971).
First published in 1903.

*T*HEORIES

The weakness of the man who, when his theory works out into a flagrant contradiction of the facts, concludes "So much the worse for the facts: let them be altered," instead of "So much the worse for my theory."

The Sanity of Art, *Major Critical Essays*; Constable (1940).
First published as "A Degenerate's View of Nordau," *Liberty* (New York), July 27, 1895.

THOUGHT

Always strive to find out what to do by thinking, without asking anybody.
If you continually do this, you will soon act like a grown-up woman. For
want of doing this, a very great number of grown-up people act like
children.

> *My Dear Dorothea*; Phoenix House (1956).
>
> To a six-year old girl; written in 1878.

TIME

There is only one way to defy Time; and that is to have young ideas, which
may always be trusted to find youthful and vivid expression.

> "Toujours Daly," *The Drama Observed*, vol. 2, ed. Bernard F. Dukore; Penn State Press (1993).
>
> First published in *Saturday Review*, July 13, 1895.

TITLES

Titles distinguish the mediocre, embarrass the superior, and are disgraced
by the inferior.

> *Man and Superman, The Revolutionist's Handbook*, "Maxims for Revolutionists"; *The Bodley Head
> Bernard Shaw: Collected Plays with their Prefaces*, vol. 2 (1971).
>
> First published in 1903.

TOLERANCE

If you make a single exception to the rule of toleration, you give away your
own case against bigotry.

> Letter to A.J. Marriott, May 1, 1899, *Collected Letters*, vol. 2, ed. Dan H. Laurence (1972).

Toleration and liberty have no sense or use except as toleration of opinions
that are considered damnable, and liberty to do what seems wrong.

> *The Shewing-up of Blanco Posnet*, preface, "What Toleration Means"; *The Bodley Head Bernard Shaw:
> Collected Plays with their Prefaces*, vol. 3 (1971).
>
> First published in 1911.

All laws act in restraint of toleration, even when they are laws to enforce toleration.

The W.E.A. [Workers' Educational Association] Education Year Book, preface to Part 1; *Complete Prefaces*, ed. Dan H. Laurence and Daniel J. Leary, vol. 2 (1995).

First published in 1918.

The degree of tolerance attainable at any moment depends on the strain under which society is maintaining its cohesion. In war, for instance, we suppress the gospels and put Quakers in prison, muzzle the newspapers, and make it a serious offence to show a light at night.

Saint Joan, preface, "Variability of Toleration"; *The Bodley Head Bernard Shaw: Collected Plays with their Prefaces*, vol. 6 (1973).

First published in 1924.

The concentration of British and American attention on the intolerances of Fascism and Communism creates an illusion that they do not exist elsewhere; but they exist everywhere, and must be met, not with ridiculous hotheaded attacks on Germany, Italy, and Russia, but by a restatement of the case for Toleration in general.

On the Rocks, preface, "Toleration Mostly Illusory"; *The Bodley Head Bernard Shaw: Collected Plays with their Prefaces*, vol. 6 (1973).

First published in 1934.

Dogmatic toleration is nonsense: I would no more tolerate the teaching of Calvinism to children if I had power to persecute it than the British Raj tolerated suttee in India. Every civilized authority must draw a line between the tolerable and the intolerable.

"Biographers' Blunders Corrected," *Sixteen Self Sketches*; Constable (1949).

Letter to Charles Henry Duffin, 1947 or 1948.

*T*ORTURE

The art of torture is the art of prolonging not agony, but ecstasy.

"On Deadheads and Other Matters," *The Drama Observed*, vol. 2, ed. Bernard F. Dukore; Penn State Press (1993).

First published in *Saturday Review*, October 31, 1896.

TOURISM

As a matter of fact, the sound of English makes me feel at home; and I dislike feeling at home when I am abroad. It is not precisely what one goes to the expense for.

Sartorius, in *Widowers' Houses*, act 1; *The Bodley Head Bernard Shaw: Collected Plays with their Prefaces*, vol. 1 (1970).

First produced in 1892.

TRAGEDY

Prometheus gains but little on Jupiter; and his defeats are the staple of tragedy.

"Satan Saved at Last," *The Drama Observed*, vol. 2, ed. Bernard F. Dukore; Penn State Press (1993).

First published in *Saturday Review*, January 16, 1897.

The only real tragedy in life is being used by personally minded men for purposes which you recognize to be base.

Man and Superman, Epistle Dedicatory; *The Bodley Head Bernard Shaw: Collected Plays with their Prefaces*, vol. 2 (1971).

First published in 1903.

There are two tragedies in life. One is to lose your heart's desire. The other is to gain it.

Mendoza, in *Man and Superman*, act 4, *The Bodley Head Bernard Shaw: Collected Plays with their Prefaces*, vol. 2 (1971).

First published in 1903.

The popular definition of tragedy is heavy drama in which everyone is killed in the last act, comedy being light drama in which everyone is married in the last act.

"Tolstoy: Tragedian or Comedian?" *The Drama Observed*, ed. Bernard F. Dukore, vol. 4; Penn State Press (1993).

Speech at Tolstoy Commemoration, November 30, 1921.

TRAGICOMEDY

This mirthless comedy, this tragedy that stripped the soul naked instead of bedizening it in heroic trappings.

The Quintessence of Ibsenism, "What Is the New Element in the Norwegian School?" *The Drama Observed*, ed. Bernard F. Dukore, vol. 4; Penn State Press (1993).

First published in revised edition, 1913.

TRAVEL

When I went to those great cities I saw wonders I had never seen in Ireland. But when I came back to Ireland I found all the wonders there waiting for me. You see they had been there all the time; but my eyes had never been opened to them. I did not know what my own house was like, because I had never been outside it.

Father Keegan, in *John Bull's Other Island*, act 2; *The Bodley Head Bernard Shaw: Collected Plays with their Prefaces*, vol. 2 (1971).

First produced in 1904.

TRIVIA

Nothing is commoner than for a man to begin amusing himself with a trifle, and presently discover that the trifle is the biggest thing he has ever tackled.

Letter to Henry James, January 21, 1909, *Collected Letters*, ed. Dan H. Laurence, vol. 2 (1972).

TROILUS AND CRESSIDA

Doubtless it washes the paint off many persons whose natural complexions are so bad that we can hardly help wishing that Shakespeare had left them as they were; but the process sets us laughing and thinking; and it may be doubted whether Homer achieved any result comparably beneficial to this.

"*Troilus and Cressida*," *The Drama Observed*, vol. 1, ed. Bernard F. Dukore; Penn State Press (1993).

Speech for the New Shakespeare Society, read in Shaw's absence, February 29, 1884.

T_{RUTH}

It may be "a sweeping assertion," but that is no objection to it if it be 99/100 true, which is as true as any critical statement—not a mere platitude—is ever likely to be. It is a sweeping assertion that every object on earth is subject to the law of gravitation, for instance.

> Letter to Francis Hueffer, January 19, 1883; *Collected Letters*, ed. Dan H. Laurence, vol. 1 (1965).

Every step toward truth (or disillusion) . . . is rather a fetter shaken off. I never gave up an old belief without feeling inclined to give three cheers and jump into the air.

> Letter to E.C. Chapman, July 29, 1891, *Collected Letters*, ed. Dan H. Laurence, vol. 1 (1965).

We do not seek for truth in the abstract. . . . Every man sees what he looks for, and hears what he listens for, and nothing else.

> Letter to E.C. Chapman, July 29, 1891, *Collected Letters*, ed. Dan H. Laurence, vol. 1 (1965).

The truth is the one thing nobody will believe.

> The Strange Lady, in *The Man of Destiny*; *The Bodley Head Bernard Shaw: Collected Plays with their Prefaces*, vol. 1 (1970).
>
> First produced in 1897.

The buried truth germinates and breaks through to the light.

> Dr. Colenso Ridgeon, in *The Doctor's Dilemma*, act 5; *The Bodley Head Bernard Shaw: Collected Plays with their Prefaces*, vol. 3 (1971).
>
> First produced in 1906

PERCIVAL: If I tell the truth nobody will believe me.
TARLETON: Oh yes they will. The truth makes everybody believe it.
PERCIVAL: It also makes everybody pretend not to believe it.

> *Misalliance*; *The Bodley Head Bernard Shaw: Collected Plays with their Prefaces*, vol. 4 (1972).
>
> First produced in 1910.

Like all revolutionary truths, it began as a joke.

> The Archbishop, in *Back to Methuselah*, "The Thing Happens"; *The Bodley Head Bernard Shaw: Collected Plays with their Prefaces*, vol. 5 (1972).
>
> First published in 1921.

The truth is sometimes the funniest joke in the world until it is thoroughly found out.

Letter to Annette Curnen Burgess, June 6, 1946, *Collected Letters*, ed. Dan H. Laurence, vol. 4 (1988).

Unconventionality

VIVIE: Oh! have I been behaving unconventionally?
PRAED: Oh no: oh dear no. At least not conventionally unconventionally, you understand.

Mrs. Warren's Profession, act 1; *The Bodley Head Bernard Shaw: Collected Plays with their Prefaces*, vol. 1 (1970).

First published in 1898.

Understanding

The only way to understand a subject is to write a book about it.

Letter to Beatrice Webb, September 30, 1909, *Collected Letters*, ed. Dan H. Laurence, vol. 2 (1972).

Unions

Trade Unionism is not Socialism: it is the Capitalism of the Proletariat.

The Intelligent Woman's Guide to Socialism, Capitalism, Sovietism and Fascism, ch. 46; Constable (1949).
First published in 1928 as *The Intelligent Woman's Guide to Socialism and Capitalism*.

Vanity

The most constant symptom of a shameful life.

"Manchester Still Expiating," *The Drama Observed*, vol. 3, ed. Bernard F. Dukore; Penn State Press (1993).

First published in *Saturday Review*, February 12, 1898.

$\mathcal{V}$EGETARIANISM

A mind of the calibre of mine cannot derive its nutriment from cows.

"Poor Old Philharmonic," *Shaw's Music*, vol. 2, ed. Dan H. Laurence (1981).
First published in *The Star*, April 5, 1890.

Of course I am a vegetarian—did you suppose I was in the habit of chewing the dead bodies of animals?

Letter to Ellen Terry, September 21, 1896, *Collected Letters*, vol. 1, ed. Dan H. Laurence (1965).

When a man of normal habits is ill, everyone hastens to assure him that he is going to recover. When a vegetarian is ill (which fortunately very seldom happens), everyone assures him that he is going to die, and that they told him so, and that it serves him right. They implore him to take at least a little gravy, so as to give himself a chance of lasting out the night.

"Valedictory," *The Drama Observed*, vol, 3, ed. Bernard F. Dukore; Penn State Press (1993).
First published in the *Saturday Review*, May 21, 1898.

My will contains directions for my funeral, which will be followed not by mourning coaches, but by herds of oxen, sheep, swine, flocks of poultry, and a small travelling aquarium of live fish, all wearing white scarves in honor to the man who perished rather than eat his fellow creatures.

Shaw: An Autobiography, vol 2, ed. Stanley Weintraub; Penn State Press (1970).
First published in "Wagner and Vegetables," *The Academy*, October 15, 1898.

I was a cannibal for twenty-five years. For the rest I have been a vegetarian.

"Who I Am, and What I Think," *Sixteen Self Sketches*; Constable (1949).
First published in *Candid Friend*, May 1901.

A vegetarian is not a person who lives on vegetables, any more than a Catholic is a person who lives on cats.

"Vegetarianism," *Doctors' Delusions, Crude Criminology, and Sham Education*; Constable (1950).
First published in *Daily Chronicle*, March 1, 1918.

A man of my spiritual intensity does not eat corpses.

Quoted in Hesketh Pearson, *Bernard Shaw: His Life and Personality*, ch. 9; Atheneum (1963).
First published in 1942.

Vice

It seems impossible to root out of an Englishman's mind the notion that vice is delightful and that abstention from it is privation.

The Author's Apology to *Mrs. Warren's Profession*; *The Bodley Head Bernard Shaw: Collected Plays with their Prefaces*, vol. 1 (1970).

First published in 1902.

What people call vice is eternal; what they call virtue is mere fashion.

Quoted in Archibald Henderson, *George Bernard Shaw: His Life and Works*, ch. 15; Boni and Liveright (1918).

First published in 1911.

Virtue

Hell is the home of honor, duty, justice, and the rest of the seven deadly virtues. All the wickedness on earth is done in their name: where else but in hell should they have their reward?

Don Juan, in *Man and Superman*, act 3; *The Bodley Head Bernard Shaw: Collected Plays with their Prefaces*, vol. 2 (1971).

First published in 1903.

Virtue consists, not in abstaining from vice, but in not desiring it.

Man and Superman, The Revolutionist's Handbook, "Maxims for Revolutionists"; *The Bodley Head Bernard Shaw: Collected Plays with their Prefaces*, vol. 2 (1971).

First published in 1903.

A practice to which nobody confesses may be both universal and unsuspected, just as a virtue which everybody is expected, under heavy penalties, to claim, may have no existence.

Overruled, preface; "Inaccessability of the Facts"; *The Bodley Head Bernard Shaw: Collected Plays with their Prefaces*, vol. 4 (1972).

First published in 1916.

People don't have their virtues and vices in sets: they have them anyhow: all mixed.

Mrs. Hushabye, in *Heartbreak House*, act 1; *The Bodley Head Bernard Shaw: Collected Plays with their Prefaces*, vol. 5 (1972).

First published in 1919.

*V*IVISECTION

Animals dislike being vivisected, but they also dislike being forced to bear burdens and draw loads. The difference is not in the pain endured by the animal, but in the fact that whereas there is no doubt that an intelligent horse would consent to do a reasonable quanitity of work for its living if it were capable of economic reasoning, just as men do, it is equally certain that no horse would on any terms submit to vivisection. On this ground the vivisector violates the moral law.

"Two Novels of Modern Society," *Bernard Shaw's Book Reviews*, ed. Brian Tyson; Penn State Press (1991).
First published in *Pall Mall Gazette*, July 15, 1885.

I regard a man who is imposed on by the vulgar utilitarian arguments in favor of vivisection as a subject for police surveillance.

"Christmas in Broadstairs," *Shaw's Music*, vol. 1, ed. Dan H. Laurence (1981).
First published in *The Star*, December 27, 1889.

*V*OTING

Unbounded hopes were placed on each successive extension of the electoral franchise, culminating in the enfranchisement of women. These hopes have been disappointed, because the voters, male and female, being politically untrained and uneducated, have (a) no grasp of constructive measures; (b) loathe taxation as such; (c) dislike being governed at all; and (d) dread and resent any extension of official interference as an encroachment on their personal liberty.

Socialism: Principles and Outlook; *The Illusions of Socialism and Socialism: Principles and Outlook*, Shavian Tract No. 4 (November 1956).
First published in the *Encyclopaedia Britannica*, 14th ed. (1929).

*W*AGNER, RICHARD

To think that this Wagner, once the very safest man in Europe to ridicule, should turn out the prime success of the century! . . . Yes, the cranks were right, after all.

"Bayreuth and Back," *Shaw's Music*, vol. 1, ed. Dan H. Laurence (1981).
First published in *The Hawk*, August 13, 1889.

W_{AR}

Soldiering, my dear madam, is the coward's art of attacking mercilessly when you are strong, and keeping out of harm's way when you are weak. That is the whole secret of successful fighting. Get your enemy at a disadvantage; and never, on any account, fight him on equal terms.

> Sergius, in *Arms and the Man*, act 2; *The Bodley Head Bernard Shaw: Collected Plays with their Prefaces*, vol. 1 (1970).
>
> First produced in 1894.

No victory is complete without the "Te Deum" by which Christian combatants assume that their God is an accomplice in their crime, and praise him for it.

> "Church and Stage," *The Drama Observed*, vol. 2, ed. Bernard F. Dukore; Penn State Press (1993).
>
> First published in *Saturday Review*, January 25, 1896.

The more destructive war becomes the more fascinating we find it.

> Andrew Undershaft, in *Major Barbara*, act 1; *The Bodley Head Bernard Shaw: Collected Plays with their Prefaces*, vol. 3 (1971).
>
> First produced in 1905.

If all the Churches of Europe closed their doors until the drums ceased rolling they would act as a most powerful reminder that though the glory of war is a famous and ancient glory, it is not the final glory of God.

> "Common Sense About the War," *Shaw on Religion*, ed. Warren S. Smith; Dodd, Mead (1967).
>
> First published in *New Statesman* (London), November 14, 1914.

War reduces us all to a common level of savagery and vulgarity whilst it pretends to distinguish us by our respective greatness.

> Letter to Siegfried Trebitsch, January 19, 1915, *Collected Letters*, ed. Dan H. Laurence, vol. 3 (1985).

It is impossible to discuss war practically without a suspension of all ordinary morals and all normal religious and humanitarian pretensions. Even that is not enough: it is necessary to set up . . . an outrageous special morality and religion, in which murder becomes duty and patriotism.

> "Is Britain Blameless?" *Complete Prefaces*, ed. Dan H. Laurence and Daniel J. Leary, vol. 2 (1995).
>
> First published as "Is England Blameless?" *Labour Leader*, February 4, 1915.

I cannot for the life of me see what claim civilians have to exemption from the risks of war. Civilians clamor for war, pay for war, send soldiers to war, express hostile sentiments and do hostile things . . . which would make a

good soldier sick, and exult when their army and navy rain bombs on
enemy civilians.

"Illusions of War," *Agitations*, ed. Dan H. Laurence and James Rambeau; Ungar (1985).

Letter to *New Statesman*, November 6, 1915.

The British blockade won the war; but the wonder is that the British
blockhead did not lose it. I suppose the enemy was no wiser. War is not a
sharpener of wits.

O'Flaherty, V.C., preface; *The Bodley Head Bernard Shaw: Collected Plays with their Prefaces*, vol. 4 (1972).

First published in 1919.

Truth telling is not compatible with the defense of the realm.

Heartbreak House, preface, "How War Muzzles the Dramatic Poet"; *The Bodley Head Bernard Shaw: Collected Plays with their Prefaces*, vol. 5 (1972).

First published in 1919.

War puts a strain on human nature that breaks down the better half of it,
and makes the worse half a diabolical virtue.

Heartbreak House, preface, "The Yahoo and the Angry Ape"; *The Bodley Head Bernard Shaw: Collected Plays with their Prefaces*, vol. 5 (1972).

First published in 1919.

War is dangerous because it is the method by which the worst men can
most easily destroy the best. By it the fools destroy the sages, and criminals
the men of good intent.

"Shaw to the World League for Peace, Geneva, September 6, 1928," *SHAW: The Annual of Bernard Shaw Studies*, vol. 16, ed. Dan H. Laurence and Margot Peters; Penn State Press (1996).

One of over a thousand statements published in facsimile by the League of Nations under the title *Pax Mundi: Livre d'Or de la Paix* (1932).

We shall make wars because only under the strain of war are we capable of
changing the world; but the changes our wars will make will never be the
changes we intended them to make.

Prola, in *The Simpleton of the Unexpected Isles*, act 2; *The Bodley Head Bernard Shaw: Collected Plays with their Prefaces*, vol. 6 (1973).

First produced in 1935.

I dislike war not only for its dangers and inconveniences, but because of the loss of so many young men, any of whom may be a Newton or an Einstein, a Beethoven, a Michaelangelo, a Shakespeare, or even a Shaw.

"This Danger of War," *Platform and Pulpit*, ed. Dan H. Laurence; Hill & Wang (1961).

B.B.C. broadcast, November 2, 1937.

If nations had any sense they would begin a war by sending their oldest men into the trenches. They would not risk the lives of their young men except in the last extremity.

"This Danger of War," *Platform and Pulpit*, ed. Dan H. Laurence; Hill & Wang (1961).

B.B.C. broadcast, November 2, 1937.

The notion that the killing of civilians, women and children is worse than the killing of soldiers can be held only by horrified people who have not thought out the subject. The object of war is to vanquish the enemy; and its method is to kill as many of them as possible. The civilian is the enemy just as much as the soldier.

Letter to an unidentified correspondent, February 5, 1938, *Collected Letters*, ed. Dan H. Laurence, vol. 4 (1988).

There must be no more nonsense about our being certain to win, and God being on our side, as in that case we have nothing to do but sit down in our armchairs and let God win.

"How to Talk Ingelligently About the War," *SHAW: The Annual of Bernard Shaw Studies*, vol. 16, ed. Dan H. Laurence and Margot Peters; Penn State Press (1996).

Written in July 1940.

The nation which is always preparing for war is like a hypochondriac who is always making his will: a dismal occupation which prevents him from doing anything else.

"The Unavoidable Subject," *Platform and Pulpit*, ed. Dan H. Laurence; Hill & Wang (1961).

Written for a B.B.C. broadcast in June 1940, but cancelled; first published in Anthony Weymouth, *Journal of the War Years (1939-1945) and One Year Later* (1948).

We always lose the first round of our fights through our habit of first declaring war and then preparing for it

"The Unavoidable Subject," *Platform and Pulpit*, ed. Dan H. Laurence; Hill & Wang (1961).

Written for a B.B.C. broadcast in June 1940, but cancelled; first published in Anthony Weymouth, *Journal of the War Years (1939-1945) and One Year Later* (1948).

Wealth

Other qualities being equal, men become rich in commerce in proportion to the intensity and exclusiveness of their desire for money.

Three Plays for Puritans, preface; *The Bodley Head Bernard Shaw: Collected Plays with their Prefaces*, vol. 2 (1971).

First published in 1901.

Weapons

To Man the weapon: to Heaven the victory.

Andrew Undershaft, in *Major Barbara*, act 3; *The Bodley Head Bernard Shaw: Collected Plays with their Prefaces*, vol. 3 (1971).

First produced in 1905.

Webster, John

The Tussaud laureate.

"Beaumont and Fletcher," *The Drama Observed*, vol. 3, ed. Bernard F. Dukore; Penn State Press (1993).

First published in *Saturday Review*, February 19, 1898; Madame Tussaud's is a wax museum in London; in act 4 of Webster's *The Duchess of Malfi*, the duchess is shown the corpses of her husband and children, which are really waxworks.

Well-made play

Sardoodledom

"Sardoodledom," *The Drama Observed*, vol. 2, ed. Bernard F. Dukore; Penn State Press (1993).

Word coined to describe the well-made play, a major writer of which was Victorien Sardou; first published in *Saturday Review,* June 1, 1895.

The well-made play is not an art: it is an industry.

Three Plays by Brieux, preface, "The Pedantry of Paris," *The Drama Observed*, ed. Bernard F. Dukore, vol. 3; Penn State Press (1993).

First published in 1911.

*W*ICKEDNESS

There is no wicked side: life is all one. And I never wanted to shirk my share in whatever evil must be endured, whether it be sin or suffering.

Barbara Undershaft, in *Major Barbara*, act 3; *The Bodley Head Bernard Shaw: Collected Plays with their Prefaces*, vol. 3 (1971).

First produced in 1905.

*W*ILDE, *OSCAR*

In a certain sense Mr. Wilde is to me our most thorough playwright. He plays with everything: with wit, with philosophy, with drama, with actors and audience, with the whole theatre.

"Two New Plays," *The Drama Observed*, vol. 1, ed. Bernard F. Dukore; Penn State Press (1993).

First published in *Saturday Review*, January 12, 1895.

*W*ILL

The strongest, fiercest force in nature is human will.

Misalliance, preface, "The Conflict of Wills"; *The Bodley Head Bernard Shaw: Collected Plays with their Prefaces*, vol. 4 (1972).

First published in 1914.

It is true that where there is a will there is a way; but the way is through knowledge; and it is surprising how often it lies just in the opposite direction to where we expected to find it.

"Why a Labor Year Book?" *Complete Prefaces*, ed. Dan H. Laurence and Daniel J. Leary, vol. 2 (1995).

Preface to *Labour Year Book,* 1916.

You know the very true saying that where there is a will there is a way. Unfortunately the good will does not necessarily find the right way. There are always dozens of ways, bad, good, and indifferent.

The Intelligent Woman's Guide to Socialism, Capitalism, Sovietism, and Fascism, ch. 86; Constable (1949).

First published in 1928 as *The Intelligent Woman's Guide to Socialism and Capitalism.*

*W*ISDOM

I am getting exceedingly wise, as I often do when I have a sheet of paper to tempt me.

> Quoted in Dan H. Laurence, "Katie Samuel: Shaw's Flameless 'Old Flame,'" *SHAW*, vol. 15 (1995).
> Letter to Katie Samuel, June 4, 1884.

It is a mistake to suppose that the difference between wisdom and folly has anything to do with the difference between physical age and physical youth. Some women are younger at seventy than most women at seventeen.

> *Caesar and Cleopatra*, "Notes"; *The Bodley Head Bernard Shaw: Collected Plays with their Prefaces*, vol. 2 (1971).
> First published in 1901.

We are made wise not by the recollections of our past, but by the responsibilities of our future.

> Zoo, in *Back to Methuselah*, "Tragedy of an Elderly Gentleman," act 1; *The Bodley Head Bernard Shaw: Collected Plays with their Prefaces*, vol. 5 (1972).
> First published in 1921.

There is great wisdom in the simplicity of a beast, let me tell you; and sometimes great foolishness in the wisdom of scholars.

> Joan, in *Saint Joan*, scene 6; *The Bodley Head Bernard Shaw: Collected Plays with their Prefaces*, vol. 6 (1973).
> First produced in 1923.

*W*IVES

The really hard position for the moment is that of the domestic woman, whose enormously valuable services, both to society and to her own household are accepted and even exacted as a matter of course, as if they were the least she could do in return for the privilege of being fed and clothed and housed and protected.

> Letter to unidentified young American woman, undated: 1895, *Collected Letters*, ed. Dan H. Laurence, vol. 1 (1965).

She would have made a most comfortable wife. Pleasant-looking, good-natured, able to see everything within six inches of her nose and nothing beyond. A domestic paragon: a political idiot. In short, an ideal wife.

> The Secretary, in *Geneva*, act 1; *The Bodley Head Bernard Shaw: Collected Plays with their Prefaces*, vol. 7 (1974).
>
> First produced in 1938.

Wives are not for conversation: that's for visitors.

> Z, in *Village Wooing*, scene 3; *The Bodley Head Bernard Shaw: Collected Plays with their Prefaces*, vol. 6 (1973).
>
> First published in 1934.

*W*OMEN

I do not know whether women ever love. I rather doubt it: they pity a man, *mother* him, delight in making him love them; but I always suspect that their tenderness is deepened by their remorse for being unable to love him.

> Letter to Ellen Terry, April 6, 1896, *Collected Letters*, vol. 1, ed. Dan H. Laurence (1965).

If we have come to think that the nursery and the kitchen are the natural sphere of a woman, we have done so exactly as English children come to think that a cage is the natural sphere of a parrot: because they have never seen one anywhere else.

> *The Quintessence of Ibsenism*, "The Womanly Woman"; in *The Drama Observed*, vol. 1, ed. Bernard F. Dukore, Penn State Press (1993).
>
> First published 1891.

The domestic career is no more natural to all women than the military career is natural to all men.

> *The Quintessence of Ibsenism*, "The Womanly Woman," in *The Drama Observed*, vol. 1, ed. Bernard F. Dukore, Penn State Press(1993).
>
> First published in 1891.

Women are human beings just like men, only worse brought up, and consequently worse behaved.

> "Unconscious Villainy and *Widowers' Houses*," *The Drama Observed*, vol. 1, ed. Bernard F. Dukore; Penn State Press (1993).
>
> Letter to the editor, *The Speaker*, December 31, 1892.

Women have to unlearn the false good manners of their slavery before they acquire the genuine good manners of their freedom.

> Mrs. Clandon, in *You Never Can Tell*, act 3; *The Bodley Head Bernard Shaw: Collected Plays with their Prefaces*, vol. 1 (1970).
>
> First published in 1898.

If women were as fastidious as men, morally or physically, there would be an end of the race.

> *Man and Superman*, Epistle Dedicatory, *The Bodley Head Bernard Shaw: Collected Plays with their Prefaces*, vol. 2 (1971).
>
> First published in 1903.

For every woman who has sacrificed her honor for a man's sake, ten men have sacrificed their honor for a woman's.

> *The Quintessence of Ibsenism*, "preface to Second Edition," *The Drama Observed*, ed. Bernard F. Dukore, vol. 4; Penn State Press (1993).
>
> First published in revised edition, 1913.

A woman is only a man in petticoats, or, if you like, . . . a man is a woman without petticoats.

> "Woman—Man in Petticoats," *Platform and Pulpit*, ed. Dan H. Laurence; Hill and Wang (1961).
>
> Speech at a meeting in behalf of the Cecil Houses Fund (which provided housing for indigent women), May 20, 1927.

The notion that the female voter is more politically intelligent or gentler than the male voter proved as great a delusion as the earlier delusions that the business man was any wiser politically than the country gentleman, or the manual worker than the middle class man.

> *The Intelligent Woman's Guide to Socialism, Capitalism, Sovietism, and Fascism*, ch. 83; Constable (1949).
>
> First published in 1928 as *The Intelligent Woman's Guide to Socialism and Capitalism*.

WORK

Nothing makes a man so selfish as work.

> Brassbound, in *Captain Brassbound's Profession*, act 3; *The Bodley Head Bernard Shaw: Collected Plays with their Prefaces*, vol. 2 (1971).
>
> First produced in 1900.

Persons who were born with a congenital dislike for honest work. I was born in that particular way myself. I wanted to do what I liked. A great many persons are born in the middle class who are in this position. They generally take up the fine arts for their living.

"Socialism and the Artistic Professions," *Practical Politics*, ed. Lloyd J. Hubenka; U of Nebraska Press (1976).

Lecture for the Fabian Society, November 23, 1906, first published in *New York Evening Post*, December 22, 1906.

*W*ORKING CLASS

What Socialist who really knows the working class is not appalled by its capacity for snobbery and humbug?

"A Socialism Program: The Gentle Art of Unpleasantness," *Practical Politics*, ed. Lloyd J. Hubenka; U of Nebraska Press (1976).

First published in *The Clarion*, August 16, 1907.

The working classes are the biggest fools I know, with the possible exception of the middle and upper classes.

Letter to Keir Hardie, undated: c. February 15, 1912, *Collected Letters*, ed. Dan H. Laurence, vol. 3 (1985).

The proletariat is not robbed by persons whom it regards as thieves, but by persons whom it respects and privileges as specially honorable, and whom it would itself rob with the entire approval of its conscience if their positions were reversed.

"The Dictatorship of the Proletariat," *Practical Politics*, ed. Lloyd J. Hubenka; U of Nebraska Press (1976).

First published in *Labour Monthly*, October 1921.

*W*ORLD, THE

God has given us a world that nothing but our own folly keeps from being a paradise.

Morell, in *Candida*, act 1; *The Bodley Head Bernard Shaw: Collected Plays with their Prefaces*, vol. 1 (1970).

First produced in 1897.

This world, sir, is very clearly a place of torment and penance, a place where the fool flourishes and the good and wise are hated and persecuted, a place where men and women torture one another in the name of love; where children are scourged and enslaved in the name of parental duty and education; where the weak in body are poisoned and mutilated in the name of healing, and the weak in character are put to the horrible torture of imprisonment, not for hours but for years, in the name of justice. . . . It is plain to me that this earth of ours must be hell.

> Father Keegan, in *John Bull's Other Island*, act 4; *The Bodley Head Bernard Shaw: Collected Plays with their Prefaces*, vol. 2 (1971).
> First produced in 1904.

z: I don't think the world is rightly arranged: do you?
a: We must take the world as we find it. It's we that are not rightly arranged.

> *Village Wooing*, scene 1; *The Bodley Head Bernard Shaw: Collected Plays with their Prefaces*, vol. 6 (1973).
> First published in 1934.

WORLD WAR I

To the truly civilized man, to the good European, the slaughter of the German youth was as disastrous as the slaughter of the English. Fools exulted in "German losses." They were our losses as well. Imagine exulting in the death of Beethoven because Bill Sikes dealt him his death blow!

> *Heartbreak House*, preface, "Evil in the Throne of Good"; *The Bodley Head Bernard Shaw: Collected Plays with their Prefaces*, vol. 5 (1972).
> First published in 1919.

WORSHIP

Is it not much more sensible to worship a sonata constructed by a musician than to worship a syllogism constructed by a logician, since the sonata may at least inspire feelings of awe and devotion?

> *The Quintessence of Ibsenism*, "The Two Pioneers," *The Drama Observed*, vol. 1, ed. Bernard F. Dukore; Penn State Press (1993).
> First published in 1891.

Writing

The writer who aims at producing the platitudes which are "not for an age, but for all time" has his reward in being unreadable in all ages.

The Sanity of Art, preface; *Major Critical Essays*, Constable (1948).

First published in 1908; the slight misquotation is Ben Jonson, "To the Memory of My Beloved, the Author, Mr. William Shakespeare."

Wrong

LADY BRITOMART: You . . . ought to know better than to go about saying that wrong things are true. What does it matter whether they are true if they are wrong?

UNDERSHAFT: What does it matter whether they are wrong if they are true?

Major Barbara, act 3; *The Bodley Head Bernard Shaw: Collected Plays with their Prefaces*, vol. 3 (1971).

First produced in 1905.

Youth

He has a hard and penetrating intellect and a remarkable power of looking facts in the face; but unfortunately, being very young, he has no idea of how very little of that sort of thing most of us can stand.

Lord Summerhays, in *Misalliance*; *The Bodley Head Bernard Shaw: Collected Plays with their Prefaces*, vol. 4 (1972).

First produced in 1910.

It's all that the young can do for the old, to shock them and keep them up to date.

Fanny O'Dowda, in *Fanny's First Play*, Induction; *The Bodley Head Bernard Shaw: Collected Plays with their Prefaces*, vol. 4 (1972).

First produced in 1911.

Zola, Emile

Zola's books, like Voltaire's pamphlets, scandalize thoughtless people; and contain episodes which can have no further or higher effect than to scandalize them. But they are securing the right of way for thinkers who will bring light and fresh air into this sanctuary.

"Asides," *SHAW: The Annual of Bernard Shaw Studies*, vol. 16, ed. Dan H. Laurence and Margot Peters; Penn State Press (1996).

Written on June 9, 1889.

His view was that if you were going to legislate for agricultural laborers, or deal with them or their business in any way, you had better know what they are really like; and in supplying you with the necessary information he did not tell you what you already knew, which included pretty nearly all that could be decorously mentioned, but what you did not know, which was that part of the truth that was tabooed.

Three Plays by Brieux, preface, "Rise of the Scientific Spirit," *The Drama Observed*, ed. Bernard F. Dukore, vol. 3; Penn State Press (1993).

First published in 1911.